A Walker's Yearbook

A preliminary walk along the newly opened Golden Gate Promenade trail, led by Bob Kane (then Commanding Officer of the Presidio) and Margot P. Doss. (Photo by Jerry Telfer, courtesy of the San Francisco *Chronicle*.)

A Walker's Yearbook

52 Seasonal Walks in the San Francisco Bay Area

Margot Patterson Doss

PRESIDIO PRESS

Walks compiled and revised from the *San Francisco Chronicle* series, "Bay Area at Your Feet."

Copyright © 1983 by Margot Patterson Doss
Published by Presidio Press, 31 Pamaron Way, Novato, California 94947

Library of Congress Cataloging in Publication Data

Doss, Margot Patterson.
   A walker's yearbook.

     1. Hiking — California — San Francisco Bay Region —
Guide-books.   2. Walking — California — San Francisco Bay
Region — Guide-books.   3. San Francisco Bay Region
(Calif.) — Description and travel — Guide-books.
I. Title.
GV199.42.C22S26944   1983   917.94'61   82-18614
ISBN 0-89141-154-2

Photographs by John Whinham Doss
Cover design by Kathleen A. Jaeger
Pastel on back cover by Jessel
Book design by Lyn Cordell
Composition by Helen Epperson

Printed in the United States of America

It's the last place. There is no place left to go.
— Lew Welch
"The Song Mount Tamalpais Sings"

Contents

CONTENTS

Introduction

WE HUMAN BEINGS, travelers and would-be travelers all, have a need for novelty. There is in us that curiosity which Samuel Johnson defined as the "permanent characteristic of a vigorous mind." It is a hunger to be delighted, amazed, bemused, confounded, taken out of self-preoccupation to test our merits against other circumstances.

This ever-recurring restlessness gets us up out of the easy chair in search of the new and strange. Sometimes it takes us onto airplanes, bicycles, ships, trains, buses, balloons, motorcycles, rickshas, hang gliders, sedan chairs, into wetsuits, onto elephants, camels, carousels and mopeds, eternally seeking otherness.

Yet the faraway countries where we usually seek otherness are losing it. They are yielding to the touristic phenomenon known as monoculture. Years ago, in a letter from Kyoto, Philip Whalen said it better and more simply. "Isn't it odd that what America has invented and has sold to all the rest of the world is nothing but 'Downtown.' Tall concrete buildings, paved streets and stoplights. Elevators and plumbing that all work . . ."

Until, finally, the place to seek otherness is right here at home. Just around the corner in the Bay Area, it awaits anyone willing to get out on foot, as I discovered to my delight long before I started writing the "walking column" in the San Francisco *Chronicle*.

That column had the most casual of beginnings. One evening I went to a PTA meeting at the old Grant School. Abe Mellinkoff, then city editor of the *Chronicle*, had a daughter in the same class as my oldest son, and we found ourselves seated next to one another. "Did you once write for the *Baltimore Sun*?" he asked after we had introduced ourselves. I admitted I had, and learned that his brother Sherman, now dean of the UCLA School of Medicine, who had been a Baltimore neighbor of ours, had sent brother Abe clippings of some of my feature articles.

"What are you doing now?" Abe asked.

I told him I was walking around exploring the town with my children.

"Ah, yes," he said in that condescending tone with which men used to dismiss anything housewifely, "but what do you do for intellectual stimulation?"

1

"Well, sometimes," I answered, "I go down to the public library to bone up on the answers to their questions."

Intrigued, he asked, "What kind of questions?"

That day Rick had asked me, "Who were the Fine Arts who lived in that Palace, Mommy?"

Abe started to laugh, then said, "Y'know, what interests your kids might interest the readers. Why don't you write up a couple of those walks and send me a list of a dozen or so more."

That was the genesis of the walking column. The *Chronicle* thought it would be of interest to the tourist (although I wrote it from the beginning to interest natives, emigrants and transplantees), so they began running the walks as a series the first Sunday in June, 1961 and terminated it the last Sunday in August.

When the boys were young, the Doss family usually stayed home on Labor Day weekends because my pediatrician husband thought the most dangerous place one could take children was on a highway on holidays. We got in the car that first September Sunday, however, driven out of our home by the telephone. There were nineteen calls before 9 A.M. that day, all asking essentially the same thing: "Where shall we walk today, Mrs. Doss?"

The *Chronicle* had about three hundred that morning, all asking the same question—which is why I have been in the paper ever after, including during what we think of in San Francisco as "the rainy season."

Initially the newspaper editors, laboring under a common delusion, thought there was one time of year, and only one, in which walkers walk. A little like the baseball or football season, I suppose. When I explained that walkers, the most independent of people, walk whenever the spirit moves them (and pointed out that everyone is a walker), they said, "But what if it rains?"

"What if it does?" I responded. "Are you made of chocolate frosting that will melt in the rain?"

But this was much too flippant, and the editors explained to to me with great seriousness that they didn't want readers calling to complain they couldn't take my walks because it was raining.

The suggestion of raincoats, umbrellas and waterproof footgear only partially satisfied them. As a compromise I proposed occasional walks especially designed to get people out of the rain.

This seemed to fill the bill, but that pioneer year we all watched both the calendar and the clouds. A wonderful thing happened. All during the rainy season, the skies miraculously cleared on Sunday, giving at least four hours of bright sunshine, certainly long enough for the pokiest walker to cover the ground I had written about. On the Sundays when the deliberate "rainy day walks" appeared in the *Chronicle*—walks around the Conservatory in Golden Gate Park, the Maritime Museum, the Academy of Sciences and such, the skies poured. It was uncanny. It happened so frequently, so predictably, that the word circulated around the newsroom that I had some sort of tap line to the elements. I don't. When people remark on the fortuitous weather for walking, I usually laugh it off by saying, "There's a genie of place that looks after environmentalists." The truth is that the Bay Area has great walking weather all year long.

It was Bill Hogan, formerly book editor of the *Chronicle*, who first told me I was writing not only a column, but a book. "If you'll gather up about a dozen of your tearsheets," he said, "I'll send them off to a local publisher in your name." That publisher's response was hilarious. Among other things, the letter said that a book of walks around San Francisco might have a market in some unforeseeable future "for the curiosity value."

After three other, and less arch, put-downs, we tried the tearsheets on the avant garde publisher, Grove Press. It is odd to think of walking, man's earliest form of transportation and the exercise favored by 44 million Americans, as avant garde, but when I started the column in 1961, it was. That first book, *San Francisco at Your Feet*, is still in print and has been revised again and again.

Even at Grove Press, the scrapbook of tearsheets lay on a desk for three months before I heard from the publisher. Barney Rosset came from New York to Marin County to testify in behalf of Henry Miller at the *Tropic of Capricorn* trial. (It's also odd to think of freewheeling Marin, which one national TV network labeled as the land of hot tubs and peacock feathers, censoring Miller.)

During the time Barney was here, my walk column on Union Square appeared in the *Chronicle*. When he read it, he said to Don Allen, Grove's West Coast editor, "Get hold of this girl, Don. I want to publish these walks." Don started to laugh. "You spend too much time in Majorca, Barney. Her scrapbook has been on your desk for months."

A book contract arrived for me within the week. Now, six books later, I still get asked a question that was put to me the week I began. "Aren't you afraid you'll run out of places to walk?"

The answer is also the same. "No, I'm not." Thanks to the readers, there have always been at least sixty usable suggestions in a basket behind my typewriter.

There are also many more places for the public to walk now than there were twenty years ago. To name just a few: the Point Reyes National Seashore, the Golden Gate National Recreation Area, the Mid-Peninsula Open Space District, the many parks added to the East Bay Regional Park system, and any number of smaller county and town parks.

The publisher of the book in your hands is jointly responsible for at least one of these wonderful new walks, the Golden Gate Promenade. Colonel Robert V. Kane was commanding officer of the Presidio in 1973 when the Golden Gate National Recreation Area was being created. In our time people rarely think of military men as environmentalists. We forget that they, too, love the land they are trained to protect. Bob Kane is one who appreciates nature and people's need to feel a part of it.

Trails in long-used populous areas don't happen overnight, of course, but this one almost seemed as if it had. One morning the telephone rang and it was Mayor Joseph Alioto asking if I would meet a boat at Fisherman's Wharf taking a press tour of the waterfront.

"But it's my birthday!" I protested. "I was going to . . ."

"I've got a birthday present for you that you'll never forget!" the Mayor said. Who can resist an invitation like that? Since he wouldn't tell me what it was, my curiosity forced me to cancel earlier plans and take the trip, if only to find out.

The present was the creation of the Golden Gate Promenade.

When we were under way in the bay, approaching the Presidio offshore of Crissy Field, the Mayor expounded on "our truly magnificent environmental treasure—the miles of dramatic shoreline along our great bay. We propose to break through these barriers and open an unbroken three-and-a-quarter-mile stretch of San Francisco's north bay shoreline to public use. . . ."

As he spoke, I heard my own words coming back to me from a report I had written long before as chairman of the Recreational

Trails Coordinating Committee, set up by the San Francisco Board of Supervisors, in which we recommended that this waterfront become a trail. I remember thinking, with the journalist's skepticism, on the snail's pace of government, when the Mayor's voice brought me up short with "and you will all be invited to join Mrs. Doss and me walking this fine new trail within two months."

The mayor was as good as his word, but he couldn't have done it without remarkable cooperation from the U.S. Army, for much of the Golden Gate Promenade runs through land that had been Fort Mason and the Presidio. Within the week, Colonel Bob Kane, Colonel John Kern, and I walked the fenced length of the Presidio from Lyon Street to Fort Point. We had the great pleasure of having a first walk on the trail that was to become one of San Francisco's most glamorous and most used walkways.

For Colonel Kane, whose retirement venture was to become Presidio Press, and for me, it was also the early beginning of a professional relationship that has resulted in publication, not only of this, but of three other of my books, *Bay Area at Your Feet, Golden Gate Park at Your Feet,* and *There There: East San Francisco Bay at Your Feet.*

Even now another splendid new walk is surfacing along San Francisco's waterfront under the leadership of Mayor Dianne Feinstein. It will go handsomely from the Ferry Building to the Bay Bridge. I am sure that it will be as much used and loved as is the Golden Gate Promenade, for San Franciscans have discovered, as I did, that the need for novelty stimulated by that sublime restlessness that gets us out of the easy chair, can be satisfied by a walk, and a look around the nearby corner can possibly be better than traveling to faraway places.

Margot Patterson Doss
May 20, 1982

January

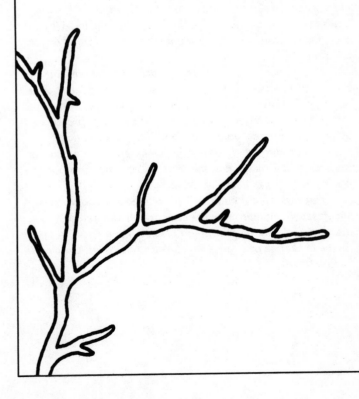

1

*Plate One in the Agenda Cochrane, the datebook my hus-
band has brought from Chile, shows a native house in the
Chol Chol region. There is a Mapuche poem with it:*

> I wish I were the sun eagle,
> I would enter the new house.
> Had I a sun crown
> I would enter from the ground
> And sit in the new house.

*Primitive or sophisticated, we all long for new begin-
nings, especially at the New Year. It is on January 1, sometimes to a throbbing head, that the false starts and indecisions
of a lifetime come back to taunt us. But not for long if one is
a walker.*

*Unconsciously the human in touch with the natural self
seems to understand that walking is a healer as well as a
pleasure. Set out for a walk and within fifty paces of getting
into a good stride one is breathing in the rhythm prescribed
by both the mystical yogic gurus and Harvard University for
the stress-reducing, heart-saving, miniretreats known as
transcendental meditation, all without lotus position hocus-
pocus, counting, or secret syllables.*

*The ideal New Year's walk for me is alongside the ever-
laving sea. No matter how brief the outing, one returns from
the shore refreshed, full of high resolve, keen again to take
up the challenge or even the dailiness of our days. Crowned
by the sun.*

Sand Dollar Beach

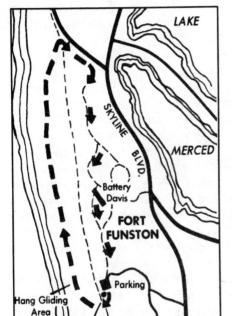

NOW THE GREAT winds shoreward blow"; wrote Matthew Arnold, entranced as we all are by the ocean in winter. "Now the salt tides seaward flow;/ Now the wild white horses play,/ Champ and chafe and toss in the spray."

The Pacific Ocean makes a great show, and never better than at the full and new moons. Walking along the waterside is also the ideal place for making resolutions for the coming year, whether you intend to keep them or not. Footprints on the sands of time, intimations of mortality and all that.

Fortunately San Franciscans are blessed with plenty of shoreline to walk. Nowhere is it more interesting than at Fort Funston, that cliffy dunescape that lies within the Golden Gate National Recreation Area at the southwest corner of the city. The choices for walking here are several. For the beachcomber, at low tide there is a broad strand that is often bestrewn with fossils after a storm. For the cross-country strider, there are looney moonscape dunes, a natural amphitheater, an old military battery, a onetime gun club, and any number of native plants to discover. For the whale watcher, there is a high overlook. For the handicapped, the halt, the lame, and the old, there is a well-paved short and completely level trail suitable for wheelchairs. Given the right winds, when you walk on the beach, hang gliders soar overhead. Climb up the cliff and there they are at eye level. Climb even higher to the top of Battery Davis and you may be above them. At any level it adds an interesting dimension to walking, and like the presence of mounted rangers, increases the safety of the walker.

My favorite of the Fort Funston possibilities is a walk that combines all the options. To make it, put on your lug-soled hiking boots and your down jacket. Then transport yourself south toward the city's charter line via the Great Highway and Skyline Boulevard. Slightly past Harding Park Golf Course and Lake Merced, watch on the west side for a road that goes uphill toward some old army buildings. Drive in and, bearing to the right, park on the concrete at the western end of the lot. (Nearest public transportation is Muni's No. 70 Lake Merced or No. 18, 46th Avenue.)

The buildings to the south of you are now in use as an environmental education center. The tall windmill nearby is an energy-oriented device to measure wind velocity. Walk toward the ocean in the area where hang glider activity concentrates. To make a reconnaissance of the beach and scan the distance for any passing pods of gray whales, walk toward the fenced overlook above the glider launching pad. On a clear day you can see the Farallones. Any beach walk should start with checking the tidebook, hopefully in every walker's jacket pocket. High tide of 6.3 one New Year's morning was at 9:37 A.M. Low tide in the afternoon was a —.5 at 4:28 P.M. To interpret these clues for the novice, from about ten o'clock in the morning until almost sundown, the tide was going out. Beaches are safer to walk on an outgoing tide, since there is less chance of being stranded.

Once you have scoped out the beach, walk back to that low wooden bridge on the overlook approach and look south to discern beyond the hang glider launching place a narrow single-file path through the sea fig. Skirt the hang glider pad to reach it. It rambles southward, then makes a sharp L-shaped turn and drops steeply a hundred feet to the beach. Once down on the strand, look back to see where you descended, then south to locate Pedro Point, parallel to Sweeney Ridge, a proposed addition to the Golden Gate National Recreation Area. As you start walking north, look up at the hang glider launching pad and the overlook to get a fix on your position. It will surprise you to see how high above they now are.

As you walk, keep your eye out for a smooth, round, gray wave-worn stone, the ideal flat shape best for "skipping the waves," one of childhood's oldest games. This is *Anorthoscutum interlineatum* Stimpson, an extinct sand dollar, that washes out of the Merced Formation from a V-shaped fossil bed that lies offshore. Fossil snails, avocado pits, and pine cones have also been found along Sand Dollar Beach, as this is known locally. Erosion produces few fossils that are pristine, but the sea has a consolation prize. This is *Dendraster excentricus* Escholtz, also a sand dollar, but not extinct.

Sandpipers, surfscoters, surfcasters, skindivers, and more rarely in winter, sunbathers, may also be along the beach. Sometimes great board meetings of bankerlike gulls congregate here. Sanderlings, like an avian secretarial pool on coffee break, skitter along the water's edge. A wedge of prehistoric pelicans may go by, stately as steamships aloft.

When you become aware that the cliffs have sloped down to the level of the Great Highway, you are parallel to the San Francisco Zoo. One long ramp goes up to the road. Near the foot of it, a broad path leads upward through the dunes. Take the path, and follow it up through a draw until you are parallel to the Fort Funston sign, then bear right on the broad old military road, a legacy from a time when this was Lake Merced Military Reservation, renamed after the earthquake of 1906 in gratitude to Frederick Funston for his helpfulness to the city.

Follow the road up to Battery Davis, with Lake Merced and all of the Sunset District and the San Miguel Hills visible on your left as you walk. (For an even better view, the spry can climb to the top of Battery Davis from its northern end.) At the first entrance, go through the massive battery and follow the trail for the handicapped as it rambles along the cliff. Natural windbreaks in the chaparral have been pressed into service by the park to shelter picnic tables and benches.

Bearing consistently south on the paved trail, you will soon be back at the overlook. If this widely varied terrain, a sample of what San Francisco was like before the city was built, was so distracting you forgot to make a resolution, here's one that's universal for our energy hungry times: Resolved: To walk as often as possible.

2

Occasionally weathercasters on the air don't know their miasma from a cold front.

Some of the best weather the San Francisco Bay Area enjoys comes in the winter months. For fourteen years I have led winter walks for the University of California Extension, and in all that time, our walkers have only been wet by rain twice. It has often rained the day before a walk was scheduled and again the day after. For any walker during winter, the clue is to seize the moment. If the sun is shining on the Golden Gate Bridge, put on your boots and get out to enjoy it.

Under the Golden Gate Bridge

U NDER THAT SWEET song in the air that is the Golden Gate Bridge, there is a spectacular path. It meanders along the face of the southern anchorage where the bridge meets

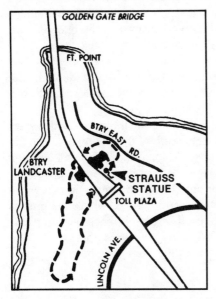

the land, revealing vistas varied and glorious at every turn. Wildflowers alternate with cypress trees close at hand. The swift-flowing water of old Papa Sacramento River meets the Pacific Ocean in the Golden Gate Strait two hundred feet below. Over-head the steely strength of the great bridge soars like a great idea newly born, while off on the horizon lie the fulvous hills of Marin, eternally serene. Walk it on a blue and gold day, and your heart will leap into your throat.

Since 1935, when bridge construction began on what was left of old Cantil Blanco, the white cliff foreshortened to accommodate Fort Point, this area has been inaccessible to walkers. Now the route has been opened to the public as a link in the Golden Gate National Recreation Area's exciting Coastal Trail, connecting the headlands of Marin via the bridge with those lovely ocean margins on Baker's Beach, Lands End, Ocean Beach, and farther south, Fort Funston. Indeed, with this link open, when the Sweeney Ridge addition to the GGNRA is a reality, one could begin walking north at Santa Cruz and go on connecting trails in county, state, or city parks or open space land all the way to Tomales Point — an odyssey about the distance of the entire west coast of Wales.

Pick a fair day to enjoy this link, a short segment of the trail one can sample in a leisurely hour. Put on your down vest or Woolrich cruiser and flat-heeled shoes, then transport yourself, preferably via the Muni No. 2 bus or Golden Gate Transit No. 64 to the toll plaza of the bridge. If you must use your own wheels, when the toll plaza parking area is full, there is additional parking designed to serve Fort Point, half a block away at Battery East, just off Lincoln Boulevard.

Once free of wheels, plow through the tourists photographing the statue of Joseph B. Strauss, chief engineer of the bridge, all set about with flowers, to read the reassuring plaque which says, "Here at the Golden Gate is the eternal rainbow that he conceived and set to form a promise indeed that the race of man shall endure into the ages." Nuclear fission, a more recent scientific achievement, may have left the eulogy dated, but not the bridge.

It is possible to reach the recent trail link through wooden steps in Battery Lancaster, immediately north of the statue, but for more diversity, bear right on the sidewalk, following it downhill through the formal flowers and a gate to Battery East Road immediately below the toll plaza. Step out onto it, and immediately you are in another, freer world, less hurried and curried, where tall grasses bend in the wind and coyote brush hides old brick gun emplacements. Bear left, and in a few steps the panorama becomes so engrossing you may miss the road that forks off sharp left. If you find yourself instead on the wide red rock road leading down to Fort Point, retrace a few steps.

Hug the fenceline. Inevitably your eyes will be drawn across the water to the Lime Point Light, Point Cavallo to the east of it, and that sheltered lagoon that is the U.S. Army's exclusive yacht harbor at Fort Baker, an ideal location for ferry landings to improve transportation within our vast park. Walk a few more steps and the guano-whitened cliffs east of Kirby Cove catch the eye, until you are under the bridge itself. Then the massive structure takes all your attention for a few moments.

When the building of the bridge was under way, deep-sea divers constructing the fender that surrounds the south pier pylon could only work four twenty-minute periods every twenty-four hours because of the velocity of the tide—four to seven and a half knots per hour. Even the trestle from Fort Point on which workers could guide the caisson into place was an engineering achievement. It was barely in place when a freighter crashed into it in a November

fog, carrying away three hundred feet. As though the fates were laughing, when the trestle had been replaced, a storm carried off even more. Like Robert the Bruce, engineer Strauss had learned the patience of a spider and came back a third time with a better plan that worked.

Follow the asphalt, observing the yellow line if a cyclist comes your way, until you reach the observation bench. Pause for a look across the strait at Point Diablo Light (the little white structure near the water), at the well-hidden fortifications at water level on Kirby Cove, and high overhead on Hill 129 the long flat batteries. When the foghorns are in play here, their different sounds define the north and south towers of the bridge and nearby points so seafarers can find safe passage in between.

Bear right when the asphalt curves up toward the bridge to admit bicyclists only to the western walkway, and chuckle perhaps at the psychologist who had to throw out an entire suicide study. He had posed a scholarly conclusion on why jumpers go off the side facing the city before learning there was then no access to the opposite side.

Climb the slight rise and Mile Rock, Lands End, China Beach, and a tree-framed glimpse of the Palace of the Legion of Honor are visible. Over all glares the Veterans' Hospital, unconscionably bright and twice as large since the new section has been completed. Go through the gate, which is supposed to be always open, and into the grove of wattle and cypress. Duddleya, Indian paintbrush, and baccharis lie above the trail as you emerge, with tidepools below and Bareass Beach barely visible around the cliff below. Cross the little bridge, go up some more steps, and the Russian Orthodox church and Washington High School are the larger buildings visible.

As we climbed the next group of stairs, former superintendent Bill Whalen, who conducted me on this walk, pointed out that the old railroad ties used for risers had come from the Belt Line tracks along Marina Green. "They would have cost us eleven dollars apiece if we hadn't saved them," he said. "The YCC built the trail and they did a good job. The kids really get involved in a project when they understand they are creating something they can bring their own kids back to see someday." The next staircase enlarges the view, which now bears a remarkable likeness to the Mediterranean coast.

Shortly the trail turns inland, crosses some historic 1906 rubble, and comes out alongside Battery Boutelle. If you were going on to Baker Beach, the route would be westerly. For this sample, instead bear left on Bowman Road, the old red rock connector for the fortifications on either hand, passing Battery Marcus Miller and Battery Cranston. When you reach the Golden Gate Bridge District's perpetually proliferating corporation yard, go up the tie steps on your right, pick your way through the parking lot, then follow the concrete steps downhill. If you came by bus, the glass-shielded waiting station for your return is about two hundred feet south. If you brought your own gas guzzler, go through the tunnel under the toll plaza and lo! there you are at the statue of Strauss, genie of the bridge, once again.

3

Brooks Atkinson, a great walker as well as a fine drama critic, once wrote of the seasons, "Although we hastily regard them as a thing apart from ourselves, we are really united to them closely. Not merely because they bring the harvest upon which we depend, or because they fertilize the soil with falling leaves and store the mountains with the water we need in spring and summer; but because as natural beings we are drawn into their movement, emotionally and physically."

Newcomers often complain that San Francisco has no seasons. We have them, although their rhythms are subtler than in the Midwest or Northeast. For walkers a temperate climate means the walking is good all year round. Winter, when there is less obscuring fog, is often the prime time for taking in a panorama from the paramount viewing places.

Walter A. Haas Playground

THEY CALL IT the million-dollar view. In these inflationary times, that's probably conservative. From the broad lawn of Walter A. Haas Park on the eastern slope of Diamond Heights, one gets at least a 340-degree sweep of the San Francisco Bay. It is, indeed, such an exhilarating prospect that walkers owe it to themselves to stroll around this ledge in the lee of Gold Mine Hill.

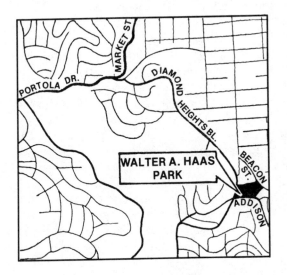

Pick a fair day to make this walk. However mild the weather may seem, take a scarf, hat, or extra windshirt. There is really no need to take your own wheels. The public transportation to Walter A. Haas Park is so good it could be included in the tourist literature we disseminate to strangers. The Diamond Heights bus No. 37 from Castro and Market stops right at the playground. The Diamond Heights bus No. 44 from Bosworth and Diamond (Glen Park BART Station) stops at the park's westernmost point, Addison Street and Diamond Heights Boulevard.

If you must take your own wheels, from downtown San Francisco head uphill on Market Street, and near its crest take the tricky left turn at the junction with Portola Drive, Burnett Avenue, Clipper Street, and Diamond Heights Boulevard. The latter looks like it is going into a housing complex. Actually, it swings right on past, passing Saint Nicholas Orthodox Church, Diamond Heights School, a recreation center, a shopping center, any number of new build-

19

ings, and Saint Aidan's Episcopal Church (which has a stunning
wall mural by Mark Adams) before it reaches Addison Street. The
Shepherd of the Hills Luthern Church is a good landmark to signal
your left turn off Diamond Heights Boulevard at Addison Street.

Park where you can. At the outset, notice the massive John F.
Shelley firehouse, home of Engine Company Number 26. Rockrise
and Watson were the architects for this big concrete monolith,
humorously labeled "the mayor's mansion" by its critics. In September of 1965 when the late mayor whom it honors was considering
buying a modest two-story house on nearby Everson Street, it made
page 4 of the morning *Chronicle*. It would have been a good invest-
ment. Comparable houses today routinely sell for $100,000 more
than Shelley considered paying twelve years ago. Vast as the view
from the firehouse is, firemen complain that despite its prizewinning
heating system, the interior is either too hot or too cold. Firehouses
don't welcome drop-in visitors, but group tours can be arranged to
see the building with a call to fire department headquarters.

Walk toward the fireplug on Addison Street and go into the
Walter A. Haas Park on the curving sidewalk nearest to it. Rain
greens the grassy areas almost overnight. On your right hand as you
walk north will be what park planners call phase one of the playground's evolution. The 2.15 acres planted and built up with berms
of earth and play equipment cost $266,000. On your left hand is
phase two, a bare hillside that demonstrates what most of this land
looked like before redevelopment of the 325-acre Diamond Heights
Redevelopment Project began in 1958. Local residents fought a
proposed fast food drive-in that would have taken the corner.
Philanthropist Haas, honorary chairman of the board of Levi Strauss
and a member of the Park Commission between 1958 and 1967,
donated $100,000 in 1975 to purchase the additional 33,000
square feet of land. It increases the acreage of the park to 3.718
acres. The second phase of construction is now complete.

Walk past the play apparatus, and soon the walk curves around
a slope that drops away sharply beyond sturdy benches, cleverly
designed with small built-in tables, ideal for chess games and intimate picnics. From the first clifftop bench, pause and assess the view
of Angel Island, downtown San Francisco, Berkeley, Yerba Buena
Island, the Bay Bridge, Potrero Hill, Mount Diablo, the South Bay,

and Bernal Heights. As you walk east, the view widens to reveal Mount Tamalpais on the left hand. San Bruno Mountain, with its stiff serpent of houses snaking erratically uphill and the perpetual red lights of the tower blinking, is on the right.

When you can take your eyes from the splendid panorama, notice that the tots sandpit you soon reach has an informal clover-leaf pattern, connecting three play areas. Look back when you are abreast of the little swinging bridge and there is Sutro Tower peering over your shoulder. Visible below is Billy Goat Hill, recently added to park property. Look up to see firehouse windows that could allow men on duty to spot a blaze before it is reported. The snapping noise you hear in this area is from firehouse flags. Fireman Jim O'Shea says in a year at the station four sets of flags are frazzled by the persistent wind. Gardeners for the park found that the wind also deposited their first efforts to plant seeds here elsewhere. That same wind may also make the air here cleanest in the city.

Come along this way morning or evening, and there may be joggers. Daytimes bring a regular coterie of mothers and small fry. When school lets out, skateboards, tricycles, and bikes appear, but the best time of all to look at the view is twilight. When there is a red sunset, evenglow often makes the Bank of America windows look like *The Towering Inferno*. Happily, a few minutes later, the city lights twinkle on below, as mellow as a Grandma Moses canvas.

4

"What makes walkers different from normal people?" This question has been put to me dozens of times. It is always a great temptation to answer flippantly that it is the world that has gone mad and walkers who are normal. I wouldn't be the first to say it.

By normal people, I presume motorists are meant. Since I'm also a motorist, my qualifications for answering could be considered objective. So here it is: The most obvious difference is that walkers are in closer touch with their environment. The world observed at three miles per hour through trees, as mankind on foot viewed it for at least ten thousand years, is not the blur viewed from behind the driver's wheel at sixty miles per hour.

Especially in the country, the walker enjoys all those rich distillations of day or night, sunshine or moonlight, windsong, stars, fog, rain, salt spray, water music. He hears the bird sing without frightening it, the whisper of trees; sees the rabbit jump without running over it; smells the flowers of spring and the freshly turned earth; perceives the wing of the Monarch butterfly.

He enjoys the changing textures in urban areas, the details of architecture, shopwindows, the human comedy. It isn't without reason that when we want to speak approvingly of a person, we still say, "He's got his feet on the ground."

Lafayette-Moraga Regional Recreational Trail

QUITE POSSIBLY THE best-used trail in the East Bay Regional Park District's 450 miles of trails doesn't run through a park at all. It runs along an old railroad right-of-way through the towns of Lafayette and Moraga.

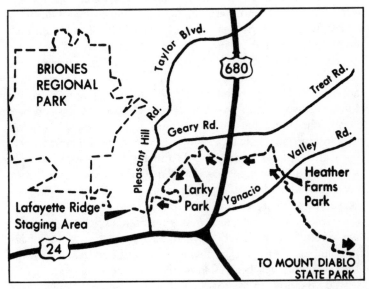

Not long ago, three dedicated East Bay walkers, Sylvia Bailes, Betty Boege, and Marie Rosenblatt invited me to take a walk with them along "our" trail. Continual enjoyment of the four-and-a-half-mile Lafayette-Moraga Regional Recreation Trail has given them a proprietary feeling about it. They are not alone in their appreciation of the trail. Approximately 120,000 people use the Lafayette end of the trail each year. Usage at the Moraga end, which includes a Gamefield exercise course, is so heavy two pairs of rings were worn out at one station in the first three years the trail was open.

"We'll meet you at the BART station," Sylvia said, and I was sold. Any trail handy to public transportation reveals good planning and so instantly goes up in my estimation.

23

To sample a section of this paragon of trails, transport yourself to Lafayette via BART. Once there, go to the south exit, known locally as "Kissing Lane" for the wives who drop and pick up their commuting husbands here with a fond spousal kiss. There is no parking on it. Walk east to the end of the cul-de-sac and take the few steps down. Go through the hiker's stile and in a moment you are at 999 Blanche Lane in front of a corporation yard for Contra Costa County Public Works Department. After passing Petar's and Flavio's restaurants, you soon emerge alongside Lafayette Sea Food Restaurant, whose outside crab pots are like a little bit of Fisherman's Wharf that has somehow strayed from San Francisco.

Bear left two blocks on Mount Diablo Boulevard, turning right alongside the Old Roundup Saloon, a brick building that started its career when Moraga Road fronting it was a logging route to the Moraga redwoods. Go past Lafayette's attractive library and bear left on School Street at the Dramateur's Theatre, housed in Lafayette's former town hall. In 1914 the brown-shingled landmark was built with a special "spring floor" to make dancing a pleasure. Its fame grew until people rode out from Berkeley and Oakland on special trains for dances. At various times the barny building has also served as library, church, and nursery school.

Look for the trailhead across from Stanley School. It goes in near 3464 School Street, marked by a barrier to automobiles. Tempting as it is to go right toward Topper Lane heading toward Moraga, for this walk bear left instead into deepest Lafayette.

You are now on the roadbed of the old Sacramento-Northern electric train, which made its last trip on February 28, 1957, a victim of the automotive industry. In its day, which started in 1918, the Sacramento-Northern was the nation's longest interurban line, running for nearly 180 miles between Oakland and Chico. The cars had red plush seats, luggage racks of brass, and natural polished wood interiors. Full course prime-rib dinners in the diner cost eighty-seven cents. The fare to ride the train was five cents.

As you swing around the curve with the trail, look underfoot for white arrows as you skirt Las Trampas Creek and approach the bridge over it. At the junction just past the blocky building, ignore the trail up Snake Hill and continue on the level. Soon you are passing Las Trampas School for the mentally retarded.

Once across Foye Street you are in one of the oldest sections of Lafayette. Some of the smaller houses began as summer cabins. Suburban backyards offer an insight into the life of their residents that once was available only to train passengers. At one point there is a tremendous bubble over a swimming pool, a trendy way to keep the water warm. Benches near a pair of tremendous pines offer a resting place. Mudwasps make free-form sculpture on the back of a house. Nearby, a "good-neighbor fence," which looks the same both fore and aft, with no wrong side, has been installed. A scarecrow in a blue parka seems to be waving at walkers from a vegetable garden. Cross Old Hawthorne Road and soon you reach an area where a spinney of fantastic big oaks gives an aura of permanence to the setting. Birds sing along the trail. Water bubbles as you near Walnut Creek.

Designed for bicycles and horsemen as well as walkers, the trail is forty to fifty feet wide in many portions, some of it on East Bay Municipal Utility District easements. EBMUD vehicles are the only ones permitted on the easement aside from wheelchairs and bicycles. The City of Lafayette, which took on the trail as a bicentennial project, and Moraga's Park and Recreation Authority contributed part of the funding to build the trail, with East Bay Regional Park District picking up the rest. The five-and-a-half-mile mark on the concrete path underfoot soon indicates the mileage from this point to Moraga. Ultimately the trail will connect three regional parks, Briones, Redwood, and Las Trampas Wilderness, as well as the two towns.

When you reach Reliez Station Road at Olympic Boulevard, you are at the formal beginning of the trail. For a return through the town of Lafayette, continue on Olympic to Pleasant Hill and bear left. At Diablo Boulevard, bear left again to reach BART.

Far pleasanter is to return the way that you came, enjoying the safe off-street removal from traffic as local walkers, joggers, schoolkids, commuters, shoppers, and toddlers have discovered to their delight. In actual usage, narrow as it is, the trail is a linear park. It is also a transportation corridor. "The city council thought it was creating a trail for fun," Sylvia Bailes told me. "It turns out to be the major route through town for walkers as well."

5

The San Francisco Bay Area often experiences a "false spring" for a week or two in winter, sometimes in January, more often in February.

In the 1950s, when ladies still wore hats, the false spring was a signal to put on a romantic leghorn straw decorated with flowers or ribbons or a chic boater, change to lighter colors, and put on a pair of white gloves when you went downtown for Monday lunch at the Saint Francis Hotel. False spring brought daphne to the downtown flower stalls and to the lapels of men's business suits.

Today this unseasonable winter warm spell is noticeable on the beaches and in the Castro District where young men bare their torsos to the sunshine. The first time I passed the extraordinary serpentine outcropping below Daphne's Funeral Home, there were a dozen workingmen leaning against it bare-chested, enjoying their lunches in the sunshine of false spring.

Rock Concert

SERPENTINE IS THE state rock of California. Most of us recognize it as a greenish rock so smooth it is silky. The geologists, however, take a closer look. They believe serpentine originally was part of the Earth's mantle that has been squeezed upward from the sea bottom along the great shear or subduction zones of the Pacific. At that time, about 200 million years ago, according to Dr. Clyde Wahrhaftig, professor of geology at the University of California, Berkeley, "the rock that is now serpentine consisted of entirely different minerals — mainly the minerals olivine and pyroxene, which are compounds of iron, magnesium, silicon, and oxygen that lack water."

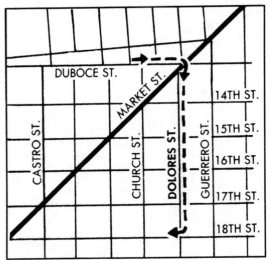

Today serpentine can be several different things, among them bastite, which are tiny flashing grains of a shiny material, and "slickentite," which swells and turns to paste under pressure when it gets wet — often the cause of landslides in California.

Don't rush right out to see if the rocks in your driveway roadcut look like paste. Instead consider a walk to see the serpentine rock wall that Dr. Wahrhaftig has described as "the most beautiful and informative outcrop of serpentine in San Francisco." The American Geophysical Union, which annually holds its winter meetings in San Francisco, makes a pilgrimage to inspect it. Many of its members believe that the rock face is so special it merits becoming a city

27

monument park. They are not the only ones. So do many residents, including Marian Isaacs of Citizens for Parks and Recreation.

To make it easy for visiting geophysicists to discover this re-markable outcropping by public transportation, the AGU published a richly illustrated paper by Dr. Wahrhaftig entitled "A Streetcar to Subduction." Its cover shows a streetcar about to be crushed at the nose by a fault. As long as the supply lasts, it is available free by writing the AGU, 2000 Florida Avenue NW, Washington, D.C. 20009. Write for this 27-page pamphlet and discover the classroom that is San Francisco.

The J and N streetcars (and the Fillmore trolley bus) all stop near this incredible rock face. Two blocks away, the eastern en-trance to the Sunset Tunnel has been swallowing streetcars into the 4,232-foot passageway under Buena Vista Park since 1928. So the ideal way to begin this walk is by public transportation.

Get off any car at the Duboce or Church Street Station and walk to the junction of those two streets. There it is on the north side of Duboce, stretching from Church to Webster streets, an excavated natural rock wall as pretty as an old Chinese scroll, with massive rocks that seem to be laid at a slant even a master stonemason could not equal. Slickentite is what seems to be the mortar. Boughs of greenery above are in the garden of the Daphne Funeral Home.

"We have to thank Nicholas Daphne for making such an aesthetically pleasing and educational stone wall," Dr. Wahrhaftig told me enthusiastically as he showed me around this fantastic rock face, "and especially for making it accessible to people to look at."

Take a good look while you are here. To geologists "an impor-tant feature of this outcrop is the gentle eastward dip of all the shear planes and the more tabular blocks." Before the theory of plate tectonics, it was believed that all serpentine was squeezed upward along vertical faults parallel to the San Andreas. This, like several other outcroppings, reveals that the upward squeezing was not ver-tical, but dipped gently eastward. If you have a powerful hand lens, scrape with a needle point one of the shiny spots in a piece of the rock lying underfoot. It will fluff up like feathers. Asbestos! Most of the asbestos of commerce is mined from serpentine.

The area Dr. Wahrhaftig would like to see as a monument park would be from the outcropping to the street, sometimes preempted by Muni for construction storage, used during the holiday season as a Christmas tree lot, and pressed into service as a parking lot otherwise. "A little judicious planting, a low hedge, and a couple of benches could transform it into one of San Francisco's bright spots," Dr. Wahrhaftig believes.

When you have examined this remarkable glimpse of the real subterranean San Francisco, walk on Duboce to Market Street where the New Mint building, a monumental fortress on its hundred-foot-high summit, stands on a trimmed-off stump of hill. The reinforced concrete and granite building designed by Gilbert Stanley Underwood was supposed to be impregnable to burglars when it was completed in 1937. Two weeks after its dedication, a pair of high school students on a lark broke into it. Turn north on Buchanan Street to see that the rear entrance on Hermann is an inviting expanse of glass. The gun tower farther down the wall is the real fortification. Medallions high on the building should interest coin buffs. They represent every coin issued by the United States until the time of completion of the building.

The Mint also sits on serpentine, part of a serpentine belt that crosses San Francisco from Fort Point to Hunter's Point. Although the exposure at Daphne's is more accessible, more photogenic, and more instructive, it is possible to see in the clumsily hewn rock underpinning of the Mint that shearing and veining dip to the northeast.

From the Mint, cross Market Street with the light and walk southwestward on it, noting on Dolores Street's boulevard strip what has been called the finest equestrian statue in the city, the California Volunteers Memorial, created in 1903 by Douglas Tilden. Then continue on Market until you are abreast of Reservoir Street. Pause and look through this one-block-long street bounded by supermarket parking to discern a charming terminal vista that ends at the austere, brick, Gothic revival Saint Francis Lutheran Church. It was called Saint Angsar's in 1907 when it was built for a congregation largely made up of Danish seamen.

Backtrack to Dolores and stroll down it to reach at 16th Street, Mission San Francisco de Asis, a two-hundred-year-old monument and the oldest man-made structure San Francisco memorializes. Built in its present design in 1782, it was restored under the careful ministrations of Willis Polk in 1920. The two-story front with a balcony and stepped columns is very different from most of California's twenty-one missions. Get there at the right time and you can still hear next door at the basilica the mass which Fr. Francisco Palou, founder of the local mission we miscall Dolores, celebrated on this site on June 29, 1776.

The name comes to us from Laguna de Nuestra Señora de Dolores, a lake that stood on the site of what is now Mission High School, two blocks farther along. Dolores Park is just across the street. Or if the bucolic is not your dish of tea, bear right on Seventeenth to reach that jumping quarter known as Castro Street. There, you are on your own. As Dr. Wahrhaftig warns, in a geologic pun, "Don't be subduced."

February

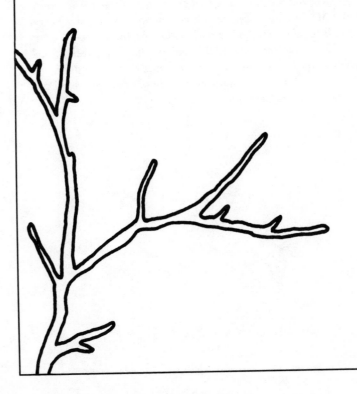

6

We don't have woodchucks in the Bay Area, so the groundhog never sees his shadow here on Candlemas Day.

Badgers are Bay Area burrowing animals about the same size as the woodchuck. Alas, the last badger known to be living wild in San Francisco was beaten to death in a chicken coop by a man in the Sunset District around 1957. We don't allow the raising of chickens in coops in San Francisco any longer either.

For the ritual Groundhog Day observer who wants to substitute a little badger watching, there are still badgers in some of the less populated areas of the nine Bay Area counties. My favorite colony of badgers inhabits the slope between the Bear Valley trailhead parking lot and the horse-breeding stables. A walker can find them along the Woodpecker Trail. They are shy animals who come out at dawn and dusk, and I wonder how long they will stay there after the new Point Reyes Visitors Center is completed.

Kehoe Beach

My life is like a stroll upon the beach/ As near the ocean's edge as I can go.

Henry David Thoreau

AFTER A LONG rainy winter, most of us are yearning to get out on the beaches. Some of those beaches, alas, are inaccessible because of slides, washouts, road damage, and such from the rainy winter of '82. The environmentalist side of me, which believes the best favor you can do a place is not to build a road to it, says, "Hurrah," for it means the marshhawks' nests will be undiscovered, the moonsnails go undisturbed, and the mountain lion left alone in its haunts. The weaker, pleasure-loving side, which enjoys sun, sand, and surf as much as the next sybarite, is a little annoyed at being inconvenienced by the elements. Fortunately Kehoe Beach, my favorite on Tomales Point, survived intact and the roads to it are in good shape.

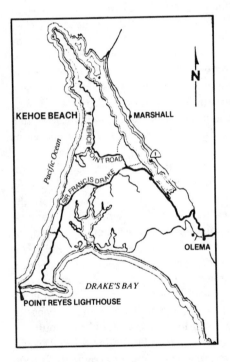

For this walk pack your picnic, and if you are interested in things botanical, bring a copy of Roxanna Ferris's *Flowers of the Point Reyes Peninsula,* for this is a haven of wildflowers. Then transport yourself north from San Francisco via Highway 101 and Sir Francis Drake Boulevard to Olema. Check into the headquarters of the Point Reyes National Seashore about a mile west to pick up a

33

trail map and the latest information on weather. Then continue
north if the day is fair, past the hard-hit town of Inverness to Pierce
Point Road. Local jokers sometimes twist the road sign, but it should
indicate that Pierce Point Road goes north. Follow it north. Kehoe
Beach is exactly six miles beyond the junction (and two miles north
of Abbott's Lagoon). A sign, a hiker's stile adjoining a ranch gate, a
comfort station, and a trash can all mark the entrance. Park where
you can along the road.

Go through the stile and look immediately for a single cowpath
that goes uphill on your right. A carpet of the fragrant Johnny-Tuck,
one of the nine species of owl's-clover, or *orthocarpus*, that grows
on Point Reyes, had covered this slope when I walked here one
February. As the trail swings around a low hill, bear left with the
fenceline. Cows pastured here are part of the herd of dairy farmer
James Kehoe. They are gentle animals, but if they stop and stare,
say "huh huh" loudly as farmers do and they usually move off.

On your left the two low hills sport leatherfern thick as hair
above rock faces carved by the wind into the lacy form known as
tafoni.

When you reach the corner of the fence, bear slightly left on
the cowpath that leads toward the next low hill. Within fifty feet, a
first glimpse of the blue Pacific will come into view as dramatically
as the raising of a theater curtain. Resist the temptation to plunge
down the valley toward the nine-foot trail visible below. Instead, for
this walk continue on the cowpath to the rocky crest of the hill. The
path winds through Douglas iris, California poppies, checkerbloom,
baby-blue-eyes, Phacelia, blue-eyed grass, cream cups, and golden
fields becoming more rich in wildflowers the closer one comes to
the sea. When the ground beneath your feet seems to become
chalky rock, much like the paloverde stone imported from Southern
California for use in rock gardens, descend from this colorful crown
of flowers on the left until you reach the tangle of cowpaths below.
Follow them around to the right. The path soon descends through
waist high lupine to the beach.

The wildflowers on the right beside the little creek the path follows, or the sea itself, may be so beguiling a first-time visitor could
easily lose the way. As soon as you reach the beach, look for a large,
immovable landmark and fix it in your memory. Sometimes flotsam
and jetsam dot the beach, other times it is swept clean.

Walk north to explore this beach. Shortly you will be under a gorgeous cliff tilted at a 45-degree angle. Water filtering from above covers the face with wildflowers and fills the shallow cave at its base with miniature stalactites and stalagmites of alum, bitter and styptic.

Continue north to find another geologic change, a granite dike intruded into the sandstone, evidence of volcanic activity millions of years ago when this peninsula stood offshore of Los Angeles. When you are parallel to the sea stacks of offshore rocks, turn back. Don't let yourself get cut off by a winter high tide.

After you have sunned, picnicked, beachcombed, or played Frisbee to your heart's content, return to the place where the trail descended to the beach, but don't climb up it. Look instead for a route over the big dune that sometimes blocks the broader ranch road to the beach. The road lies about a hundred feet south of the path through the wildflowers.

Climb the dune to the road and you are immediately in the midst of a kitchen midden, or Indian mound. One hundred thirteen Indian sites have been identified on the Point Reyes Peninsula, and archeologists exploring Kehoe Beach believe it was the site of an Indian village for more than three thousand years.

Bear, elk, wildcat, mountain lion, antelope, wolf, coyote, pheasant, black grouse, wild geese, pigeons, turkeys, and crested partridge were all once common here. Old accounts say Indians often slew elk by driving them over the cliffs. Tule elk, incidentally, have been reestablished in the National Seashore farther north, on the tip of Pierce Point.

Follow the lagoon back toward the road. Red-winged blackbirds will fly from the tule rush as you walk. Hawks may soar overhead. Canaries dart. A turtle ambles across the path. Point Reyes may be nicknamed "The Solemn Land," but on a sunny day, the way to Kehoe and back can seem like the Elysian Fields.

7

The young plum tree in our garden, which gets more sun than its older parent, usually blooms the first week in February, a glorious cascade of white flowers, the first fruiting branches of spring. Each year since we have owned our house on Russian Hill, the parent tree has given us a good crop of little red-skinned yellow fruit, bland to eat out of hand but tart made up in jam.

Winifred Allen of Belvedere told me long ago that it was the Mirabelle, a wild plum that originated in France, and that it has no enemies but man. For this reason, she said, Luther Burbank used the Mirabelle as a parent in many of his plum hybridizations. It also seems to be the plum the Chinese use for making dried salt plums, those white-rimed, hard morsels called *see muy* that the children of Chinatown love. One year we had five little Chinese girls raiding the tree. If ever I am not spry enough to pick up the plums, there is the way I can distribute the fruit without waste, for the Chinese are every bit as frugal as the Scots.

My Scottish genes rebel against wasting a single plum. So each year I have made plum jam. The tree is generous. There is always plenty of jam to give my sons, my neighbors, my editors, my film crew, and any number of friends.

One of the friends with whom I shared plums was Imogen Cunningham. The tree seemed to foster our friendship. While Imo lived, her Green Street house number was the same as our Greenwich Street number, to the eternal confusion of the Post Office. When she remailed my missent mail, she usually jotted a note on the back of the envelope about some recent column I'd written.

When our sons were young, they hand-carried her missent mail to her, together with whatever was in bloom or bearing in the garden. Plum blossoms went in the spring with her mail, fruit in the fall. Imo was also a jam maker. She claimed the Scots had originated the art. In my storage shelves, there are still a few empty jars with her neatly typed labels on them. I also recall the inevitable time she said to me, "Margot, don't send me any plums for jam this year. My canning days are over."

"Oh Imo," I protested, "surely you're not going to leave us yet?"

Yes," she said, very matter-of-factly, "I've made up my mind to go soon. My work is done and I'm tired."

And of course she did go within a few weeks. It was a happy friendship, shared on many levels, but I miss her most when the plum trees are in bloom.

Edgewood Avenue, San Francisco

THE LACE-EDGED VALENTINE called Edgewood Avenue in San Francisco bursts into pagan pink glory each year one mild day irrespective of the Weather Bureau, the vernal equinox, the groundhog, or the calendar. Walk along this two-block ledge on the edge of the greenbelt then, and winter is dead as a dinosaur.

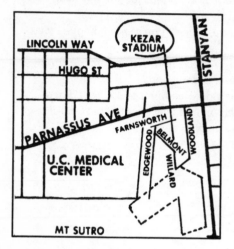

See it in bloom with sunshine filtering through the pale pink plum blossoms onto the red brick of the paving below and you will never forget this double lane of stately old houses. It becomes a red-carpeted aisle transmuted into timeless beauty fit for an emirate, a head of state, a potentate. Through the alchemy of color it could be a backdrop for Makarova in tutu pirouetting on the sunlit bricks. Kiri Te Kanawa bursting into "Cosi fan Tutte" would seem appropriate.

Farnsworth Lane is the special secret place to come upon this remarkable spun sugar fantasy. Many vantage points look down on a vista. Farnsworth Lane looks up.

To reach it, get off the No. 6 Parnassus or No. 43 Masonic Muni bus on Parnassus at Willard Street. Walk uphill on Willard about eighty feet. Farnsworth steps slip off uphill inconspicuously between two short squat obelisks—looking exceedingly private. They are public. Start up them and you climb to an unexpectedly green world of treetops. The hectic street below and the bustling University of California Medical Center nearby recede magically out of sight and sound as you ascend.

At the apex, step out into the roadbed of Farnsworth Lane, which forms a short platform at the foot of Edgewood. Look uphill.

When the *prunus pissardi* and *prunus bleiriana* trees that line either side are in bloom, Edgewood is a love song to every beholder.

At any time of year Edgewood is handsome. This is no accident. Families whose homes face on Edgewood planted the purple-leaved plums because they liked the color interplay when this was an unpaved red rock road, part of a horse trail that led up into the hills of Rancho San Miguel. The trees cost six bits apiece and were planted ten feet apart at the urging of Rose Levy, a dedicated gardener who lived on the east side of the street. A strong neighborhood association fought long ago to resist paving of any kind. Red brick was the happy compromise. When the sun picks out the rich pattern of the brick in counterpoint with the redder leaves or the pale pink blossoms, who can doubt their wisdom.

A former newspaperwoman, the late Fran Grubb, who grew up here, once wrote me that it was a joyous place for a childhood. "Our garage was a stable with a hayloft where we kids created and performed in plays. Admission 25 pins or a nickel. . . . In the middle of Edgewood lived Mrs. Philippine 'Schotzie' Retenmeyer. To a child's eyes, she was a real beauty. She owned the Samarkand Ice Cream Company, but we loved her for her glamorous appearance and charm, not only for the ice cream, though she was generous with it and it was delectable. Her house had a circular wrought iron stairway, which was most unusual."

Another remarkable house on the street was that of Meyer and Rose Levy. "Each room was decorated in the manner of a different country, a Turkish sitting room, Chinese living room, American Indian play room, Spanish garage and so on."

It was something of an artists' and writers' area as well as a doctors' row. Agnes Danforth Hewes, who wrote historical novels for young people; Hearst columnist Elsie Robinson; Margaret Parton, author of *Laughter on the Hill*; artist Rosebud Preddy; sculptor Chris Mueller, Sr.; and actor Holbrook Blinn were among the talented residents.

Then as now Edgewood had a special world of nocturnal wildlife in Sutro Forest, which hugs the avenue on the south side as part of the park department's internal greenbelt, and on the west is where Ishi the Indian made his final home. The last free coyote trapped in San Francisco came down from the ever-diminishing Sutro Forest in 1927 and was caught on the lawn of what was then called the Affiliated Colleges. Raccoons and skunks are still nighttime visitors. On hot days, a few of the San Francisco garter snakes, an endangered species, come out to warm themselves in Edgewood gardens.

Stroll up the street to its end, for this is a place for leisurely perambulation. Probably nothing closer than Prunus Walk at Dumbarton Oaks, Washington, D.C., has quite the same heady exuberant pink ambiance.

To get the fullest pleasure, walk up the shady side of the street to the tall stand of eucalyptus. This greenbelt area is so lively with growing things it could hardly be called a dead end, though there is no through road here for cars. The sure-footed may want to essay the footpath through the greenbelt. By bearing consistently right, the path through the forest will bring one out at a U.C. parking lot. Downhill through trees immediately behind the houses makes a loop back to Farnsworth Lane.

More entrancing is to return on the sunny side of the street three-quarters of the way. Bear right on Belmont to see how the plum tree persuasion has expanded. Bear right again on Willard to Woodland to enjoy more of this sunny pocket on the eastern slope of Mount Sutro. Woodland returns to Parnassus. (This route can be used as an approach for those unable to climb steps.)

Inspired by the effect of Edgewood Avenue's annual two-week Valentine, residents on adjacent streets have also chosen the purple-leaved plum as their street trees. Although some of the homes are more modest than on doctors' row, the pink of the trees in bloom gives a festive air to the whole community.

It is an area so neighborly it annually closes off streets for a block party. Like their neighbors on Edgewood, citizens along Belmont and Woodland believe that beauty is not only its own reward, but like liberty, well worth the extra effort.

8

Two Northern California events sometimes happen in the rain. Both of them attract thousands of tourists. One is the Crosby Golf Tournament at Pebble Beach. The other is the Chinese New Year Parade in San Francisco. Golfers and parade watchers don't seem to care. They come rain or shine.

The axiom in San Francisco is "If you don't like the weather, wait three days." For a walker, it may be only a question of waiting three minutes for a change. Or of transporting oneself a mile or two away. Like the Mission District, Chinatown weather is better than more westerly parts of the City.

For tourists, Chinatown also offers an instant mini-vacation. It is often the highlight of a San Francisco visit, especially for the food. One time I served as a "sightseeing expert" at a dermatological convention in the new Moscone Center. The name of a good Chinese restaurant was the request almost everyone made. San Francisco has several hundred of these, covering thirty-two separate Oriental cuisines at last count, so this is not as easy to answer as one might expect. Since we also had a restaurant expert at the convention booth, I passed these queries on to him.

One persistent doctor came back, asking me what he should order at the Chinese restaurant.

"Didn't you ask the food critic?" I asked him.

"Oh, yes," said the doctor, "but I wanted a second opinion."

Chinatown

IN OLD CHINESE calligraphy, the character "to walk" originally resembled a crossroad. Now it looks more like two road signs, according to Gordon Lew, publisher of the bilingual weekly, *East-West*, who thinks, "The slanted one was probably damaged by a near-sighted motorist who wanted to read the sign but was a little slow on the brakes."

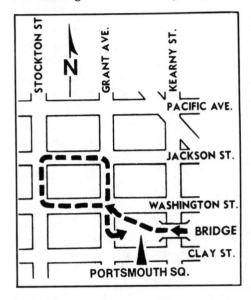

Logically enough, the character for pedestrian is "walking person"; for a planet, "walking star"; and for a priest, "walking feet," referring to the traveling monks of old China. "Walk," however, also means a business firm, possibly because such firms were destinations for a walk. So a bank is a "money walk," and of course every Chinese hopes the bank won't. Because the thunder god is walking around, in Chinese the word is actually "walking thunder." The folklore is that you can tell from the loudness whether the thunder god is walking toward or away from you.

Gordon Lew also tells a great walking story: "Once someone asked a wise man, 'If a man comes up and says there is a pot of gold somewhere, should I ignore him or should I hurry there to find out if he's right?'

" 'If you ignore him, you may miss something valuable,' said the wise man. 'If you rush over, you may be disappointed when you find there is no gold. So why don't you try WALKING there?'

" 'But if there's no gold, wouldn't I still be disappointed?' " To find the wise man's answer, see the end of this walk.

43

Meantime, to begin it, get off the No. 83 Pacific or the No. 30 Stockton Muni bus in "Little Hong Kong," as Chinatown's busiest crossroads, Broadway and Stockton, have been nicknamed. Make your way along Stockton Street, bearing south. Often it teems with shoppers six abreast, but traditionally the Chinese spend the first days of the New Year in family seclusion.

At the outset, notice Acme Center, whose frozen specialties are visible through the window, so you needn't enter if they don't have what you seek. As with many Hong Kong shops, it is half the size of an ordinary shop. Head south on the east side of Stockton for this first block, to get a distant perspective on the fish, fruit, pastry, vegetables, and meat shops. The fronts of many open totally to the street and their wares spill out. Usually aswarm with people of both genders, carefully selecting each kingfish, each bitter melon, sometimes each water chestnut or each long bean. From this aspect, the ubiquitous shopping bags sometimes seem to be pulling the people, rather than the opposite.

At Pacific, cross to the west side of the street and join the throng just for the fun of it. "Color was everywhere. A thousand little notes of green and yellow, of vermilion and sky blue assaulted the eye," Frank Norris wrote of Chinatown in *Blix*. "Here it was a doorway, there a vivid glint of cloth or hanging, here a huge scarlet sign lettered with gold, and there a kaleidoscopic effect in the garments of the passersby." The melange is still the same. Piles of oranges, pomelos, and tangerines; red and gold paper streamers; flowering tree branches; kumquat and azalea plants on sale for Chinese New Year intensify an already lively bourse. New shops, such as Kay Wah Pastry, the Bon Vivant, Lun Wah and Sun Sang markets, interspersed with such older ones as On Ning Tong Herb Shop, Wing Fat, or Fong Creamery tell the story of the resurgence that has followed the passage in 1965 of the Immigration and Nationality Act amendments. Chinatown, almost bursting at the seams with new energy, has some of the ambiance of a boom town. Big, green potted plants with congratulatory red streamers traditionally indicate a new business.

As you reach Mandarin Towers, Chinatown's first high-rise apartment building, you are nearing the portion of Stockton that publicist Charlie Leong calls The Street of Celestial Wisdom because of the schools, churches, civic groups, and Chinese institutions centered on it. The Presbyterian Church in Chinatown, which dates from 1907 at this site, has the largest tree on the street. Saint Mary's Catholic Center across the street is also an old-timer.

At Clay Street you reach the Kong Chow Building, which houses the new post office. If it is between 1 and 4 P.M., go into the discreet foyer and take the elevator to the Taoist Kong Chow Temple on the fourth floor, where seventeen gods sit on the altar. Chief among them is Kwan Ti, god of war and peace. Recreated after more than a hundred years on Pine Street, the temple, designed by architect Ed Sue, also has a fascinating view of the cityscape. Inspect the altar and its offerings, smile at the toy motorcycle that stands alongside the god's horse among other pets, note the ancestor's room behind the main altar and observe the fireplace for sending prayer papers to heaven, then go out on the Stockton Street balcony. Unexpectedly, both Angel and Yerba Buena islands are visible. So are both levels of the Stockton Street tunnel. Next door, the Chinese Six Companies is informally known as the city hall of Chinatown. Central Chinese High School and Kuoming Tong are other institutions in the block visible from the balcony.

If you are game for more walking, Grant Avenue, Chinatown's main street and the tourist trinket trail, is one block downhill. Loop back on it to your point of origin for this walk. The wise man's answer, incidentally, is, "If there is no gold, you may enjoy your walk, which will always bring you good health for good health is better than gold."

9

Not long ago Richard Hart and I went for a walk around the San Francisco Zoo with our Evening Magazine *film crew to see what was gnu. Zoo director Saul Kitchener showed us the Wolf Woods, the Musk Ox Meadow, the beautiful old Dentzel carousel and the Gorilla World, all of which have been renovated as part of the master plan that will ultimately make the entire zoo much more woodsy and natural.*

He also told us a surprising story. He had been invited to go as a consultant to a major Texas city that was planning to create its own version of Gorilla World. Saul described the educational panels that are located on the periphery of San Francisco's prizewinning Gorilla World. The Texans became alarmed. There was no way they were going to tell the story of evolution at their zoo.

Around the Zoo

IN XANADU, WHAT did Marco Polo do? He went to the Zoo. King Hud of Liang and King Wan kept up with Kublai Khan. They too, Mencius tells us, each had a zoo. Hatshepsut, Hannibal, and

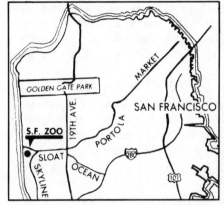

Shalmanazar II each kept a zoo. And so, fellow citizen, do I and you. When all else palls, what do we do? What else? We go to the Zoo.

When spring has almost sprung, there is a great deal new to see at the San Francisco Zoological Gardens. From aodad to zebra, the primal urge is stirring. Usually there is a new baby hippo, and other fledglings, kits, cubs, calves, and pups are due to struggle onto this turf any moment. The turf itself is greener and more gardenlike than in the past, with concrete disappearing in favor of leaf and stem. If you haven't been out to zoo for a while, it is time to consider a walk around this classic.

To make this walk, consider an approach through the area zoo director Saul Kitchener considers the prettiest, with a look at Wolf Woods en route. The No. 18 and No. 10 buses go right to the main gate at 45th Avenue. The L streetcar comes within a block. (There is also plenty of peripheral parking for those addicted to their own wheels.)

Pay up your two dollar fee (with a nod to Jarvis-Gann as you unzip your purse), go past the San Francisco Zoological Society gift shop, which now occupies Mother's House, and bear left at the playing field. At the next junction, take a right toward Monkey Island, whose resident colony of sixty or so spider monkeys was born here. To the constant delight of San Franciscans, it has been thriving since the 1940s, shortly after the island was completed by the WPA. Like people, many of the monkeys seem to like the rain and perform outside whatever the weather. Bear left and make a quarter circle around the island, then take the walkway that goes off toward the waterfowl lake, noticing among others if you will "a curious bird, that red, long-legged flamingo, a water bird, a gawky bird, a singular bird by jingo" as Lewis Gaylord Clark described it.

As you cross the little stone bridge, if you are a birdwatcher, look for a belted kingfisher or a black-crowned night heron, who often fish a stickleback out of the little stream. Like the resident pair of red-shouldered hawks who sometimes take a pigeon off the monkey cages, these wildlings know a safe hunting ground when they find it.

Bear left away from the aviary for the moment, and circle uphill to find Wolf Woods, where a bright and curious trio of timberwolves check out all comers on the path. Worth a look is the explanatory kiosk nearby that exonerates in simulated headlines and news copy much of the so-called wolflike behavior mistakenly attributed to wolves. One of the columns purports to be by the well-known columnist "Herb Canid."

After you have discovered how interesting these misunderstood animals are, return downhill to the aviary and go in. Once inside birds will be all about you, including the baby blue crowned pigeon, whose hairdo is rather like Einstein's. "We've had grand success breeding birds in this setting," Kitchener says, "including the nene goose of Hawaii, which was almost extinct, and the Rothschilds mynah bird of Bali." As you near the exit, look up into the light fixture where the red-cheeked bulbul nests—a mere handful of twigs and feathers.

Just outside the door are the California sea lions and harbor seals. New babies arrive here annually in June and July. Bear right at the polar bears, cross the creek again, and there you are at a grassy meadow, a favorite for picnicking, and behind it, the gala gold umbrellas of the recently refurbished Zoo Cafe. Swing past it to come upon a stunning scene for which our zoo is world famous, a meadow where Asiatic axis deer, black buck, and antelope browse beyond a long border of rockroses.

At the mall the elephant house, known among zoologists for its vast colony of bats that hangs out here too, faces the lion house across a reflecting pool. Bear left shy of it to swing around the hoofed animals, including the waterbuck, which seems to have a target on its derriere. Although it looks as though it was designed as an aid to amateurs on safari, the target actually helps protect the waterbuck by concealing him in the brush. The smaller animals are the little barking deer, or muntjac. Continue on to see the baby black rhino, born December 8, 1979. He is the fourth for Papa Stonewall, son of Stonewall II, grandson of Rhinestone and brother of Flint Stone. Stroll on a few more yards to see the capybara, who has a scent gland on his nose, the better, perhaps, to smell himself. This big rodent was a gift to the zoo from PUC czar Dick Sklar.

The fun at the zebra pen is to look at the stripes as though they were fingerprints. No two zebras are ever identical. Look for the tree here where the crowned cranes roost, even as they do in Africa.

If Peter Matthiessen's unusual quest for the snow leopard left you thinking you might never see one of these rare animals, take a good look at a nearby cage. The snow leopards like San Francisco's weather so well they breed here. So do the reticulated giraffes, the Colobus monkeys, which look like they were designed by Cecil Beaton for a production of *My Fair Lady*, the musk ox, and any number of other jeopardized species.

If the zoo doesn't seem to be curried to within an inch of its walls, it's because there is an attempt to naturalize it. Plants growing near cages, for example, are often food plants, placed to give the nearby resident a treat to grab. Others are planted to soften the old stark walls, pits, and ledges.

As you near the familiar gorilla cages, look to your left. In the area where the miniature railroad had been a longtime favorite, there are now two handsome additions. One of them is a big meadow surrounding a lake, where walkers can stroll over the musk oxen browsing below; the other is a half-acre tropical paradise for gorillas, the largest in any zoo in the world. Both are designed with ramps and overlooks to bring the walker as close as safely possible to the animals. The miniature railroad will be reinstalled with a longer ride.

If you want to adopt an animal, stop in the Zoo Society's trailer, hard by. Fifteen dollars takes a llama, $25 a liontailed macaque, $500 a Barbary ape or Laysan teal duck, $2,000 a black jaguar, or $10,000 a grizzly or a gorilla. You don't get to take him home—just know that he'll be cared for here as your very own.

March

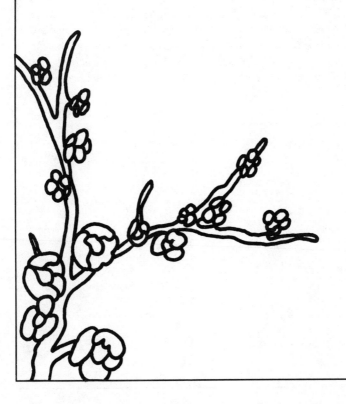

10

"The hounds of Spring are hot on Winter's traces" is a line from a popular song lifted from Swinburne that comes to mind when March winds howl in our fireplace chimney. The Bay Area may not have snow as the East Coast and Midwest do, but we certainly get March winds. These are not trade winds. They are westerlies. Sometimes they leave the air so sparkling clear the roads on Mount Tamalpais or on Mount San Bruno seem to be etched in drypoint. Looking out of a window at them, a walker yearns to be out, afoot and light-hearted.

It was on such a day that I first went for a walk in Pacifica. Unpretentious Pacifica has many of the qualities that gave "crazy owld, daisy owld" Telegraph Hill its livability early on. By the year 2000 artists and novelists will probably be discovering it. Twenty years later, so will the haut monde.

San Pedro Valley County Park, Pacifica

GOING OUT, I found, was really going in," John Muir once wrote. He meant, of course, going into that complex eco-system of which Man is essentially part. A great new place to understand it is the Valley View Trail in San Pedro Valley County Park, a thousand-acre jewel dropped like a scarf on the Coast Range. Located in Pacifica's Linda Mar area along two forks of San Pedro Creek abutting the San Francisco water-shed lands on Whiting and Fifield ridges, it may well become an important entry point for the south-ern section of the Golden Gate National Recreation Area.

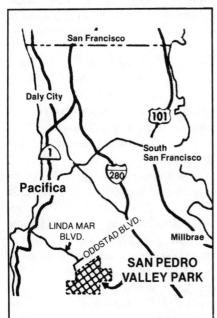

Steelhead still come up San Pedro Creek to spawn. A bobcat family ranges the upper reaches of its steep canyon sides. Red-tailed hawks soar overhead. If there is sun anywhere along the coastside, one is likely to find it here. Valley View Trail, a footpath on the San Pedro canyon's northeastern slope, gives a broadening look at the burgeoning Linda Mar and Park Pacifica communities with each ten-foot rise, then swoops down into a little wilderness to make a 2½-mile loop from the valley floor to the canyon heights. Well enough designed to make the gradual climb seem easy, it can be traversed by the average walker in a pleasant two hours.

To make this walk, transport yourself south from San Francisco fifteen miles via Route 280 and the Cabrillo Highway, Route 1. Turn east on Linda Mar Boulevard and drive uphill to Oddstad Boulevard, which crosses Linda Mar like a T. Bear right on Oddstad about a hundred feet, and turn into the park at Rosita Road. Pay your two dollar parking fee, and find a place to park near those odd supports that fill the adjoining field, all that is left of a former landmark here, the architecturally spectacular Saint Peter's Church, which disintegrated not long ago from a terminally leaky roof. Parishioners now meet in less lofty quarters visible to the left and deserve a word of thanks for their persistence. Without them, this beautiful valley would not be a park.

Put on your lug-soled boots, then look for the farthest trailhead in the northeast corner of the lot. Cross the bridge over the south fork of San Pedro Creek, pausing to look for fingerlings if it is late enough in the month, and bear left. The picnic tables and rest rooms stand on land that grew pumpkins, squash, and artichokes not long ago. Roses and periwinkle along the creekside are remnants of the Weiler Ranch, which farmed this valley last.

The second bridge you cross spans the middle fork of San Pedro Creek. Fish population inventories conducted by the California Department of Fish and Game indicate that of 125,000 eggs laid on the unsilted redds of San Pedro Creek by a scant 30 female steelheads to reach these gravelly shallows, fewer than 3 percent of the 2,500 young fry to reach the sea survive to return. "We hope to see an increase in fish," Ranger Monica Michaels told me, "but any little catastrophe, such as a fire in Linda Mar, that released chemicals into the storm drains or a single barrel of spilled solvent, could wipe out the total population."

The brick building on the left is the North Coast County Water District purification plant. Cross the Weiler Ranch Trail, a nine-foot-wide gravel road, alongside it and look for the Valley View Trail sign on the uphill side. A two-foot-wide footpath, it takes off uphill on the slope overlooking the grassy green meadow.

No one knows exactly where the followers of Captain Gaspar de Portola made their two-day camp alongside San Pedro Creek in November of 1774, but certainly the scouting party first to see San Francisco Bay had a glimpse of this canyon as they climbed to Sweeney Ridge. The Portola party, incidentally, walked overland from Baja California. They never *landed* in Pacifica no matter what erroneous signs along Highway 1 may mislead you to believe.

As you climb, the nearer homes visible are in Park Pacifica development, with the old Linda Mar neighborhood, one of nine villages incorporated into the growing megopolis known as Pacifica, coming into view a little higher. Most of the area in San Pedro Valley west of Highway 1 at Linda Mar Boulevard was a large seaside lagoon a scant quarter century ago.

San Pedro Mountain, elevation 1,050 feet, is the eminence to the south nearest the sea. Montara Mountain, whose North Peak is 1,825 feet and has the radio repeaters on it, is visible directly across the canyon. What seems to be a crack coming down from North Peak is actually Brooks Falls, a Bridal Veil-style waterfall at its best in rainy springtimes.

When you reach the broad Crest Trail, a firebreak, cross it and stay with the Valley View Trail, which almost diminishes to a cowpath here. Be alert to cross the firebreak twice more as Valley View Trail heads inland. Douglas iris, ceanothus, and coyote brush grow here and the bright eyed may spot the Mission Bells fritillaria. Ferd Simon, of Pacificans United to Save the Hills, or PUSH as it is locally known, conducted me on this walk and looks forward to a time when a side trail will connect Pedro Valley Park with the Portola Discovery Trail on Sweeney, the next ridge north.

Soon the trail plunges downward through chaparral. Before rounding the first switchback, look west for a great panorama of the Pacific, defined by Pedro Point on the south, Rockaway and Mori's Point on the north. The grassy meadow below is Middle Valley, to be used this summer for day camping. When you reach the bench almost at the valley floor, you are once again at the Weiler Ranch Road Trail. For quick return, bear right along it, and one level mile later, after passing fields lush with California poppies, you will be back at the parking lot.

All of this land was once part of the 8,928-acre Rancho San Pedro granted to Francisco Sanchez. His adobe home still stands downhill at the junction of Linda Mar Boulevard and Adobe Drive. A fine example of authentic Monterey architecture, it now houses a museum, also operated by the San Mateo County park system. As you make your way back to Highway 1, stop if you have the time. It will give you more of a feeling of historical continuity with our agrarian past than almost anything else can.

11

Two fine lighthouses have become hostels recently. One is the Pigeon Point Light; the other, Montara Light. They stand about twenty miles apart. Pescadero's Pebble Beach lies between them, one of a chain of San Mateo County State Beaches along this stretch of coastline.

For the distance walker or for a bicyclist this trip can be truly memorable. European bicyclists seem to have discovered its pleasures much more than Americans. The last time I stopped at Pigeon Point Hostel, there were two French, two Swedish, four German, and a mixed party of Czech, Yugoslavian, and Polish visitors.

Pebble Beach to Bean Hollow

Imagine a dozen females, some in bloomers, and some with-
out; some with long, some with short dresses, high boots and
low cut gaiters, straw hats, green veils, bandanas and the in-
evitable Shaker—lying about in every conceivable position,
some on the knees and hands, others flat on their stomachs,
with hands busy, feet stretched out, and heads half buried in
holes they have made in the beach—were there but some
wreck in sight it would have the appearance of a number of
bodies washed up by the waves....

—Alta California, May 1867

THIS EARLY ACCOUNT of California's golden girls was describing Pebble Beach "where agates, opals, jaspers and carnelians of almost every conceivable color...with a natural polish imparted by the action of the waves" were once found in great abundance near Pescadero.

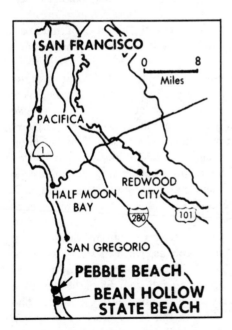

Today Pebble Beach is one of that lovely chain of San Mateo County State Beaches that stretches along fifty miles of coastline from Thornton Beach just south of San Francisco to Ano Nuevo Beach almost on the Santa Cruz County line. Each beach has its own distinctive character, along coastline that reminds many travelers of Cornwall near The Lizard. My favorite stretch of trail along them goes for one delightful

57

mile between Pebble Beach and Bean Hollow State Beach. En route
the walker will see families of harbor seals, colonies of sea and
shorebirds, a wealth of tidepools and of wildflowers.

To make this walk, transport yourself south from San Francisco
via Routes 28, 35, and Highway 1 until you are at the shore about
thirty-five miles away. When you see the sign west of the highway
indicating Pebble Beach State Park, stop, park, and look around.
This was once the site of "Coburn's Folly," a tremendous hotel built
in 1892 by pioneer Loren Coburn, once owner of both the vast
Butano and Punta del Ano Nuevo ranchos, in expectation that the
Ocean Shore Railroad line would someday serve it. He waited in
vain. The Ocean Shore, whose slogan was "It Reaches the Beaches,"
never spanned the coast between Tunitas Creek and Davenport
Landing, despite its promises, leaving Coburn with a posh resort
that was almost useless in the preautomotive days. Ultimately it
burned, but not before a bitter suit against his neighbors in Pescadero, which brought him damages of $1,000, left him the most
hated and ostracized old man on the coast. With no Coburn descen-
dants left in the county, fortunately the animosity is now only a
memory.

Put your dog on the leash, then look for the trailhead at the
south end of the parking lot. Just past the portable privies, follow
the single beaten path along moorlike greensward through seaside
daisies, lizardtail, wild buckwheat, seathrift, and the rich purple of
Douglas iris. Ignore the numbered posts, whose self-guided infor-
mational booklets are a casualty of inflation, and enjoy what you
can see. Off to your right the tidepools, often fringed with basking
harbor seals and their charming pups, are equally splendid, with
waterfalls splashing dramatically over the reef offshore as each
wave crashes upon its rocks.

Because the fragile intertidal zone is the home of seaweeds,
barnacles, anemones, urchins, sponges, jellyfish, snails, seaslugs,
chitons, limpets, starfish, blennies, and hundreds of other small
creatures, no invertebrates, according to Section 51 of the California
Sportfishing Regulations, may be taken along here. Pokepolers find
the monkey-faced eels abound in the rocky crevices, however.
Birders spot red-billed oystercatchers, curlews, killdeer, godwits,
helldivers, murres, pelicans, cormorants, gulls, and any number of

"peeps," as little sandpipers and sanderlings are known, along this rich beach.

So fascinating is the shorelife that unless a noisy vehicle passes you may feel yourself in wilderness on this cleverly sited trail. Little bridges span the gaps small rivulets carve on their journey to the sea. Checkerbloom and wild strawberries thrive. In September of 1979, walkers along this trail found a totally different scene as the community and media discovered a rare blue whale deposited in a little pocket known locally as Fiddler's Cove. After zoologists had determined that she had died of old age, bones and specimen samples were hauled off to the University of California at Santa Cruz, according to Charles Jones, a Pescadero author of *When the Whale Came.*

Look south as you approach Bean Hollow to discern Pigeon Point Light House, which now contains the newest hostel in the American Youth Hostel chain. At its dedication, State Director of Resources Huey Johnson and approximately two hundred other bicyclists who left San Francisco by bicycle at 8 A.M. arrived at Pigeon Point by 2 P.M. Dangerous as it looks, in 1869 steamers were loaded by capstan from a heavy wire cable and slings, two hundred feet in the air above the water at Pigeon Point. At that time supplies came in and lumber went out that way, for there was no road along the coast.

Cut from the path to the sand when you are near Bean Hollow, originally Arroyo de los Frijoles, if the tide is low. To know when you are parallel to the parking lot, keep your eye peeled for picnic tables. The way back to Pebble is the way you came, but you won't be bored. There is so much to see along this lively shoreline, making the walk back an hour later is a whole new shell game.

12

"Strawberry Fields Forever" was a songwriter's view of heaven in the sixties. More recently, reporter Jerry Carroll writing on death in the San Francisco Chronicle indicated that accounts of forty-one people who had been pronounced dead and later revived "ranged from views of a pleasant road ending at an old farm gate and meadows dotted with flowers to billowy clouds and light pulsating with exquisite music." The Elysian Fields. Or heaven by any name.

Wildflowers are cast like a mantle on the meadows and hillslopes of California every spring. If the "out-of-body experiences" of people who have lived after their transcendental experiences are any indication, heaven is very like the earth as we prize it most.

With each passing year, alas, fewer and fewer such heavenly hillslopes and open spaces are un-built-upon.

Botanical gardens may not be everyone's idea of heaven, but they are dependable places to see wildflowers. The time may come when they are the only places to see some varieties. How odd of Mankind to destroy what seems to be a universal idea of heaven. Are we forever chasing ourselves from the Garden of Eden?

The Wildflower Botanic Garden

THE FLOWERS THAT bloom in the spring, tra la, are doing their annual thing, tra la, over in the Regional Parks Botanic Garden in Wildcat Canyon, Berkeley.

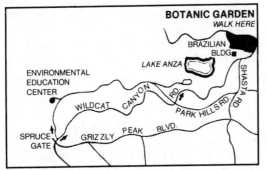

Although the name doesn't reveal it, the garden is devoted to California's native plant species, with nothing in view in its creek-carved slopes save trees, shrubs, and flowers indigenous to the state. Kids have nick-named it the Wildflower Garden. To better acquaint the walker with the rich variety of wildlings that bloom here, a Rites of Spring celebration is often under way in the East Bay Regional Parks, with lectures, exhibits, and a three-month schedule of wildflower walks throughout the many East Bay parks. Just as birders take as a goal the sighting of one hundred birds, the Rites of Spring suggest a wildflower "life list," with much the same goal.

One of the Rites of Spring festivities, entitled "Where to Find Wildflowers," is a well-correlated display of bas relief topographic maps of the state keyed to photos of wildflowers in bloom and to a chart showing where in the nine regions of the wildflower garden to find them growing. What this means is that the walker can stop in the Tilden Botanic Garden Visitor's Center, scope out the display, then walk out into the garden to inspect that rare elusive wildflower one may never otherwise see. Or if you think you have spotted a rare owl's-clover (which looks nothing like owls nor clover), here's an opportunity to check whether it grows in the place you found it. When I went, to my great delight the rarest wildflower in the state, the Franciscan or Presidio manzanita, was in bloom. So was the Point Reyes wallflower, a rarity that usually requires a six-mile hike out Tomales Point to find.

There were also silktassels, giant shooting stars, barberries, wake-robin, yellow bush poppies, and any number of flowering currants in bloom, sending their pink electrical charges out in showers. If you haven't walked there for a while, now is the time for a visit to the wildflower garden in Tilden Park.

To make this walk, transport yourself to Berkeley and thence to the Spruce Gate entrance at the junction of Grizzly Peak Boulevard at Spruce Street and Canon and Wildcat Canyon roads. Take Wildcat Canyon Road downhill and to the right, past the Brazilian Building, curving east to the little parking area just across the road from the fenced Botanic Garden. If you had to pay seventy-five cents to go through the turnstile last time you were here, it will come as a pleasant surprise to find that the garden is once again free. The fee, necessitated by Jarvis-Gann, came off thanks to the efforts of a dedicated group of volunteers from the California Native Plant Society who raise funds for this purpose now with rare plant sales in April and October.

Walk in, bear left to the visitor's center, register, and if you can take your eyes from the compelling view through the garden doors beyond, go into the gallery on your right to see the display. When W. E. Hutchinson visited Wildcat Canyon in 1914 around this time of year, he wrote in *Byways Around San Francisco Bay:* "It was the season when the flowering currant puts on its gala dress of pink blossoms and the banks of the creek for a long distance were like a flower garden. On higher ground the beautiful Zygadene plant, with its pompon of white star shaped flowers and long graceful leaves grew in profusion. Maidenhair ferns, the only variety we saw, sent forth their delicate streamers from every nook and cranny, forming a carpet of exquisite texture."

Today, if anything, the canyon is even more exquisite. Built after mounds of dirt had been shoved downhill by the WPA during construction of the eighteen-hole golf course uphill, it has been transformed into a microcosm. One can stroll from the desert to the seashore by way of the Santa Lucia Mountains, the Channel Islands, the Pacific rain forest, or the redwoods.

When you have absorbed the exhibit, go out onto the overlook just outside the center. The commanding drifts of creamy yellow visible on the simulated sea bluff across the creek are the Point

Reyes wallflower. Before you go off for a closer look, glance to your left where waterfalls of Wildcat Creek tumble melodically out from under the road. Tempting as it is to go there immediately to look for maidenhair fern, bear right instead. When wildflower buffs Sue Dalcalmo of Lafayette and Myrtle Wolf of Claremont conducted me on this walk one rainy day, they laughingly told me the tubular plastic covers over the cactus in the desert area, where the finest collection of California cacti in the world is concentrated, were to keep plants dry, not sterile. Wire and plastic cages are to protect tasty plants from rabbits, deer, and birds.

Swing down into the foothill section (numbered 4) via the descending ramp and stroll along the stream until you reach the stone bridge. Save crossing it for later, however, and go up the steps, then across the lawn to reach the Channel Island area, where unusual plants from our newest area to become a national park are sure to be in bloom. The giant shooting stars with their blooms in clusters as big as primroses are worth a digression anytime.

Swing past the grove of ironwood trees, and as you come down the hill, notice the cabin off to the right in an area old-timers refer to as the vegetable garden. Botanist James Roof lived here, sans plumbing and electricity, growing his own food when he was director of the garden. Present husbandman of the garden is Wayne Roderick, known among horticulturists as a botanical historian. "Be sure to look for the pink sand verbena," he advised me as we started out. "You know it was the first wildflower described from the West Coast. By LaPerouse about 1777, as I recall."

Bear left toward the retaining wall from the vegetable garden. It will lead through Santa Barbara County ceanothus, past dwarf ninebark in bloom, and finally a big nutmeg tree. Then take the bridge across the creek to reach the seabluff, a vignette of Point Reyes above the lighthouse, where rose rockcress may be in bloom among the lichens. When you leave this fetching cliff, follow the creek northward. If it seems open for a rain forest, relax. This is the area, formerly much overgrown, that treetopper Ted Kipping cleaned up, pruning so artfully it is hard to believe anything has been removed.

Leave the rain forest and swing uphill through the incense cedars, noting en route the western leatherwood near the stone garden shack. Then curve around to your left to the redwood grove. In a good year for violets they are rampant in the redwoods. Ginger growing with it hides its flowers under the broad leaves. Once past the pond, start downhill, noting the plant nurseries as you come back toward the creek.

If this museum of living specimens challenges you, consider the further pursuit of baby-blue-eyes or Johnny Tuck at the Environmental Education Center, near the Little Farm at the northern end of Tilden Park. Here the Knouse collection of wildflower photos may be on display, correlated like the visitor's center display to the places plants were found in the wild and where they can be seen in the wildflower garden.

At either place, before you leave, look in the racks near the entrance for a log of other Rites of Spring events. There will be ranger-led wildflower walks throughout all of the East Bay Regional Parks during the three spring months. Given the right amount of sunshine after the rains, a walker could fill in a hundred wildflowers on his life list in a couple of rambles in spring.

13

The big ugly trench created by the Army Corps of Engineers to tame Corte Madera Creek could have been attractive. Certainly the flood control channel in San Antonio, Texas, has shown that such watercourses need not be cold, sterile, Bauhaus-cum-Nazi architecture. The Corps of Engineers, however, hasn't changed its flood control design in more than a hundred years. A walker can see the prototype for that trench in several places in the Presidio. One of them on Lover's Lane is crossed by the oldest footbridge in San Francisco.

The other is on Battery East Trail at the approach to that wonderful tunnel that pops the walker from the line of fortifications through to a handsome overlook of the Golden Gate Bridge. The channel design is less offensive when it is unfenced and small enough to leap. In its larger version, for Marin County especially, there should have been canoe ramps, meanders, variety of facings, rocks, plantings that were more than cosmetic.

Ross and Kentfield

"MUST I LEAVE thee, Paradise . . . these happy walks and shades?" Milton wrote. There are old residents of Ross or Kentfield who are sure he was writing about Marin, although he died long before the county was named. Certainly the trees are many and shady there and the walking happy indeed. Mrs. Miniver in garden gloves, trug basket over her arm, would feel as much at home in either place as she would on the lanes of jolly old England.

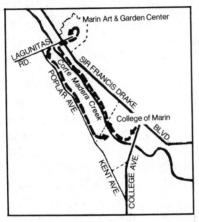

One of the best walks to sample these contiguous communities begins at what was once Ross Landing and follows Corte Madera Creek from Kentfield to Ross Common. To make this walk, dress carefully for it in your Ivy League casuals. Then transport yourself to the junction of Sir Francis Drake Boulevard and College Avenue, preferably via Golden Gate Transit. This is the College of Marin campus, thanks to the generosity of Mrs. A. E. Kent, who donated the land on the west side of College in 1908 for a recreation area known as the Tamalpais Centre (sic). Much of this land is now the campus. If you had come along this way in 1857, however, it would have been a busy shipping point named for founder James Ross. Flat-bottomed schooners came to Ross Landing to transport potatoes, bricks, and wood to San Francisco.

By the time a narrow gauge railroad came huffing through Ross Valley in 1875, the name had been changed to Tamalpais. Residents of the town of Ross, known even then to be thorny, thought there would be less confusion with their name. Kent, Kentwood, and finally Kentfield were subsequent names for Ross Landing.

Once parked, seek out Corte Madera Creek, which crosses College Avenue beside the bus shelter, a long block south of Sir

Francis Drake Boulevard. A Class I Marin County Recreation Department hiking and bicycle trail, a link in the Cross Marin Trail between the Larkspur Ferry and Tomales Bay State Park, follows the fenceline of the creek. When you reach it, bear right in a gentle northwesterly direction.

When Marin Junior College opened in 1926, with 85 students, there were 6 faculty members. A barn served as gymnasium, and classes were held in a redwood shingled house. Today the College of Marin has 371 on the faculty, counting part-time instructors, and several of the twelve major buildings are prizeworthy.

Soon after you pass Parking Lot 11 and the COM police office, the trail assumes its general character, vines struggle up the chain-link fencing, great old trees lean over from the backyards on either side and shrubs ramble beside old gardens. On the hated trench in which the Army Corps of Engineers has trapped the creek, graffiti burgeon. As you glimpse the private lives revealed in various back-yards—a dog being curried here, a boy repairing a bicycle there, a man washing his car in another—you feel like a ghost train out of the past on this straight and narrow track. Some of the back gardens ignore the creek and trail, consciously screening them out. Others, like the one numbered 306, treat it like a front entrance, complete to handsome fence, footbridge, and flagpole with a lanyard for pennants.

Look through open spaces between houses for an occasional glimpse of insulators on the telephone poles along Kent Avenue, which look like contemporary sculpture from this aspect. At an area where clematis and star jasmine sprawl on the chainlink fencing, a ramp will take you up beside the Kentfield General Hospital. Cross toward the caged platform tennis court and the trail reasserts itself.

"Thanks Homecote spray paint" or "Latin American Solidarity" and "Keep Russian Traitors Out" or, more boldly, "Ross Snobs Suck," say the graffiti on the far wall of the sunken creek trench.

When you reach a point where the creek suddenly becomes natural, with untrammeled banks teeming with wildlife and froggy music, you are in Ross. It is also the scene of a classic confrontation between bureaucracy and the citizenry. Led by Marty Kent Jones, a group of citizens stopped the Army Corps of Engineers trenching of Corte Madera Creek here about ten years ago.

The post office, established in 1887, is now housed on the site of a former train station dead ahead. Since there is no mail delivery in Ross, residents come in daily to pick up their mail here. Walk around in front to enjoy the bulletin board, a record of rank, swank, and status. Where else can you see a commercially printed twelve-by-nineteen-inch handbill complete with photograph offering $150 for the return of Digger, a golden retriever. Walk around to the far side of the post office to wander for a while in the charming formal garden hedged hard by. It will bring you out at the corner of Lagunitas Road and Poplar Avenue. Bear right for one block, and you will pass Ross City Hall, with a Bufano statue on the front lawn, and reach Sir Francis Drake Boulevard. Cross it and you are immediately at the Marin Art and Garden Center, a ten-acre showplace that includes two outdoor theaters, a plethora of winding paths, an octagonal library housed in what was once a pumphouse, and a handsome serpentine wall commemorating a much loved conservationist, Mrs. Norman Livermore.

When you have explored it, return to Ross Common on the far side of Poplar. In horse and buggy days, coachmen in livery often met the afternoon trains here as local residents returned from Montgomery Street or Union Square in the City. Ross School abuts the common.

Cross Poplar to peer into the windows of One Ross Common. A visit here or to Harriet Webb's any year could turn one out with this year's newly stylish "preppy" look. The handful of surrounding stores have a carefully nurtured "country village" ambiance. Sam the Butcher is a real meatcutter, but the Ross Garage is a garage no longer, but a rabbit warren of boutiques and restaurants. The little town also boasts a goldsmith, a poodle groomer, an antique store, and a hairdresser.

Cut through the Ross Garage's elegant side garden to discover an old gas pump used as a garden artifact and beyond it formal steps leading to the creekside trail for quick return to your wheels. Of course, if you would rather see the fronts of those houses that back on the trail, you can stroll down Poplar Avenue. At the Kentfield city limits, it becomes Kent Avenue. By either name, it will bring you back to the College of Marin via a lane of simple cottages that have been summer homes, have housed servants to tidy up the big estates back in the hills, and have now become as chic as any London mews.

April

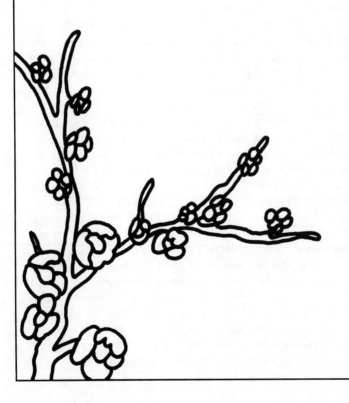

14

Springtime is moving time too. The need to find new digs hasn't troubled us for a while, but it wasn't so long ago that San Francisco landlords looked on our four small sons with dismay. One landlord doubled the prospective rent on sight.

It was still possible then for a growing family to afford a private home, so in desperation one spring we decided to buy. We found two houses we really liked. One was on the fringes of Mill Valley, the other in San Francisco. Both had qualities we sought—enough bedrooms, a fireplace, a south-facing garden, no front lawn to mow, doorframes tall enough to admit a six-foot-five-inch man comfortably.

We liked the plan of the city house best, but it also cost about ten thousand dollars more, a sum that is laughable today. It was ten thousand dollars we thought we could not afford. We sat down with a pencil and paper and soon realized that suburban living would also require two cars—one for the breadwinner, the other for our busy household.

It soon became clear that we could easily save ten thousand dollars in five years simply by not owning car number two. As it happened, we saved much more by buying the city house. Everything we needed in life was within easy walking distance or accessible by public transportation. My husband loved the walk to his work. The boys walked to the homes of friends, to Sunday school, to school, to dancing class, to birthday parties, music lessons, swimming lessons, to the beach, to the park, to the playground, to the grocery store.

They also became explorers. One day, Number One Son discovered the warehouses and waterfront that lay just beyond the next hill. He came home excitedly and said, "Think of it, Mother! Some of those big old buildings are so full they are spilling bags of beans right out into the street!"

Today the sparkling new Levi's Plaza has replaced "those big old buildings spillings bags of beans."

Levi's Plaza

SAN FRANCISCO HAS a wonderful new waterfront walk. Its heart is the eleven-acre Levi's Plaza, where the low, terraced red brick buildings are scaled to a six-foot man on his own two feet, where one-quarter of the area is generously given over to well-planned open space, where San Francisco Bay seems to be part of the city, so close at hand you could reach out and touch it—a soft, inviting place that makes working, walking, and indeed, living, in the city seem once again an eminently pleasant idea.

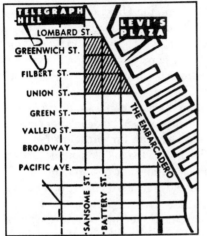

"We wanted it to be warm as a college campus," Peter Haas, president of Levi Strauss & Company and scion of one of the city's most philanthropic families, said as he showed me the prospect from his new office terrace. "Levi's used to have its warehouse and office on Battery Street before moving farther downtown. We used to ship out of here. For us, it's like coming home again."

To make this walk, put on your favorite faded old Levi's, transport yourself, preferably by the Muni No. 32 or No. 42 bus lines, to the corner of Sansome and Lombard streets, and prepare to be agreeably surprised. This former warehouse district is already home to several hundred people at Telegraph Landing and will soon be home to hundreds more as new apartments are completed.

At the outset, look around. At one time Telegraph Hill was round on this side; the place you are standing was almost two hundred feet higher and there really was an artillery battery on Battery Street. When the sheer cliff to the west was blasted away by Harry N. and George F. Gray to create fill for the long-gone waterfront extension known as East Street North, whole lots toppled, taking homes

73

with them. Feeling ran so high two people were shot to death, one of them contractor George Gray, before the dynamiting was controlled. Residents of the hilltop have been united protectively as a community ever after.

Before the Embarcadero and its piers were built, sailing ships used to nuzzle up to Pier 27, fronting the One Lombard Building, which began as an icehouse. They were loaded from the open warehouse doors. "During construction we found permafrost at the lower levels from long storage of ice here," architect Pat MacLeamy of Hellmuth, Obata & Kassabaum, who designed Levi's Plaza, told me.

Snuggled in under the cliff on the west is 101 Lombard Street, a new garden complex of apartments created by developer Gerson Bakar, who once fought to help keep the Embarcadero Freeway from snaking along this way. Six units in the building are decorated by Miles Sandstrom. With special permission one may go in and view them for an elevated look at the area first if you wish, or save it for the end of this walk.

Then walk south along Sansome Street to reach Building B of Levi's Plaza at the Greenwich corner. For reference, look uphill to locate the Greenwich Street steps, then about a hundred feet from the corner, bear left at an angle through the arcade that suddenly opens between what seems at first glance to be another warehouse. Actually it is the back door of the plaza. Designed as a little neighborhood shopping center, it will have a bank, a drugstore, a deli, and a bar. A sudden glimpse of a flowing fountain beckons one into the open space beyond. Watch those two sets of shallow steps as you descend into the broad corridor. Just before you leave the building, pause a moment to look uphill on your right. There the arcade unexpectedly soars to two stories, revealing Coit Tower in all its glory.

As you emerge into the sunlight, the fine old Italian Swiss Colony warehouse, whose cornices and balustrades have recently been facelifted and earthquake-proofed, is on your left and houses a restaurant facing the plaza. Centerpiece of this urbane part of the plaza is a fountain with many flowing faces. Walk up into their midst via the stepping-stones to enjoy the music of the water, then loop back via stones through the lawn area to return to the paved center of the plaza.

Look upward to enjoy the expansive glass-roofed atrium that ties together the two halves of Building A, the Levi Strauss headquarters, whose stepped-back, zigzagged terraces, as classic as a Hopi cliff dwelling, seem to reflect the hillside homes above. Walk toward it, but stop on the red brick walkway mid-plaza to discern the Filbert Street steps on the right and below them the plaza's main entrance from Sansome Street. Displays from Levi's historical collection are rotated through the atrium. Cafeteria on the left as you face the building is for employees only.

Bear left on the brick paving, which is actually Filbert Street, now a pedestrian-only way, toward the second fountain surrounded by berms of earth and green lawns off toward the bay. Enticing as it seems, resist it for a moment, and once across Battery Street, walk south again to follow another arcade under a bridge connecting the two halves of Building C. When you emerge at Union Street, bear right until you can see the little Cargo West Building, an historical landmark, which has been surrounded by the larger building as sensitively as a jewel in a fine setting. The setback facing the neighboring Ice House Alley is another delicate architectural touch. "We think the spaces in between are every bit as important as the buildings themselves," architect MacLeamy told me.

Retrace your steps along Union Street toward the tugboat lying at Pier 19 at the foot of the street. Then, just shy of the Belt Line railroad tracks, cobbles and a sweet jolt of greenery make an introduction to the plaza again. Bear left, and try to puzzle out, as I did, why the Port Authority refused to allow developer Gerson Bakar permission to plant between the tracks, although it was offered at no cost to the city. Another few feet of green along this border of the broad Embarcadero would help reduce smog, traffic noise, and pollution, and increase the walker's enjoyment.

When you are again parallel to Filbert Street, go down the steps on your left until you are abreast of the fountain, then bear right. Like the rest of the plaza landscaping, the fountain was designed by Lawrence Halprin and interprets a Sierran headwater source, with a mountain stream coursing down through a little natural amphitheater disguised as a mountain meadow. Both stepping-stones and bridge cross the stream. Take your choice, then continue northward to linger on the second bridge overlooking a little island that could easily serve as an impromptu stage. All that is missing in this charming conceit of meandering mountain rill are water plants and trout. On the opposite side of the bridge, the creek seems to join the bay. Actually its waters are recycled back to start their melodic little journey again and again.

Idle in this welcome green oasis. The restaurant at its end is Mildred Pierce's, reminiscent of an earlier, lustier waterfront made more romantic by the passage of time. To complete this walk, cross at Greenwich Street and go back to Sansome past the Bay Club to complete a loop back to 101 Lombard. Or if you find yourself rubbing your eyes in disbelief that new construction and building could be this generous, walk this walk again. It's better the second time.

15

Spring for young San Francisco fishermen usually happens the day fishing begins on Lake Merced. The sports pages of the Chronicle *announce it, and traditionally the lineup is six deep around the borders on opening day. At one time the crowds grew so great that parts of the shoreline on Lake Merced have now been placed off limits to protect the banks from overuse.*

Lake Merced

If he be an honest angler, may the east wind never blow when he goes a fishing.
— *The Compleat Angler* by Izaak Walton

ALTHOUGH THERE WERE no glaciers in San Francisco, Lake Merced, a remarkable natural V-shaped eight-acre lake in the southwesternmost corner of San Francisco best known to hundreds of young Nimrods as our "backyard fishing hole," was glacially formed during the Pleistocene.

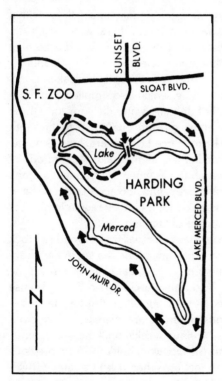

Sound impossible? Then consider a paper published a few years ago by geologist Neil E. Fahy in which he postulated that the formation of Lake Merced began during the last of the four interglacial periods. According to "Origin of Lake Merced," printed in *California Geology*, "A series of poorly consolidated sands, called the Colma Formation, were deposited as the glaciers melted and subsequently released water causing sea level to rise above its present height. The sands of the Colma Formation crop out around Lake Merced, in Colma Valley, extending as far as McLaren Park three miles to the east and as far as the Cliff House three miles to the north.

"When the glaciers advanced again for the last time and sea

level was lowered, the natural drainage flowed westward across this relatively level surface to the sea. . . . A northwest flowing stream drained the region now occupied by the Westlake district of Daly City. A southwest flowing stream drained the area of the Ingleside and Sunset districts of San Francisco. The streams meandered through their valleys, joined, and flowed west into the ocean."

And there you have the two arms of Lake Merced. Wave action depositing a big sandbar that dammed the streams did the rest, shutting out the Pacific Ocean.

More recently its history has been equally unusual, for within recorded time, Lake Merced has contained both saltwater and fresh. The switchover happened between 1869 and 1895 and according to Dr. R. C. Miller of the Academy of Sciences, small fishy animals adapted to both environments now live in the springfed lake.

For a look at this unusual place, which also supplied San Francisco with 3.1 million gallons of drinking water daily for forty-three years, transport yourself, preferably by Muni bus No. 29 to the south end of Sunset Boulevard at Lake Merced Boulevard. Like its name, Laguna de Nuestra Señora de la Merced, the Lake of Our Lady of Mercy, is a good bit smaller than it was when the Spaniards drank from it. At present it is thirty feet deep, had 386 acres under water at last count, and is a standby reservoir for the city. It regularly supplies sprinkling water for the golf greens of Harding Park.

Beyond the parking circle, the walker will find a broad red rock path. Follow it across the footbridge, one of the few left in San Francisco. From the middle of the bridge is a great place to inspect the north flange of the lake, or if you have a California fishing license with two trout stamps affixed in your pocket, to fish for the limit — five trout. About thirty thousand trout are planted before trout season opens, and plantings continue weekly until the season ends December 31. Dinner for one, the rare wary holdover from previous seasons may run to fourteen inches. When it isn't swamped with fishermen, the bridge is an ideal place to linger, dream, and muse.

Once the mystery of water reflection wearies, follow the path uphill. It emerges in Harding Park, an eighteen-hole golf course open to the public that is looking great since a recent grounds renovation under the Title II program. Walk around in front of the clubhouse to continue on the road that leads westward between the two flanges of these old, drowned stream valleys. At the first turn of the road, look to the right to see one of the few remaining marshy arroyos within the city where migrating waterfowl can find food and shelter. It is here that marine biologists can also find the relict fauna of Lake Merced as reported by Dr. Miller. Rowboats are moored in the next inlet.

The Lake Merced boathouse, completed in 1959 by the Recreation and Park Department, is the next building one encounters. For many years the bar and restaurant were leased as a concession to Aurie Kuntz, who operated this fringe of the lake as a private playground when it was still owned by the Spring Valley Water Company. Now Frank Mehl rents the sailboats and rowboats and sells fishing licenses and bait. The new Parcourse is the gift to the city from Perrier, currently the chic choice in many a cafe.

The Children's Pier is the special pontoon located near the boathouse and reserved for kids under sixteen. It was renamed and rededicated in 1978. Look on the flat rock overlooking the pier for the seven-pointed, star-shaped gold plaque that honors Police Officer Douglas Gibbs, killed in the line of duty October 1977.

At Skyline Boulevard, bear north toward the San Francisco Zoo, keeping your eye peeled for mushrooms if you are mycologically informed. Soon you will find yourself back at the point of origin for this mile-and-a-half loop. If you are eager for more walking, keep right on going around the five-mile shoreline loop that encircles the lake. En route, historians can see where Rivera y Moncada camped in 1774. Engineers will find, at 17 feet above sea level on the site of the old Spring Valley pumping station, a pumphouse that lifts water in a 105-foot rise from Crystal Springs at 280 feet to Sunset Reservoir. They will also find a water main that crosses the lake to provide a causeway that is a favorite with bank fishermen.

With persistence and perseverance one can also find across the highway near the apartment complex that calls itself Lake Merced Hill, the approximate site of the last duel-to-death in San Francisco. Two obelisk-shaped markers and a tablet label the little dell in which the antislave Senator David Broderick was fatally wounded by that terrible-tempered Southern gentleman, Judge David Terry. Old-timers in the neighborhood dispute the actual location, but the entrance path is off Lakeview Drive and El Portal Way.

16

Cherry blossom time becomes more important in San Francisco yearly. The Japanese community sponsors an annual Cherry Blossom Festival that includes what I think of as the best parade in the city. The cherry trees in containers at Nihon Machi are handsome, but they can't compare with the bigger trees in Sidney Walton Square downtown. For sheer numbers of trees however, Golden Gate Park now has even Washington, D.C. beat.

Cherry Blossom Walk

The cherry-flowers bloom;
We gaze at them,
They fall, and . . .

Onitsura

AND . . . THE WORLD seems a better, happier place for a moment. Which is reason enouch to hie oneself to Golden Gate Park, which now has close to two thousand cherry trees along its meadows and drives, for a cherry tree walk.

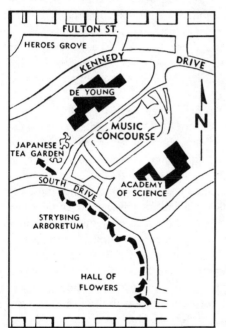

Half of the flowering cherry trees were a bicentennial gift from Emperor Hirohito and the government of Japan. The others have been given to the city during the last ten years by Ikebana International, which has just planted its thousandth tree with a *Senbonzakura* celebration.

In Japan, *hanami*, or cherry blossom viewing, is a national pastime that almost amounts to a mania. From March through May, Japanese newspapers give daily listings of trees in bloom all over the country. At least fifty major resorts, whose only raison d'être is a distinguished old cherry tree or lane, meadow, or mountainside of cherries, are listed in the official government guide to Japan. A dozen or more trees are so remarkable they have additional listings under their own names. More than fifty varieties of cherry grow in Japan, including the *kiku sakura*, which has a chrysanthemumlike flower

83

with two hundred petals, and a *kongo sakura*, whose flowers are yellow. Devotees of *hanami* start their pilgrimages to these trees when the first bud breaks, working their way as the season progresses from Nagasaki or Shimonoseki, to Kyoto, to Nara, to Yoshino, and finally to Tokyo, visiting the famous trees as they come into bloom. The romantic pattern for cherry bloom watching is to take a picnic, a candle-lit lantern, and your light-of-love and plan to watch from beneath the tree as dusk falls with petals sifting gently downward.

The more venerable the tree, the better, of course. Japan has one tree, named Yamataka Jindaisakura, which is reputed to be 1,800 years old, and 400-year-old trees are not uncommon. While San Francisco can't boast any cherry trees as old as redwoods, the first trees planted in 1969 by Ikebana International along South Drive have now attained substantial size and make for the best show.

To make this walk, transport yourself via the No. 44 O'Shaughnessy, No. 72X Sunset Express, or No. 71 Haight Muni buses to the corner of Ninth Avenue and Lincoln Way. At the outset, go into Strybing Arboretum through the main gate. Notice immediately inside in the median strip the new Knot Garden of Herbs, half of another bicentennial project. Pass the information kiosk and the last ornamental gate to find its other half, a fan-shaped counterpart. Both are colonial classics, much like those at Williamsburg, Virginia.

Bear left behind the Helen Crocker Russell Library. Within a few steps you will be at the Takamine Garden, a memorial to Dr. Jokichi Takamine, a chemist noted for his work on adrenaline. By no coincidence, he was the man who assisted President William Howard Taft in bringing the first cherry trees to the Potomac Tidal Basin in Washington, D.C., a project that has grown to six miles of trees. The Takemine Garden here in Strybing is a gift from his daughter-in-law Katharyn Hedland, now remarried.

As enchanting as the arboretum is at this time of year, for this walk save it for later. Retrace your steps back through the main gate and continue along South Drive. You will walk in glory all the way when the cherry trees are in bloom. As you stroll, observe how the four trees on the east side of the drive have been planted with taller green trees behind them. When Faye Kramer, a founder and former president of Ikebana International, conducted me on this walk, she pointed out that the trees are the single-petaled akebana, which the Japanese consider most beautiful and fragile, grafted on sturdy mountain cherry rootstock, which resists most pests. "They have been artfully planted in groups of random numbers to give a natural feeling, such as one might find in the wild," Mrs. Kramer said. "The Japanese prefer to see cherry trees on the side of a mountain or meadow surrounded by green."

The northeast corner of the intersection with Middle Drive would be ideal for *hanami,* with its solid wall of green behind it. The next groups are visible alongside the sign for the Garden of Shakespeare's Flowers. Look for a path at your feet that seems to go nowhere to find where the thousandth tree was planted. Amateur archeologists will recognize the path that ends at the fence as the first main entrance to the arboretum, phased out by the more impressive gate near the Garden Center. Slender striplings on the side of the path nearest the street are the tipoff.

"The Tokyo police force have the sakura, or cherry flower, as an emblem on their badges," Mrs. Kramer told me as we approached the Japanese Tea Garden, "which doesn't seem effete to them because the samurai identified with the cherry blossom too." Go as far as the Strybing rear gate and cross South Drive at the crosswalk. It will bring you out at a path that leads through a splendid stand of cherries toward the side gate of the tea garden, where the most venerable of all the park sakuras grow. After visiting it for the springtime jubilation, if you aren't sated, there are still another thousand trees scattered at various parts of the park: a large group near the Rose Garden, another near Stowe Lake, many more along South Drive near 19th Avenue, many at Marx Meadow, and by Spreckels Lake, North Lake, and Middle Lake. One group of commemorative cherries has been planted in the Fuchsia Garden behind McLaren Lodge in honor of two plantsmen, Arthur Menzies and Norvell Gillespie, and park commissioner John Conway. Three more memorial trees have been added for Mayor George Moscone, Congressman Leo Ryan, and Supervisor Harvey Milk.

Don't count on a seat in the tea garden teahouse in cherry blossom time. Better do as we did and end this walk with a beer at the House of Piroshky, Ninth Avenue between Lincoln Way and Irving. I can vouch for the mushroom piroshky.

17

The pleasures of walking are legion—to name a few: the companionship of a dog; health and exercise; birding; the acquaintanceship of trees, shrubs, and flowers; the gathering of driftwood, shells, and seaweeds; rockhounding; scientific observation; romance; sightseeing; vamping; and marketing. All are reason enough for taking a walk. So is architecture. Its pleasure is intended to be public and pops up in some unexpected places in the Bay Area. One of them is the wine country.

Saint Helena's Stone Victorians

TWO POINTS IF you can identify "The County of Stone Bridges." Right the first time! It's Napa County. Best known for its vineyards and wineries, Napa County also has some remarkable stone buildings of native basalt and sandstone. The greatest concentration of them is within an easy six-block walk in the charming little town of Saint Helena.

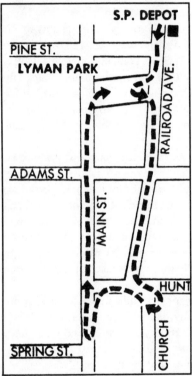

Next time you feel the urge to visit the wine country, consider an architectural walk through Saint Helena as well. Toward that end, Napa Landmarks, Inc., with the help of a grant from the National Trust for Historic Preservation, has published a handly little book called *Architecture Napa, A Guide to the Land, the Buildings and Styles of Napa County* to be used with its three walking route leaflets, one each for Saint Helena, Calistoga, and Yountville.

According to *Architecture Napa* most of the stone buildings are Richardsonian Romanesque. "H. H. Richardson, an architect working in the east, popularized a style derived from Romanesque architecture and characterized by massive stone and heavy arched openings. The Christian Brothers winery, built in 1889 from local stone, is an outstanding example of this style." The 1880s, after winemaker Andrea Sbarboro had imported to Asti many Swiss and Italian stonemasons, were the heyday of stone quarrying in Napa. Skilled Chinese laborers, also imported to construct wine cellars and aging caves, worked side by side with them.

The result in Saint Helena is a Victorian Age Main Street unlike any other in the Bay Area. To make this walk, write first for your guide to Napa Landmarks, Inc., P.O. Box 702, Napa 94558, where the one-page walking guide leaflets are available for 60 cents and the little architecture handbook for $4.95. Proceeds from the books help fund the Napa County Preservation Assistance Program.

Then, guide in hand, transport yourself north from San Francisco via Highway 101 to the Vallejo-Napa exit onto Highway 37. From 37 go north on the Wine Way Highways 12, 121, and finally 29, which becomes Main Street in Saint Helena. Since this walk is on paved street sidewalks, and is level enough for wheelchairs, any good walking shoes will do. Once within the little town, drive through it to Pine Street, take a right one block to Railroad Avenue, and find a place to park along the street near the Southern Pacific Depot.

Get out and prepare to enjoy the lazy pace and hometown flavor on foot. Author Robert Louis Stevenson, who spent a nine-week honeymoon on the slope of Mount Saint Helena, is probably the most famous person to arrive at the depot, point one on the architectural tour. The second station to be built along Railroad Avenue, it was part of the Napa Valley Railroad in 1868. Now it belongs to Southern Pacific, which makes its money on freight rather than passengers. By 1908 there was also an electric train running down Main Street.

Start walking south and the next significant building is Johnson's Depot Saloon, known in the great railroading days as "Babe's Place." The wooden part dates to 1868; the stone portion, originally the John Ramos Sherry Factory, to 1877. Sherry was "baked" upstairs in containers so heavy they bent the floor joists.

Cross the street to Lyman Park to see one of the most charming band concert gazebos, built around 1922. Throughout the twenties and thirties, concerts were held in the park every Wednesday evening. Earlier, a German turnverein and, in 1899, Saint Helena's first public high school stood on the spot. Also worth seeking out for the fun of it is a stone "horse and dog water fountain" that was moved here from Oak and Adam streets, a victim of the horseless carriage.

Point three is the handsomely renovated Pritchard Building at the northwest corner of Adams and Railroad, whose unlikely past includes service as a feed mill, warehouse, coal bin, and roller skating rink. Diverting as the bookstore now housed in it may be, continue on Railroad Avenue to see The Hatchery, midblock, which has also been recycled. In its time it served as a foundry to make wine crushers, as a power plant, a glove factory, and as the hatchery that gave it its present name. Stevenson buffs may defect for hours on discovering the Silverado Museum collection devoted to Stevensoniana. Gourmets also make a note for later visiting of La Belle Helene and the Miramonte Restaurant, both on Railroad Avenue, whose French chefs have become known for nouvelle cuisine.

Architecture aficionados will want to bear left on Hunt Street and cross the railroad tracks, taking a right down Church Street to find a stone warehouse with a crenelated roof edge. The oldest part, built in 1878, looks newest because of stuccoing. Other portions were added in 1881 and 1889.

Retrace your steps to Hunt Street, bear left, and go the long block to Main Street where the Wonderful Drug Store, another native stone building, constructed in 1891, once held the best soda fountain in the West. Look in the sidewalk for the name. GAR, by the way, doesn't stand for Grand Army of the Republic, but for George A. Riggins, who owned the Wonderful. Look up and down Main Street at the electrolaires. These festive streetlights first saw the light at the 1915 Panama-Pacific Exposition in San Francisco.

Bear left on Main to inspect the oddly hip-roofed Noble Building, which is Dutch colonial, unlike most of the local stone buildings. Luther Mark Turton was the architect. It was once the train depot for the electric train, but has housed a furniture store, an undertaking parlor, and a chicken hatchery in the past.

A. Goodman, a pushcart peddler who began his career on Main Street door to door, realized his fondest ambition when he built the double facade building for his dry goods store across the street. Now it houses The Compleat Winemaker and a bar. When you have noticed it, reverse direction and walk northward on Main to find six more unusual stone buildings, among them the Saint Helena Star building; the Masonic Hall, a fine example of Victorian with heavy Eastlake influences; and the IOOF building, all with brick facades over stone. Most charming on the architecture tour for many will be the little "Honeymoon Cottage" of southern belle Sally Wall.

Saint Helena has much more to see and discover, including

the Beard Building, constructed in 1974 to blend with the rest of the street, as well as six excellent wineries, a great olive oil factory, and an outstanding wine library. Wander as you will, for it is hard to get lost in this paragon of places, and the greatest delights of all are the ones you find yourself.

May

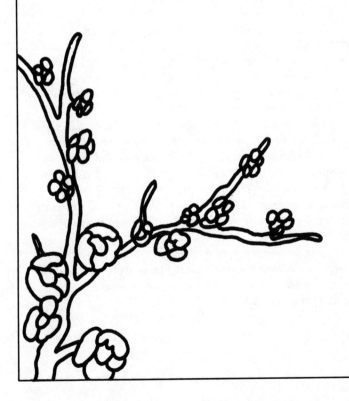

18

We rented a house on the upper slopes of Mount Tamalpais while its owner was on sabbatical some years ago. It is a spectacular house designed by Bob Marquis. At that time there were no houses higher on the mountainside. Looking down on it from the Twenty-Minute Trail around the crest, or from the Double Bow Knot, the house, its studio and garage grouped around a swimming pool, looks somewhat like a miniature Japanese village. From within, its vast expanses of glass reveal each passing cloud and bird. A storm experienced there is more spectacular than any television show.

One of the pleasures of living there was watching the Sierra Club classes practice belaying up a sheer rock face. Another was a mysterious little group of people, Indians I think, who came once by moonlight. I saw light reflected from a large lens or crystal as they made special ceremonial gestures and then disappeared.

One morning chittering noises in the manzanita bushes outside the bedroom window awakened me. At first I thought birds had arrived to raid the berries. But no, it was chipmunks holding a breakfast party. How they feasted! Sitting up in bed, I felt like a privileged host. Then I must have made a revealing movement, for in the flick of an eyelash they were gone, running off in silky ribbons to a safer bush farther away.

Birds came next morning. When I wakened to chirping, expecting chipmunks again, instead there were pine siskins, fox sparrows, and white crowns, a few at a time, gleaning what the chipmunks had left.

Matt Davis Trail

"TAKE AWAY TAMALPAIS and what is left of Marin County would hardly fill a wheelbarrow," Albert S. Evans, editor of the San Francisco *Daily Alta* wrote in 1869 after his first visit to the mountain.

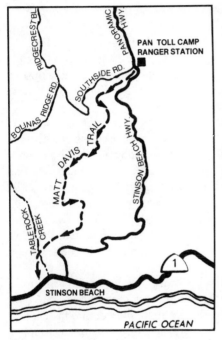

"The mountain itself is rugged and rough," he reported five years later. "Small parties occasionally visit the mountain during the summer months . . . but the character of the trail is such that the majority of them are satisfied with the view from halfway up." It must have been quite an odyssey. At that time the best place to ascend was from San Rafael, reached by boat. The first road over the mountain wasn't built until 1884.

The view from halfway up the mountain is still satisfying, especially looking west at the limitless horizon that is the blue Pacific. One of the great trails on the mountainside today, high enough up the slope to offer a pleasant variety of terrain, is the Matt Davis, the lifetime work of a humble San Francisco carpet layer. The countryside was almost as rugged as Evans had described when Matt Davis began spending his weekends creating the trail that bears his name. Most of the expenses were paid out of his own pocket, with help in the last few years before his death in 1940 from the California Alpine Club and the Tamalpais Conservation Club. Trailbuilders Roy Winne, Fred Sandrock, and Harold Atkinson have turned their hands to improving the trail from time to time since then. More recently young people from the California Conservation Corps have given the Matt Davis Trail a complete overhauling.

The trail actually begins a quarter mile up Throckmorton Ridge from the historic Mountain Home Inn site, a spot established in 1912 as a sandwich counter and rest stop along the Mount Tamalpais and Muir Woods Railway line. When Matt Davis began his work, like other visitors he came from San Francisco by ferry and train. In the late winter or early spring when Fern Canyon Falls are roaring with water is the best time to enjoy the eastern length of the trail, between the approach to East Peak and Bootjack Camp. In May my choice is the last lap, from the Pan Toll Ranger Station, the state park headquarters, to Stinson Beach.

To make this walk, take a friend or more, but not your dog, and transport yourself northwest from San Francisco via the Golden Gate Bridge, Highway 101, Shoreline Highway, and Panoramic Highway. A tollhouse once stood across the highway from the Pan Toll Ranger Station. Oral history has it that the tolltaker put a skillet on the nearby fencepost whenever he wasn't present. In those days, no one cheated. It just wasn't done.

Golden Gate Transit provides good transportation to Pan Toll, especially on weekends, and makes the uphill return easier if you time your walk right.

Once at the station, cross Panoramic Highway and walk uphill on the narrow path that climbs to a trailmarker at the first curve on Southside Road. Plunge downhill from the marker into the chaparral, round the curve, and you are in a serpentine outcropping. Pause a moment to locate Southside Road above, bound for Rock Springs, and Panoramic below, winding down to Stinson Beach. The Matt Davis Trail is so cleverly sited that walkers will not cross either again. Only the sharpest ears will be aware of the roads from the trail.

Seven canyons are crossed by the trail, which loops through the oak, bay, manzanita, and fir trees in a great scalloplike festoon. In the depths of each one is a stream, usually dry at this time of year, but discernible in the clever engineering of stone runoff channels. Tarweed makes the pungent odor along the meadowside approach.

After leaving the fourth canyon, one emerges from the forest on a grassy knoll. Take the upper trail. Don't smoke on the trail al-

though California chaparral is fire-climax adapted, evolved through milennia of natural fires long before the white man came. Nomadic Indians often set fires as well to drive out game. Like his resistance to acceptance of predators in the natural scheme of things, the white man, you and I fellow walker, resists the naturalness of fires, largely because of the potential threat to us or to property.

You soon come upon a trailsign indicating the westward route to Stinson Beach. Follow it and once again you are in forest. Notice how well footbridges have been constructed and natural embankments shored up with railroad ties. Later in the steeper sections of the descent, old sapling logs have been used for handrails.

When you reach the sign for Table Rock, pause and go out on the rock for two special surprises. The first is a stupendous broad coastal view, revealing all of Stinson Beach and its sandspit below with Bolinas visible on the cliffs above Bolinas Point and Duxbury Reef beyond the lagoon. Surprise number two is the music of the surf and the counterpoint of a waterfall below Table Rock. Thousands of hikers have paused here for their picnic lunch, as Matt Davis himself often did. If you forgot your sandwich, relax. Stinson Beach is only fifteen minutes away.

Go downhill, looking up at the waterfall as you round Table Rock, then follow the trail on the near side of the creek through the woods to emerge near the streetsign for Belvedere and Buena Vista avenues. Take the road to the left, and you plunge down into the happy holiday world of Stinson Beach, a town whose only raison d'être has been pleasure. The bus back up to Pan Toll stops in the Stinson Beach parking lot. Formerly a state park, it is now part of the Golden Gate National Recreation Area.

19

"At last they came to where Reflection sits — that strange old woman who . . . steals light out of the past to shed it on the future," Olive Schreiner once wrote.

That's how museums seem to me — places where light from the past is shed on the now — which of course was future to the past.

The Miwok Museum has grown out of Marin County's overwhelming urge to know more of the past of its land. In the days of the Indians, there were several hundred Indian villages in Marin, 119 of them on the Point Reyes Peninsula alone. The museum itself sits on one such site, and many of the artifacts in its collection were dug in the adjacent oak grove.

There is hardly a place in the county where fishing weights, charmstones, beads, or arrowheads have not been spaded out of the ground at one time or another by a gardener. Visit almost any old Marin garden and there is usually a metate or hammerstone tucked in somewhere among the cineraria. To behold one of these treasures is to draw aside for an instant the curtains of the past. Inevitably it sets the finder to pondering. Who used it? How did it get there? How was it made?

The place that has the answers is the "hands on" collection at the Miwok Museum. Here one has not only the thrill of touching another culture, but the even greater appreciation of skill that comes to the visitor who returns to become actively involved. Among other things, volunteers at the Miwok Museum can learn to drill those beads, chip those arrows, weave those baskets, and even to cook as the Miwoks did.

Miwok City Park

MIWOK CITY PARK in Novato is best known for the Marin Museum of the American Indian, a remarkable ethnographic and artifactual collection of Native Americans.

Many of its artifacts were excavated on the site, a former Miwok village. First-time visitors happening upon this rapidly growing collection may become so entranced with its richness that they never discover the hidden thirty-five acres of additional parkland adjoining the museum. It stretches back along the shoreline of Novato Creek and up an unspoiled hill to provide some of the most pleasant walking in the area.

To make this walk, transport yourself north from San Francisco via Highway 101 to Novato. The museum is located at 2200 Novato Boulevard at San Miguel Way. There are two ways to approach. One is the poky milk-route along South Novato Boulevard, which affords interesting glimpses of the new and old Novato side by side. It's a chance to see how Novato, fastest growing city in Marin, has come to be second in size only to San Rafael and may soon outstrip it. This route will take you right to the door of the museum. The other is a more rapid chute, San Marin Drive, through an affluent enclave totally constructed by one developer. If you choose this route, bear left for one very long block when you reach Novato Boulevard.

Park and walk toward the museum building, which once stood on the downtown Novato site of the Crocker Bank and was given to the city in 1973. It is open Sundays from 1 to 4 P.M., weekdays from 10 A.M. to 4. For this walk, save its attractive displays of Indian life, geologic specimens, and historical collections until last. Continue past the building to the grove of huge old bay and oak trees on the creek bank beyond.

Go under the trees into the deep shade of the creek bank and pause a moment. It almost has the feeling of a house. If the blackness of the earth underfoot seems unusually sooty, your instincts as an archeologist are sound. This is the area that was excavated in the late fifties to yield many of the beads, charmstones, fishing weights, and metates inside the museum.

Walk toward the picnic tables (which can be reserved through the Novato Recreation and Park Department for special occasions) and continue along the creekside until you run into deeper wildwood, then bear left. Cross the paved bicycle path and skirt the brush, crossing on the lawn until you are parallel to 59 San Miguel Way.

You will then be at a concrete footbridge. A sign to the right points to the Miwok Trail. Go out halfway on the bridge and pause to look both up and down the creek, happily saved from trenching by the U.S. Army Corps of Engineers some years back. Notice the tot lot near the sandy beach on the left. Children play here as Indian children once played while their mothers did the family washing in Novato Creek.

Watch out for the steep step as you come off the bridge. If you smoke, from here on leave your cigarettes in your pocket. About fifty feet beyond the bridge, bear right. Soon the broad footpath emerges from the streamside willows. Take another right at the next fork, and within a few feet you are in dry open meadow where brodeia and amole grow. About a hundred feet farther pause to look back toward the Sweetwater Ranch. By another name it is the undeveloped O'Hare Park. San Marin High School is also visible. The broad highway you see looking west is Novato Boulevard on its way around Little Mountain to Stafford Lake.

Continue climbing and soon you are in an airy grove of coast live oak, black oak, valley oak, and a number of hybrids of one or another. At the crest, walk out to the right into the grassy flat, trampled by the deer who sleep here, to look down on "The Valley of the Gentle Seasons" that lies below, sheltered on the opposite side by Big Rock Ridge. Lucas Valley is beyond the horizon line. Look to the left to discern Mount Diablo and San Pablo Bay. Since the weather in Novato is reputed to be the best in the Bay Area, this is visible most days.

Return to the trail and continue along the footpath. Barbed wire on the left is a reminder that this was once part of the old Oliva Ranch. Soon the trail swings around overlooking Oliva Drive, once the road to the ranchhouse. Now it threads its way through Park Haven, a townhouse development. As the trail descends, look on the downhill side for a tangle of pipes and the concrete platform that once supported old redwood water tanks. Mount Burdell, and the TV transmitter on it, is visible through the trees on the right.

As you pass the fallen trees, notice the blue elderberries nearby, a useful plant to Indians. "We dry them to use in our student pro- grams," museum director Virginia Hotz, who conducted me on this walk, said. "The Indians also used them for split-stick rattles, for courting flutes, whistles, and gambling staves."

The big metal-covered barn visible below, formerly the red- wood barn site of the ranch, is now used by the Northwoods Bow- men for an indoor archery range. Farther along, the sharp-eyed can look through the trees on the slope far beyond the valley to spot an intrusion of Sonoma volcanic rock, which looks like a broad scar below the ridgeline. Red-tailed hawks often soar near it, riding the thermals. A great blue heron flew over as we walked and quail scur- ried off the trail.

Go downhill at the next fork. In a trice you are back at the bridge. Cross it and you have left rural California for suburbia. Bear left on the sidewalk toward the bollards and as you follow the asphalt (abreast of 51 San Miguel Way) back into the trees, look on your right for an oak used for storage by the acorn woodpecker. Next landmark along the trail is a little redwood grove, usually much in need of mulch.

When you reach the tule and cattail pond, a part of the native plant garden, you are back at the museum where all the pleasures of the collection await. Browse to your heart's content in this friendly place before hurtling back into the hurly-burly of the present day.

20

Putting on a pair of Clark's cushion-soled chukkas, or desert boots, for this morning's walk around the volcanic preserve, I am reminded that an editor friend who recently vacationed in New Orleans told me a pair of their cousins, called Polyveldts, saw him through miles of walking comfort during Carnival and Mardi Gras.

Cowboy boots and the kind of black leather ankle-high shoes that old Italian gentlemen wear are what Richard Brautigan walks in, and he's a man who doesn't own a driver's license and doesn't plan to get one. Since ours is a repressive age that wants everyone ticketed and catalogued, he carries his passport for identification.

Robert Sibley
Volcanic Regional Preserve

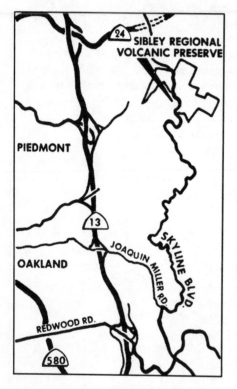

T EN MILLION YEARS ago, the San Francisco Bay Area had its own Mount Saint Helens. No, it was neither Tamalpais nor Diablo! The cauldron that spewed out molten lava, mud, and ash to form the East Bay hills is located in Oakland, in the park recently renamed Sibley Regional Volcanic Preserve in honor of its geologic importance.

Two volcanoes have been located within the preserve in an area that may well have been mapped as "intensively as any area of comparable size in the world." Although students of geology at U.C. Berkeley have been mapping the terrain from as early as the days of Professor Andy Lawson, it is only recently that the owners of the land were formally notified of the extraordinary nature of their holdings.

The notifier is Stephen W. Edwards, a graduate student in the department of paleontology and part-time gardener with the East Bay Regional Parks Botanic Garden, who mapped the park "for fun" one fall to improve his mapping skills. "While I was doing it," he told me as we walked along the trail toward Roundtop, "I found a couple of volcanoes and other volcanic evidence."

To enjoy the "volcanic walk," wear your hiking boots and bring a sunhat or wait for a cool day. Your dog is welcome on a leash, but no cigarettes. Transport yourself east from San Francisco via the Bay Bridge and Highway 24. Go south on the Warren Freeway to Redwood Road, then uphill on Redwood to Skyline Boulevard. Bear left on Skyline past its junction with Joaquin Miller Road five miles to the Sibley Regional Volcanic Preserve entrance.

Park and walk toward the display board visible from the entrance, which now bears a volcanic map and description of the exciting past of this land during the Miocene. When you have absorbed it, go up the paved trail beyond an automotive barrier of rough-hewn planks. "Professor Garniss Curtis, who did the potassium-argon dating for Olduvai Gorge, was really the discoverer of the volcanic vents," Steve Edwards told me modestly enough. "He verified the origin. All I really did was let the EBRPD know what a geologic treasure the public has here."

About the time you approach a Y, a water tank becomes visible ahead on the slope of Roundtop. Bear left and head for the tank. The other trail goes up 1,763-foot-high Roundtop, whose views unfortunately are obscured by a Monterey pine forest.

The little path you cross may look like a deer trail at first glance, but it is actually part of the East Bay Skyline National Recreation Trail, a thirty-one-mile ridgetop route for walkers that links Chabot, Redwood, Roberts, Huckleberry, Sibley, Tilden, and Wildcat regional parks, as well as several open space and EBMUD preserves. If you are planning to walk the Skyline some weekend, file this tank as a trail landmark in your memory bank.

"Most nature lovers hate the kind of scars building such a reservoir leaves on the land," Steve Edwards said as we neared the tank, "but EBMUD has done the geologist a service here, and so has Kaiser Sand and Gravel in the quarries we will see later, by revealing vents, outcrops, and other geologic features that are usually out of sight underground." Walk past the tank to the fence to discover you are looking west toward Mount Tamalpais. The big valley immediately below is underlain by riverbeds of the 10- to 12-million-year-old Orinda Formation where fossil mastodons, hipparions, camels, and prongbucks have been unearthed. Due north is the main ridge of the Berkeley hills, underlain by lavas. Eucalyptus trees below, whose leaves seem speared on dead trunks, are survivors of a killing frost a few years ago. Originally planted by Oakland real estate magnate Frank Havens, of the Mahogany Eucalyptus and Land Company, they were intended as a lumber crop. Havens's bubble burst, after he had planted thousands of trees between 1910 and 1913, when he learned he had the wrong tree. The quick-growing blue gum was not the valuable lumber tree used in Australia. When you have admired the view, go behind the water tank to see a 15-foot-thick dark grey basalt dike that cut through brown volcanic mudflows. "You are looking at a feeder into the volcano that shaped the Berkeley hills," Steve Edwards says. "It may not look beautiful to you, but so much is revealed here in cross section that for a geologist it is paradise."

Retrace your steps back to the broad gravel trail and bear right, and right again at the fork. When you reach the gate, open it, go through, and reclose it to keep cattle in. You are still within the park. East Bay Regional Park District permits grazing on many of its lands to minimize fire danger. As you round the next curve, don't be alarmed if you smell skunk. The little blue flower underfoot is *Navarettia squarosa*, better known as skunkweed for the perfume it emits when trod on.

About twenty-five feet short of the next fork, which comes from above, look on your right at the small bare cliff to discern the pebble conglomerate of the Orinda Formation and a fault running at an angle toward the right. Bear left at the next fork. Soon you will reach a quarried area where a magnificent outcrop shows the Moraga Formation reverse faulted over Orinda mudstones. After you have puzzled it out, retrace your steps again and do a right turn with the trail. The fence on the right is a boundary of the park. From this unexpected view area, the south half of pastoral Siesta Valley and Highway 24 are visible. Walk to your left to the old quarry here to see volcano number two revealed against the far quarry wall like a map. Four other volcanoes have been located on the adjoining ranch — private property geologists hope will one day be added to the park. As you look across the quarry at the massive grey volcanic plug, you are seeing, not upended strata, but the units of basalt that pulled apart as layers when the hot lava flow cooled. A complex vent, it too was one of the major feeders for lavas that support the

Berkeley hills. Don't be tempted to take the footpath along the left wall of the quarry unless you are spry.

Once again retrace your steps back to the trail and bear right at the next fork to see a cliff of tuff, or volcanic ash, before returning the way you came, for another look at the parking lot display board. It will help any novice absorb the message in the stones.

"Any chance of a repeat performance?" I asked Steve Edwards as we cooled off from our walk by the park fountain. "Not likely," he said. "The subduction process that caused Roundtop to clear its throat of magma has moved northward. That's what is causing all the activity at Mount Saint Helens."

21

It gets harder every year for me to drive south from San Francisco along El Camino Real, along the Bayshore Freeway, or even along Highway 280. The memory of open shoreline, of acres of waving grasses, of marshland from which birds arose by the thousands like a cannon shot, of fruit trees in bloom, of one lone tannery, of a big red barn in a vast field — all now replaced by slurbs or miles of industrial slum — is painful to me. The loss eats at my soul. The quality of life here has become so diminished by population pressures, it sometimes seems almost unbearable.

The same shock of loss came to me when first I traveled the Tokaido Road in Japan after having enjoyed Hiroshige's ukiyo-e prints of the fifty-three stops, each a day's journey on foot, between Tokyo and Kyoto.

Yet we have seen in San Francisco that it is possible to reverse the process of deterioration of a place. Ghirardelli Square is a good example, for this was once industrial waterfront, just as surely as the area bordering the "bloody Bayshore." Perhaps the children who enjoy the Coyote Point Museum will make a comparable turnaround down the Peninsula when they are grown.

I hope I live long enough to see the Bayshore become rural again. Only the old really know how the quality of life has diminished, tarnished, cheapened, since the advent of the automobile.

Coyote Point Museum

IMAGINE YOURSELF AS a drop of water, rained down into the Santa Cruz Mountains and launched on a journey to the sea. If the possibilities sound exciting, the new Coyote Point Museum, in San Mateo County's wonderful oasis, the Coyote Point Park, is for you.

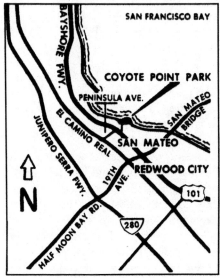

To make this walk, transport yourself seventeen miles south from San Francisco via the Bayshore Freeway, Highway 101. Take the Peninsula Avenue exit at Burlingame and follow the park signs east. Approaching from the south, Poplar Avenue offramp is the key that unlocks this treasure trove. Be prepared to pay a two dollar parking fee per car and, unless you go on Friday which is free, another dollar per adult or fifty cents per child for six- through seventeen-year-olds at the museum door.

Park and walk uphill toward the handsome new Douglas fir building designed by Palo Alto architect John W. Stypula. It is so sensitively placed among the tall eucalyptus John McLaren planted long ago, it looks as though it had been there forever, or conversely, had popped up overnight like a mushroom. Actually it has been twelve years in the planning and building and cost $1.9 million in federal, state, county, and private money.

Once at the entrance, go in, walk through the broad blue-carpeted corridor toward that inviting panorama of bay water and bridge framed by trees visible through the big window at the end. En route you will pass classrooms and auditorium on the one side, a museum shop on the left. Tempting as it is to head up immediately on the stairway on the left, forbear for a moment to look out the window toward the upper right to discern the big bee-tube. This is a private transparent entrance to the museum for a resident hive whose honey will be harvested and ultimately offered for sale here.

As you climb the stairs enjoying the two-story view window, if you feel islanded, your instincts are true. Coyote Point was an island that until 1933 sheltered "Indian Joe" Evencio, the last Costanoan Indian on the Peninsula. Tidelands were filled to make more land where the golf course is today. Quonset hut and other temporary buildings used by the museum were part of a U.S. Government Merchant Marine Cadet School once located on Coyote Point.

At the upper landing walk straight ahead before entering the exhibit hall for another look into the humming bee-tube. Then as you approach the showroom, be prepared for a surprise.

The big airy room, clean as a Shaker meetinghouse, is the point at which you turn into that drop of water, for you arrive, cloud-high, at the uppermost of four descending levels. Bare oak floors treated like a basketball court to withstand abuse are connected by ramps leading downward. Overhead, poet Gary Snyder's voice is caught on paper: "air, fire, water and Earth is our dancing place now," he says on the story board. Black Elk speaks too: "To the center of the world you have taken me and showed the goodness and the beauty and the strangeness of the greening earth, the only mother."

To one side is a biosphere, a slice of the earth created in decoupage by volunteers, members of the museum association or of the Junior League, which has long contributed its support. "Nature to be commanded must be obeyed," enjoins Francis Bacon near the rock that depicts earth, under a lotus form that represents the sun, by the introductory exhibit, "A Place Called Earth." To get more local, go around behind the next panel for "A Place Called San Mateo."

Next level down, the scene stealers are sculptured oak trees and redwood trees, whose startling dimensions look like they were conceived in a giant kaleidoscope, rather than a seed. When you stand under the conifers, look up for a great illusion. Under the wagon-wheel oaks, walk toward the wall on your left to discover some live animals, including the bees, some termites, and woodrats in the display on communities and ecosystems.

Ease on down the ramps as you will. By the time you reach the lowest level you will have passed through the coniferous forest (designer Gordon Ashby's interpretation) and grassland on your way to the coastal scrub on one side of the gallery, and through broadleaf forest, chaparral, and finally baylands on the other. You'll also have a new understanding of Man's place in the natural world. "Human Impact" cases, funded by a grant from the National Endowment for the Humanities, are displayed with each of the six biotic communities to demonstrate historical use, environmental concerns, and some future possibilities.

Level three has another scene stealer, the food chain pyramid, an arresting tower of power done in soft sculpture that depicts the diet of a red-tailed hawk for one year — 1,069 mice, 98 small birds, 20 gophers, 18 rabbits, 15 squirrels, 15 shrews, 9 game birds, 7 snakes, 4 rats, and 2 weasels, to be exact. It also shows how the hawk's diet feeds itself awaiting his dinner — as graphic a biosystem as one could envision. Be sure to walk to the opposite wall and take the steps down for the thrill of walking over "the marsh" on the lowest level. Then cross to find the tule pond and walk through the aquarium behind it. There are, naturally enough, plenty of other drops of water to merge with on this journey to the sea.

"It is my hope that the exhibit will provoke people to do something in their own lives that moves them closer to an accord with nature . . . make changes that allow them to live in harmony with natural processes," Gordon Ashby said of his aim for the museum. Whether they do or not, the message is so subtle, they'll enjoy the walk.

22

"For God's sake, let us sit upon the ground/ And tell sad stories of the death of kings," wrote William Shakespeare in King Richard II, when wars were small, courage a viable virtue, and personal glory still a possibility.

Enamored as we've been of the dollar, for a long time the United States has swept death, courage, and sentiment under the rug of disinterest. But things don't go away just because you don't look at them. We need our parades, retreats, and reveilles. We need all our rituals celebrating heroism if only to remind us how foolish wars always are.

Presidio Walk

THERE WERE SPANISH-AMERICAN War veterans in the Armistice Day parades of my childhood. With a band behind them playing "The girl I left behind me . . ." they marched,

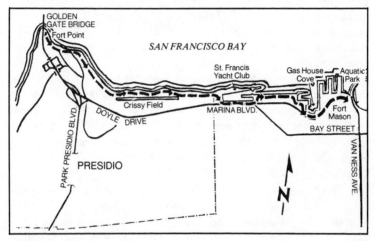

maybe exaggerating their limps a little, a meager grove of old gnarled ambulant trees, like Birnam woods coming to Dunsinane sans camouflage.

The ranks of World War I veterans were longer. And sprightlier. "Pack up your troubles in your old kit bag . . ." their marching bands played. Or "Goodbye Broadway, Hello France." Sometimes, remembering what it was like to be a doughboy, they sang, ". . . and the caissons go rolling along," and, "It's a long way to Tipperary . . ." The crowds lining the length of Lombard Street to see the men parade from Fort Mason to the National Cemetery in the Presidio sang along with them. Women, widowed perhaps, would sometimes brush away a poignant tear when they sang, ". . . though our lads are far away, they dream of home."

To keep Memory Lane at arm's length, the Sixth Army pipe band, stalwart six-foot giants made taller by their shako hats, would liven things up with "K-K-K-Katy" or "Mademoiselle from Armentiers, Parlez-Vous?" Especially if there were a visiting contingent of Forty 'n Eighters from the Rainbow Regiment with a motorized cattle car in the parade.

There was always one group of marchers that puzzled me. They were the telephone operators, a group of stately ladies in long skirts. Not nurses, not Red Cross workers, and not quite soldiers. The band behind them would usually play "How You Gonna Keep 'Em Down on the Farm, After They've Seen Paree?" or sometimes, more appropriately, "Hello Central, Give Me No Man's Land." For these were the "Hello Girls," General "Black Jack" Pershing's elite multilingual corps of telephone operators, many recruited out of San Francisco.

They puzzled Congress too. There were only eighteen of the telephone operators left, three of them from the Bay Area, when the United States finally decided they were soldiers after all and provided honorable discharges for the "Hello Girls" sixty-one years later. To honor the Female Telephone Operators Unit of the Army Signal Corps the Presidio Museum opened an exhibit of memorabilia of their service.

The museum is a good walk in itself anytime, but for old times' sake, consider a stroll through the Presidio, along part of the old Memorial Day Parade route. Weekending motorists pushed the parade off Lombard, which is, ironically enough, a military highway, so forgo this part and begin at the Lombard Street gate on Lyon. At the outset, for historical perspective, walk one block south along the handsome Presidio wall, to play detective for a moment and see where the D-car street railway once entered the Presidio. It takes a sharp eye to discern mends in the wall. For a nickel the D-car offered a thirty-minute scenic trip from the Ferry Building, but it is better remembered for its Lothario motorman, a bigamist known as the "Ding-Dong Daddy of the D-car Line."

As you stroll back to the main gate, look across the street at the little cluster of shops. Before Prohibition, it was a row of saloons and gambling houses. One memorable night in 1898 the Tennessee Regiment, about to leave for the Philippines, rioted here in protest when the proprietor of a gin mill was discovered using loaded dice. They proceeded to set fire to the place and to burr the threads on water hydrants. Their revenge was complete as they sat along the stone wall, shouting the rebel yell while frustrated firemen vainly tried to couple hoses. As a result of the demonstration, San Francisco fire trucks carry threading tools and fireplugs have a locking device.

Take a good look at the fine old bronze cannons, captured during the Spanish-American War, and much like the ones that guarded Castillo de San Joaquin, the Spanish predecessor to Fort Point in 1776.

As you walk through the handsome Lombard gate, try to envision how the ladies wept and sighed as the First California Regiment marched through here to board the troopship *City of Pekin* at Fort Mason, bound for the islands. Watchers whistled in admiration when the Twentieth Kansas, Colonel Frederick Funston in command, marched out, each man wearing a tremendous sunflower issued by the citizens of Kansas who came to see their men off to war.

Eucalyptus trees along the wall date from 1880, when the post agronomist ordered planting of the once-bare Presidio. Go through the gate until you reach Letterman Drive, the first right turn. This land was horse pasture for the cavalry until the earthquake and fire of 1906 when hundreds of tents sheltered the homeless. Tide flats lay below where Crissy Field is today.

When you reach the tricky junction near the Military Police Station, continue on Presidio Boulevard into the trees. Land downhill beyond MacArthur Avenue on the left is still known as Tennessee Hollow for the encampment of that much-admired regiment. Cordell Hull, secretary of state in Franklin Roosevelt's cabinet, was a captain with the Tennesseeans here.

Houses lining the approach and either side of Funston Avenue are excellent examples of military Victorians, most built around 1862. At Funston you have reached Alameda Gate. Go into the little boulevard circle planted with ceanothus to locate markers for the Presidio Historic Trail and the Ecology Trail identifying this as the former formal entrance to the Presidio headquarters. Bear left along the charming little company street, observing as you walk how gracious the setting is for having a planter strip of grass and street trees between the sidewalk and street. At Moraga Avenue, bear right, past Pershing Hall, to reach the Chapel of Our Lady. One of the four bronze markers delineating the original Spanish Presidio's four corners is located inside the now-expanded chapel.

Continue on Moraga to reach the Officer's Club, which conceals a part of the adobe wall of the Spanish commandancia within. Fun for kids is to discover the names of the cannon guarding it.

Cross to Pershing Square where Old Glory waves on the site of the home of General Pershing, which burned while he was on duty overseas, killing four members of his family. Old bronze cannons, which like those by the officer's mess once overlooked the Golden Gate, surround it. Daily salutes are fired from the seventy-five-millimeter guns.

When you have read the many markers, follow Sheridan Avenue northwestward, away from the Parade Ground, to reach the National Cemetery. Traditionally the Memorial Day and Armistice Day (now Veteran's Day) parades have been timed to reach this point before 11 A.M., when a moment of silence commemorates both the signing of the Armistice that ended World War I and the valiant soldiers who died in that conflict. Who remembers the ends of subsequent wars?

When the last bugle note of taps dies on the breeze, follow Lincoln Boulevard eastward pass the Parade Ground to Funston to reach the first post hospital, built in 1857, and now the Presidio Museum. "J'ecoute," the Hello Girls used to say when they answered the phones near the battlefields of Ypres and Verdun, "I am listening." For all their valor, it took a long time before anyone listened to them.

June

23

Walkers are freer of stress than the sedentary. Stress, according to Dr. Hans Selye, the famous endocrinologist, is the "non-specific response of the body to demands made upon it." In other words, stress is the stuff that ulcers and heart attacks thrive on.

When we walk, to quote anthologists Sussman and Goode, "we make a frontal attack by way of the muscles on whatever is disturbing the mind."

First the muscles smooth out the tensions through a rhythmic pattern of contracting and relaxing. Then the nerve ends send a message back to the central nervous system saying everything is A-Okay. When these comforting signals reach the conscious mind, they have a liberating effect.

It is no coincidence that the breathing and rhythm of walking are simulated in the use of a mantra during meditation. For example, try repeating over and over the mystic syllable "Om," which is known as the universal mantra. It soon sounds like the tolling of a big bell as you breathe in, like the echo of a clapper as you breathe out. It is very like the vibrations and rhythms of a comfortable relaxed stride.

Either way one can drain off stress, anxiety, anger, or fatigue. A walk itself may not solve anything, but it lets the storms of the body and mind blow themselves out.

Roberts Recreation Area — An Open Secret

ONE OF THE best kept secrets in the East Bay is the urbane eighty-eight-acre Thomas J. Roberts Recreation Area. If you are looking for a great place to take an outdoorsy dad for a barbecue, swim, or walk, this is a candidate. Only the aficionados know of its swimming pool, picnic areas, softball field, outdoor dance floor, children's playground, and well-kept trails through redwoods and chaparral. It is a jewel of a park surrounded by other parks. The vast 2,074-acre Redwood Regional Park clasps it like a lover on three sides, while Oakland's Joaquin Miller Park nudges it on the west.

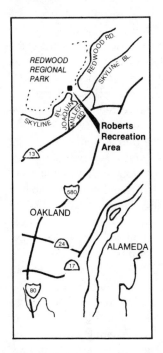

The first park to be "adopted" under the East Bay Regional Park District's innovative adopt-a-park program for industry to help relieve the funding pressures brought on by the 1978 tax cutbacks, Roberts Recreation Area is under the protective wing of Kaiser Aluminum & Chemical Corporation. The informal partnership has brought some great improvements, some needed repairs, some excellent maintenance, enthusiasm, and during summer, good free transportation for kids to the gate.

To make this walk, transport yourself via BART to the Fruitvale Station. Ask for a transfer, then look nearby for the AC Transit shuttlebus named "Bus-ter Roberts," not the best pun, perhaps, but one the kids enjoy. It runs between 11 A.M. and 6 P.M. The transfer slip lets BART riders of all ages ride free on the shuttle. Thanks to Robert's adoptive parent, East Bay kids can board the shuttle free any-

where along the route—Fruitvale and Lincoln avenues, Joaquin
Miller Road and Skyline Boulevard.

If you must use your own wheels, transport yourself to the East
Bay via the San Francisco-Oakland Bay Bridge. Take Route 24 to
the Warren Freeway, Route 13. Follow 13 south to Joaquin Miller
Road, bear left, or east, on Skyline Boulevard to the well-marked
park entrance on the east side of the boulevard.

Once there, pay the modest fee at the kiosk. Happy shouts will
tell you where the swimming pool is located at the north end of the
parking lot. Walk past it at the outset toward the service yard at the
north extremity of the entrance road. Go around the garage to the
left. At its end, look for a grassy trail that goes downhill past an automotive barrier. This is an access to the Graham Trail, which makes a
pleasant loop around the heart of Roberts Recreation Area to give
the walker a sample of its pleasures and possibilities.

Follow the trail downhill through the purple periwinkle, a hint
of the longtime human occupancy of this land. Once part of the vast
Rancho de San Antonio, the redwoods you walk through were
logged as early as 1840, many by adventurers and seamen who had
jumped ship. By 1852, Thomas and William Prince had established
a steam-driven sawmill, one of many to work in the East Bay redwoods, about a mile north of the first junction you reach. Bear right.
Tall as they are, the redwoods on either hand are second growth.

Within fifteen years of the Gold Rush, the redwoods that had
guided early seafarers safely through the Golden Gate and San
Francisco Bay were gone, including a tree that may well have been
the biggest coast redwood of all. The stump of this giant, $33\frac{1}{2}$ feet
in diameter, was discovered in 1855 by Dr. William P. Gibbons, one
of the founders of the Academy of Sciences, on a walk through
what is now the Redwood Regional Park.

"Over a miniature valley on a space not exceeding three acres,
I have counted not less than 150 stumps," he reported, "the small-
est of which is 12 feet in diameter. Three fourths of them exceeded
16 feet and one fourth 20 feet in diameter from three to six feet
above the level of the ground." This cemetery of trees made a conservationist of him instantly. "Even the melancholy pleasure of
seeing the ruins of this forest," he wrote, "will be lost in a few years
unless some protective influence be extended over it."

Gibbons was far ahead of his time. The protective influence he

longed for finally came in 1951 when the eighty-eight acres of
Roberts Recreation Area was purchased by the EBRPD from
rancher Elsie Brougher. Plum blossoms in the park reveal in springtime where her orchard stood near cutover land once used for cattle
grazing. The park name commemorates an early park commissioner, locomotive engineer, fireman, and labor leader, "Tommy" J.
Roberts, who served for twenty-seven years as business agent for
Local 39 of the Stationary Engineers Union. He died in 1958 at the
ripe old age of ninety-five after watching Oakland grow from a town
of 5,000 to 400,000.

It is hard to believe such a city is close as one comes through
the tall *Sequoia sempervirens*. Wild currant, starflowers, ceanothus,
lupine, leatherwood, and cleavers grow along the trail. Deer and
raccoon tracks cross it among the horses' hoofprints. Don't resent
those horsedroppings. All the East Bay Regional Park District's
gravel trails can be used jointly by both horsemen and hikers. This
one, the Graham Trail, like the Dunn Trail that adjoins it, was
named for a member of the Metropolitan Horsemen's Association.
Since the horse is a skittish and easily panicked creature, if you are
new to joint-use trails, when you meet a horse on the trail, good
hiking manners require that the person on foot step off the trail and
stand still until the horse passes. If there is poison oak at the trailside,
just stand still.

Soon the trail leaves the trees and opens into chaparral. Mount
Diablo and the valley between seem an infinity of open space, visi-
ble at some turns. Voices may come across the valley immediately
east from the West Ridge Trail, a portion of the East Bay National
Skyline Trail, which runs along the next fold in the Coast Range.
More likely you will hear sightseers admiring the view from Diablo
Vista, immediately uphill on your right, once the site of a pony ring
and now a favorite picnic place.

After you round the open knoll, the trail forks. Bear right, uphill
past the car barriers. In the length of a city block you are at the Roberts lower parking lot. Go over to its south edge to discern the baseball field, then cross to the western periphery to discover the dance
pavilion in its contemporary guise as a volleyball court. Picnic areas
in the redwoods behind it were once an informal amphitheater for
dancers.

When you have enjoyed this evidence of an earlier time in

park planning, recross the parking lot and follow the steps uphill to reach a broad lawn and beyond it the Children's Wading Pool and play area, with its big contemporary toys made of logs.

If the day is warm, the swimming pool and all its refreshment awaits just beyond. A suntrap on the north side is there to lure tanners. The swim is an easy, lazy way to end a walk, unless those enticing aromas of barbecue wafting through the trees drive you to distraction . . . but of course, you brought your own.

24

John Kieran, a New York naturalist, once wrote, "Comfortable footwear is at the bottom of every enjoyable step along the road. If the shoe doesn't fit, no sensible walker would think of wearing it."

You can't put the same shoe on every foot, nor give the same answer to the question, "What are the best shoes for walking?"

Most of the shoes on the six shelves in my closet are low heeled. The vacation shoes, mostly designed for warm weather walking, are my favorites. Sandals that have trod not only Ocean, Stinson, Thornton, Kehoe, Limantour, Bolinas, Carmel, and San Gregorio beaches, but the red dust of India, the black sands of Hawaii, and the muck of Thailand's rice paddies. They stand beside rope-soled espadrilles that bear smirches of bunker oil from the strands of Santa Barbara, Tenerife, and Dakar, alongside alpargatas from Guaymas and squeaky huaraches whose soles have been reglued a dozen times since they scuffed through Sonora and Chiapas. None has heels higher than half an inch.

On vacations, almost everyone walks twice as far each day as at home, and this is best done on a low heel.

San Gregorio Beach

AMONG THE JOYS of rambling southward along wonderful Highway 1 are the nine San Mateo State Beaches. Of these, one of the pleasantest is San Gregorio Beach, carved through high cliffs by the eight-mile-long San Gregorio Creek, whose far reaching tributaries drain fifty square miles of rugged mountainous country.

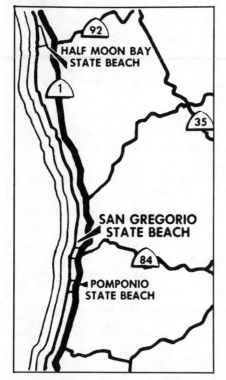

The burgeoning coastside megapolis thins out a little after one passes Half Moon Bay and the terrain gets steeper, as the pioneer Ocean Shore ("It Reaches the Beaches") Railroad learned to its dismay in 1898. It never did reach San Gregorio by rail. Instead, passengers were transported from the last railstop at Tunitas Glen by Stanley Steamer. The ride must have been marvelous. One left the depot at 12th and Mission streets at 8:30 A.M. and went by rail through scantily populated coastal towns and seaside meadows to Tunitas Creek. There one transferred to the ten-passenger steam-powered automobile stage for the trip to San Gregorio and points as far south as Santa Cruz. En route, according to the Ocean Shore Railroad ads, one passed through "the most fascinating scenery in California. Cliffs, bluffs, beaches, rocks, redwoods, gardens and marine scenery."

It is still fascinating. To make this walk today, transport yourself, a few friends, swimming gear, and picnic south from San Francisco

122

via Highway 1 about eight and a half miles south of Half Moon Bay. Look for the familiar state park sign, then pull off the highway, park, and walk down to the beach. On the cliff a busy concessionaire, with his truck backed into an unusual corral whose low walls make a counter, is often doing a land-office business in farm fresh eggs and soft drinks. Sometimes the population sounds like Chapultepec Park.

As you reach the beach trail, notice the cautionary sign, which warns against dangerous surf, sleeper waves, a backwash, and rip currents. There is also a big, warm, safe lagoon, fortunately, as scores of children seem to have discovered.

In 1769 when Gaspar de Portola and his party of explorers came this way, there was an Indian village on the lagoon. The Portola party, including Father Crespi and Miguel Costanso, made camp about a league from the mouth of the creek, remaining there for two days for the benefit of the sick and weary in their party. Crespi was so impressed by the Indians and the land, he proposed San Gregorio as a mission site.

By 1839, the four square leagues of land called Rancho San Gregorio had been granted to Don Antonio Buelna, who also owned another land grant on the present site of Stanford University. The road he built to connect the two vast ranches, now called La Honda Road, was the first one over the peninsula mountain range to the coastside. Stanford students have always found it easier to reach the beach than the early loggers who hauled logs out of San Gregorio Basin between 1855 and 1910. From 1855 when the Templeton Mill opened, and 1908 when Burt Week's Shingle Mill was rolling, there were twenty-five lumber mills that thrived in the deep, remote redwood canyons of San Gregorio. Eight-, ten-, and twenty-ox teams struggled out of the forests with the big redwood giants. Some of the logs were so tremendous they had to be horsed up out of canyons, using cables wound on a spool powered by a donkey engine.

Once on the beach, walk back up the canyon a short way. The old settlement of San Gregorio once had a Chinese village along the creek where laundry was done for lumbermen in waterside washhouses. Shacks that marked the village have floated off in high water and heavy seas long since.

A famous resort, San Gregorio House, a frame hotel overlooking the creek, was the first of many to blossom for vacationers on the San Mateo coast. In "California for the Sportsman," published by the Southern Pacific Railroad in 1911 to lure passengers to the state, San Gregorio was touted as one of the great fishing places for Quinnat and Chinook or King salmon throughout June, July, and August.

Stroll back to the beach to explore its strand or to sift through the sand for miniature shells or the occasional quartz pebble. If the beach is too crowded, don't be tempted to stray to the north, a private nude beach, unless you are prepared to pay the entrance tab. Instead, do what San Mateo residents do: Drive a mile and a half south to the next beach in the chain, Pomponio, named for a renegade Indian who terrorized the coast during the Gold Rush years. Like each of the San Mateo beaches, Pomponio has its own character. Some photographers claim it is the most photogenic on the coast, with a marshy lagoon, nicely curving estuary, and high cliffy backdrop. Pomponio also boasts a small-mouthed slimy cave, much too small to house the sea monster reputed to haunt this coastline. The monster, a smaller Loch Ness lizardy type, is supposed to haunt a cave farther north between the private Marin's Beach and Tunitas Beach. Early mariners described him with a head "high as the mast of a fishing boat" followed by a loopy series of oily humps. Leaping porpoises or schools of seals sometimes give the same impression.

If the little ranch town of San Gregorio seems more entrancing, look for the La Honda Road immediately across from San Gregorio Beach. Once so populous it had a branch of Levy Brothers, it now keeps only the Peterson & Alsford General Store and a small post office in business. The Stage Road took its name from the first stagecoach to come to the coast. San Gregorio House, almost as ghostly, is still behind the service station south of the highway, a private residence whose 1850 glories are almost forgotten.

25

We seem to have forgotten that people got along very well indeed for five thousand, and possibly ten thousand, years without the gas-guzzling automobile. How did we do it? Simple enough. We planned the requisites of life—homes, schools, shops, churches, theaters—all to the scale of a six-foot man, a five-foot woman, and growing children all dependent on their own two feet for transportation.

For example: When William Penn created the public school system in Philadelphia, he specified that a school should be located every six blocks. The distance from a child's home to school under this plan averaged three blocks. At most it was six. It was such a good system other cities in the United States adopted it. Whatever you think of busing kids to school—and I happen to think it solves nothing—busing deprives kids of the pleasure, the habit, the exercise, and the casual education gained from walking to school.

A return to William Penn's system, which already exists geographically in a majority of American cities, automatically cuts out the need for schools (read "taxpayers," please) to spend money on gas, vehicles, drivers, car insurance, and roads. It is money that once went to educating kids, rather than getting them to and fro, which they could do on their own two feet.

In the process of walking to school, kids socialize, get to know their own neighborhoods, learn a little local geography, sometimes make friends with shopkeepers, postmen, and patrolmen also walking a neighborhood, watch the changing seasons as plants and trees go through the annual succession of bloom, observe the pattern of the community, in short, learn the ebb and flow of the world.

Sonoma's Architectural Heritage

TIME LIES SWEETLY on sunny old Sonoma. The great trees of its eight-acre plaza, largest of its kind in California, rustle in the drowsy afternoons of summer. Bees buzz in the salmon-colored Sonoma rose. Lovers picnic on the grass. Children play near the city hall in its center. Old men nod on the shady benches. So peaceful a place hardly seems to be the stage for that comic opera we called the Bear Flag Rebellion. Yet a marker in the park indicates this was the scene of it on June 14, 1846, a scant 135 years ago.

Like the plaza, the surrounding blocks of the National Historic Register Area are rich with the story of the past. Mission San Francisco de Solano, restored to its adobe heyday era, the Monterey-Colonial barracks where General Mariano Vallejo housed his Mexican troops, many of the fine old adobe buildings within the mile-square area laid out by Vallejo, still stand. So do some interesting farmhouses, false-front pioneer buildings, hip-roofed cottages, great old Victorian Era homes and churches. To make it easier for the visitor to find Sonoma's architectural and historical treasures, the Sonoma League for Architectural Preservation has created a fine walking tour of the old town heart. Cleverly enough, the tour begins in Vasquez House, 129 East Spain Street, headquarters of the League, where booklets describing each site and locating it on a map are available for a modest sum.

127

To make this walk, put on your citified walking shoes and warm weather clothes. Transport yourself north from San Francisco via Highway 101, the Black Point Cutoff, Highway 36 to 121, and thence by 12 to Sonoma Plaza. Once at the plaza, bear right to First Street East. (First Street West is the other side of the plaza.) Bear left, and look for a public parking lot north of East Spain Street just behind the barracks building. Once parked, walk back toward the plaza, but leave it for last on this stroll. Instead look for El Paseo opposite the mission on East Spain Street.

Go into the Vasquez House, a steep gabled one-and-a-half-story house of wood that was built in the early 1850s for General "Fighting Joe" Hooker and once stood on the other side of the plaza. Pick up your copy of the guide in the charming little shop, then go out to find that Number 2 site is the Blue Wing Inn, also known as Sonoma House, a two-story adobe believed to have been built by Vallejo to house officers and travelers.

Resist the temptation to cross immediately to the beautiful low-lying mission and bear right instead for a block and a half along East Spain Street to see, among other interesting houses, the Ray Adler adobe at number 205. Built in 1846, it is almost unchanged from the time when it served as the Officer's Mess for the Stevenson Regiment.

After a look at Site 6, Lewis Adler's first store and the Pioneer Saloon, number 256, which once stood across from the Blue Wing Inn, backtrack to Second Street East and cross to number 196, the Castagnasso Farm, almost a picture of the rural ideal only a block and a half from the heart of town. Behind its picturesque gambrel-roofed farmhouse, barns, and grounds looms the volcanic Schocken Hill, where much of the stone visible in Sonoma was quarried. The little house at 147 was quarried from rubble of Schocken's Quarry, Number 10, for example.

At Mission San Francisco de Solano, all that survives from earliest mission days is the bell and a portion of the padre's house. The church itself, California Historical Landmark No. 3, built in 1849, was rebuilt in 1858 after a big earthquake and weakened anew by the quake of '06. Go in, for the pleasure of its deep, cool interior and displays. Kids especially will enjoy the burros out behind the mission and the awesome cactus hedge.

Cross First Street East and you strike a rich lode in this bonanza of history. Hard by Sonoma Barracks is the Toscano Hotel, which began as Nathanson's General Store. Next to it is the hotel annex, now an office of the State Department of Parks and Recreation, but originally part of the servants quarters, standing in front of the Indian Kitchen next door. The Servant's Quarters, Site 16 on the tour, is all that remains of Vallejo's Casa Grande, the home where all of his children were born. Fire destroyed the rest of the building in 1867.

The high quality of Sonoma Jack at Sonoma Valley Cheese Factory, 2 West Spain Street, has made architectural purists accept the inharmonious Art Moderne building housing it in this ancient village for almost forty years. Site 18, an adobe that began as Salvador Vallejo's home, has been the Swiss Hotel since the 1880s. Hundreds of visitors pour through the doors to see the three dollar bill on the backbar and try the Hair of the Bear sherry.

Before the walker has finished rounding the plaza and its nearby periphery, he will have visited a total of fifty-six buildings, at least a third of them adobe. One of my favorites is the Nash-Patton adobe at 579 First Street East, Number 36 on the heritage tour. It was here that John H. Nash, the first American to be alcalde, or mayor, in Sonoma under Mexican rule, lived. It was also the place where General William Tecumseh (Marching Through Georgia) Sherman arrested him in 1847 because he refused to turn over his office to the American-appointed alcalde, Lilburn W. Boggs.

Another of Sonoma's architectural gems is the Carpenter's Gothic Cottage at 564 First Street East, Site 37. Once you've seen all the charmers on the tour, come back to the plaza to linger awhile in this cool oasis. It wasn't always as relaxing as it is today. In Vallejo's time, forty Mexican cavalrymen from San Francisco's Presidio drilled on it. So did one hundred Indian soldiers. Horse races and dog and 'coon fights were held here. Soil from the plaza was dug out to build the surrounding adobe buildings, and for years the chuckholes left by such diggings remained to plague the unwary who might cross the plaza by night. It had other stirring chapters in its long, eventful life, too. One of them was the incursion of the Sonoma Valley Railroad, which put its tracks down Spain Street and preempted the plaza for a depot and roundhouse, carbarns, brickyards, and such. It took a suit against the railroad to oust the iron horse and its droppings in 1890. Credit the hardworking ladies of Sonoma Valley Women's Club for making the plaza parklike.

If this urbane little circumambulation whets your appetite for more walking, look on the map for directions to Lachryma Montis, the redwood Gothic Revival home of General Vallejo. As a bonus, a secondary route takes off from the parking lot to this handsome home via the walking trail alongside the Northwestern Pacific Railroad tracks from Depot Park. Go the other way and you reach Sebastiani winery along the tracks.

26

The colors of animals, even domestic animals, are so subtle, fashion designers could make their reputations emulating them. What could seem more sophisticated in a color scheme than the Siamese cat. That distinctive dark set of gloves, ears, and tail, that tawny back and head could have come out of the swankiest Parisian salon. Yet it has a purpose. Look at a Siamese asleep in the sun. With its dark feet tucked up against its body, it seems to be only a shadow of a round rock. Instant camouflage.

Champers, my white Alsatian, has a champagne-colored ribbon along his pelt that could hide him as a sleeping mound of wind-discolored snow in the mountains of his origin. It works equally well on a white rug.

Wild creatures are even more remarkable. Blue butterflies frequent the blue flowers — chicory, thistles, lupine, clover. White moths hover over the white yucca flowers. Canaries flit among the yellow lupines.

It takes a sharp eye, but sometimes the walker who pauses for rest awhile will have the pleasure of such discoveries if he is quiet. Tennessee Cove is dependable for this. Bobcats like to sleep on the south-facing slope high up on the right as one walks toward the ocean. Their camouflage colors are evolved for chaparral. Watch for them before you are in view of the lagoon near the ocean.

Tennessee Valley

T ENNESSEE VALLEY, ADDED last year to the National Register of Historic Places, is a beautifully unspoiled bucolic strath that leads through 1,268 acres of gently sloping hill-

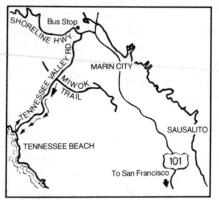

sides to a secret little beach within five miles of San Francisco. Acquired by the Golden Gate National Recreation Area in 1976, it is only accessible on foot, by way of a 1.6-mile trail. Wildflowers shyly dot the meadows along a path that meanders like the creek through land level enough for the tiniest tot or a spry grandparent. All of which makes it a great place for a walk, picnic, or even a last day of school party.

For this walk leave your dog at home. Transport yourself, picnic, and wind shirt north from San Francisco. Take the first offramp beyond Sausalito, labeled Shoreline Highway-Stinson Beach and Highway 1. It slides under the freeway, rounds a curve, and reaches Tennessee Valley Road quicker than you can Flopsy, Mopsy, and Cottontail. Bear left on Tennessee Valley Road and drive as far as you can. Golden Gate Transit Buses No. 10 and No. 20 stop near the junction of Shoreline Highway and Tennessee Valley Road. From there it will be about a mile and a half to the trailhead, just below the Tennessee Valley Stables, a boarding and horse rental facility.

The ornate Marincello gate, which once stood here in anticipation of a community of twenty thousand homes long since thwarted by conservationists, has been removed by the Park Service. Park your car near the trailhead. Look about to locate the Miwok Trail, which crosses nearby, for future reference, but for this walk, go through the hiker's stile across the cattleguard on the paved road you just left.

132

As you begin this walk, look uphill on the left above the ranch buildings to locate a green ledge along the hillslope. Geologist Salem Rice, who has been mapping this area, has identified this as part of the first road to exist in Marin County and would like to see it given an appropriate historical marker.

If you had come along this way one sunny Sunday in 1849, you might have seen Charles Lauff, Charles Alban, and 300-pounder George Brewer in a buggy being drawn along the road pell-mell by a runaway Alasan horse. Marin's pioneer buggy ride, recorded in Munro-Fraser's 1880 *History of Marin County,* "went up hill and down dale, over stones and through chaparral, hither and thither, during all the bright and merry hours of that happy Sabbath day, recking not nor caring for aught beneath the sun. The buggy, which was worth three hundred dollars in the rosy morn, was not worth a shilling in the dewy eve. Its first day's use in Marin county was its last."

You might also have scared up a grizzly or an elk. In 1916, recalling a bear hunt on Christmas Day, 1847, in which he was the guest of William A. Richardson, Lauff wrote, "As we passed into the Tennessee Valley, the hillside was white with bones of elk, deer and wild coyote, killed from time to time for their hides." Even earlier, Lieutenant Joseph Revere, a nephew of the famous silversmith who "spread the alarm through every Middlesex village and farm," participated in a comparable hunt in which the grizzly was flayed, its lard rendered on the spot, and carried back to what is now Sausalito in a blanket born by four of Richardson's vaqueros.

Not surprisingly, this area was known as Elk Valley before it became Tennessee Valley, following the wreck of the sidewheel steamer *Tennessee* March 6, 1853. The creek alongside the road is still called Elk Valley Creek. It soon joins Tennessee Valley Creek. At some points along the trail, water courses merrily on either side. Barns visible near the Bettancourt house, largely hidden by trees, are used for rangers' mounts. Like many other homes within the GGNRA, the owner has lifetime tenancy.

The second stile is to keep cattle from straying. Continue along the roadside path. Soon there is a choice of staying with the road or leaving it for the footpath through the meadow. If it is dry enough, the meadow is more fun.

Cross the stream, and fifty feet along you reach the junction with the Pacific Coast Trail, an extension of the Golden Gate Promenade that continues all the way to Tomales Point. Continue through the meadow. After you pass the "Johnnies-on-the-Spot" as rangers call the portable privies, look uphill on your right where bobcats sometimes snooze in the sun, as seemingly innocuous as housecats. Also unusual along this length of the trail are the bright yellow flowers of a miniature iris locally known as "golden-eyed grass."

One of the pleasures of this trail is to come up over a little rise and see the water of a lagoon lying unexpectedly ahead. Created by damming around 1947 to supply water for cattle and for duck-hunting, the lagoon is often alive with migrating birds. In summer, gulls frequently float here, washing salt from the runnells along their beaks. At the weir, the trail crosses the stream again and reaches the next surprise, the pebbled beach. Like Rodeo, the next beach east, jade, jasper, serpentine, and carnelian are among the pebbles.

Although the ship never sailed again, six hundred passengers came safely ashore here from the *Tennessee*. Among them were William T. Coleman, who later organized San Francisco's two vigilante committees; James Stuart, the miscreant who became the first man to be hanged in San Francisco; a hero, Chief Mate Dowling, who jumped overboard with a line tied to his waist and struggled ashore to secure a breeches buoy for saving passengers; passenger agent Thomas Gihon guarding fourteen chests of gold bound for Wells Fargo; and a Hudson Bay factor, sixty-three-year-old Peter Ogden, who also had several thousand dollars in gold coins in his locked valise. Since the valise was too heavy for him to carry very far, Ogden unlocked it, put dirty clothes on top of the coins, let some half-worn shoes hang out, and hoping that thieves would believe it contained nothing of value, set out for Sausalito. It worked. When he returned, trunks nearby had been rifled, but the satchel was untouched.

Park historians and archeologists who excavated the beach after last year's storms found more than three hundred artifacts from the *Tennessee* and possibly a few from the schooner *Fourth of July*, wrecked here in 1849. To continue the excavation, volunteers led by historian Jim Delgado are selling T-shirts imprinted with a picture of the *Tennessee* to raise funds.

If the tide is low enough, from the water's edge look to the right to see an "eye" in the cliff, possibly started by a stake or deadeye driven into the rock to try to save the *Tennessee*.

Find a place to enjoy your picnic, or sun awhile and enjoy the illusion of vacationing miles away from the city. Then to return, the stroll back is the same route you came.

July

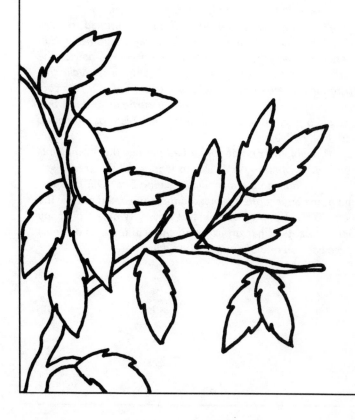

27

A tentative finger of fog pokes under the Golden Gate Bridge, probing toward Alcatraz. That's the sure sign that summer weather has reached the Bay Area. It will probably burn off by 10 A.M., leaving the whole region in glorious California blue and gold sunshine. By 3 P.M. it may come inching back. Within a day or two the "hand of God" cloud formation will be caressing the Marin Headlands. Given a few more days, San Francisco may be blanketed in fog nightly as the summer pattern sets in. Then it becomes "the cool grey city of love" that poet George Sterling enjoyed.

Not everyone likes it. Mark Twain is reputed to have said, "The coldest winter I ever spent was a summer in San Francisco." Whether he wrote it or not, it dramatizes the truth. When every other part of the country is sweltering, swimming in every pond, relishing watermelon for its cool sweetness, watching the girls in their summer dresses, San Francisco puts on a jacket, orders a hot pizza or warms up with Irish coffee.

Probably no one ever handled the weather complaints newcomers often make as well as wonderful Winifred Allen. When her husband, Harry, was building Sea Cliff, prospective home buyers often remarked that they could not see the view. "This is one of our sil-l-lver days," Winnie would say with a sweep of her arm toward the windows. "You must come back on one of our gol-l-lden days."

A Grove of Writers

OUTSTANDING TREES WERE so highly regarded not so long ago that they were often named for outstanding leaders —presidents, statesmen, generals, senators, pathfinders, writers.

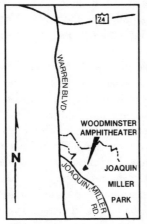

Nobody has named any trees for presidents or generals lately, but a tradition of planting trees as "living monuments" to writers, which began in 1930 in Joaquin Miller Park in Oakland, is once again being carried on by the California Writer's Club. Appropriately enough, the two redwoods planted there last year were dedicated to the "Poet of the Sierra," Joaquin Miller, whose home the park once was, and to Mark Twain, who may well be America's greatest humorist. The trees replaced a pair named earlier for the two men but removed to make way for the Woodminster Outdoor Theatre, an open-air amphitheater also dedicated to California writers. The plan is to honor additional writers annually.

The trees named Miller and Twain joined an auspicious hillslope grove in the park celebrating writers associated with the Bay Area: Robert Louis Stevenson, Kathleen Norris, Jack London, John Muir, Father Palou, Bret Harte, Edwin Markham, Edwin Rowland Sill, and Charles Warren Stoddard, to name a few. Planted between 1930 and 1956, the dates of each tree are known, making it possible to see how much growth each redwood made in a defined time, which makes for interesting walking.

The literate, who know that the word "academy" means a grove of trees, first and foremost, can have the fun of punning on schools of philosophy, as well. Plato and Socrates may not be here, but the grove certainly represents a group of learned men.

A great way to make this walk is to plan to spend a warm summer evening in the park, picnicking and later attending a summer musical under the stars. Telephone 531-9597 in advance for reservations.

139

With your picnic packed, dress in warm weather clothes and bring a warm jacket to wear around finale time. Then transport yourself to Oakland, preferably with the aid of AC Transit's 15A bus. Via your own gasoline, cross the Bay Bridge and take Highways 580 and 24 heading for Walnut Creek. From 24 turn south on 13, the Warren Freeway, to Joaquin Miller Road, making a left turn uphill on Upper Sanborn Drive into the park. Pay the parking fee and leave your wheels in any of the nine parking lots the ranger sends you to.

At the outset, go into the big circle of seats known as "The Cathedral in the Woods" to locate your seats and enjoy the vast view that forms a backdrop for the stage itself. If a plane passes overhead from Oakland Airport, relax. During performances planes are rerouted elsewhere, a bit of interagency cooperation San Francisco's park department and airport might emulate at Stern Grove. Notice the legend on the proscenium arch "Dedicated to California Writers," then go out the exit to the left of the orchestra pit as you face the stage. Walk past the building to the south edge and look for a path beyond the stage door. Step into the trees and instantly you are in a magical world where a twin recurving Beaux Arts stairway designed by Howard Gilkey descends gracefully enough for a fairy-tale princess or Busby Berkeley musical extravaganza.

The three big trees immediately on your left are named for poet laureate and librarian Ina Donna Coolbrith, journalist Charles Warren "In the Footprints of the Padres" Stoddard, and Bret "Heathen Chinese" Harte, the man who made the West romantic. Trees on the opposite side of the path nearest the building whose architect was Ed Foulkes, designer also of the Tribune tower, are named for Edwin "The Man with the Hoe" Markham, and journalist John "The Mountains of California" Muir.

Step out below the big water bowl just under the balcony of the art deco building to locate on the far side of the dry cascade the trees named for Edward Rowland "Lord Be Merciful to Me, a Fool" Sill and journalist-archeologist Charles Fletcher "My Cigarette" Lummis. Of these, all but Muir were planted October 15, 1930. The tree named for the great conservationist was planted September 26, 1931.

Return to the south staircase and go down the steps. Biggest tree on the left is named Hubert H. "History of California" Bancroft. On the right, feminists and women's libbers will be pleased to find Gertrude "The Conqueror" Atherton and Mary Hunter "Earth Horizon" Austin. Across the creek from them stand Robert Louis "The Silverado Squatters" Stevenson, Jack "Cry of the Wolf" London, and George "Cool Grey City of Love" Sterling. Analogists might chuckle that London seems to be a stauncher tree than Sterling.

Continue down the staircase, and after locating Father Francisco Palou, chronicler of the first Spanish explorations of San Francisco Bay, and Herbert E. Bolton, once professor of history at the University of California Berkeley, look for a family group of trees named for novelists Frank, Charles, and Kathleen Norris. Circular benches on either side of the path are also named for poets. Notice brass plaques. The big circular Gertrude "Handbook of Californiacs" Mott Fountain at the foot of the cascade, dedicated June 2, 1955, was named for a wife of an Oakland mayor and the mother of a young landscape designer, William Penn Mott, whose work here preceded a long career of public service in California parks. If you were one of the many couples who have been married at the scenic spot between the Mott Fountain and the adjacent Coolidge Pool, this is the place to let the old nostalgia burn.

Go all the way to the bottom at Joaquin Miller Drive to discover the most recently planted trees. Then as you climb back up the opposite side, look left through the trees to discern California Historic Landmark No. 107, "The Abbey." It was Joaquin Miller's home when the surrounding sixty-five acres he owned were known as The Hights.

As you climb back up through the trees, try to envision a five-foot-tall blonde lady with a heart-shaped harp, tripping up this stairway like a zephyr. Daughter Juanita Miller, who gave The Hights to Oakland, held an annual day commemorating her father at Woodminster from 1930 until 1967. Her lighthearted spirit still lingers as tangibly as the trees.

28

There wasn't another soul in sight when we started to film a segment on the Old Bale Mill near Saint Helena, California, a few miles east of Jack London Park, for the KPIX-TV Evening Magazine. Soon a car pulled up and a boy of about five came dashing up. He pulled on the corner of the plaid cape I wear on the airwaves.

"What did the cow's tail feel like?" he demanded.

This was wine country and there wasn't a cow for miles. What did he mean? Then it dawned on me that he must have seen an earlier program we had done on the air about the Earthquake Trail in the Point Reyes National Seashore where a cow is reputed to have fallen into a crevasse during the 1906 earthquake. So I told him, "It's not a real cow's tail, you know. It's just a statue made of metal, and cold to the touch."

"Did you ever feel a real cow's tail?"

I had.

"What did it feel like?"

I let him grasp my wrist. "That's what the long part feels like." Then my hair. "And that's what the curly part on the end feels like—except you have to imagine it full of wet mud." He pulled his hand back so suddenly, you knew he was feeling the mud.

About that time the cameraman, Scott Gibbs, must have been showing some displeasure at the interruption, for the mother called her son away. "Mommy," he shouted happily as he went dancing off toward her. "She's not just a picture! She's a real person! She has hair like a cow's tail."

142

Ranch Trail:
Jack London State Park

"WHO WILL REAP what I have sown here in this almighty sweet land?" Jack London wrote of Beauty Ranch, his 1,400-acre Sonoma County spread where he raised pure-

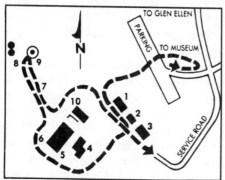

bred livestock. "You and I will be forgotten. Others will come and these, too, shall pass, as you and I shall pass and others take their places, each telling his love, as I tell you, that life is sweet."

And sweet indeed it is in the wine country, where the Jack London Historical Park at Glen Ellen has been expanded from its original thirty-nine acres to eight hundred. The walker who goes to enjoy it will find in addition to the long-established trail to the Wolf House ruins and London's lava rock-covered gravesite, new trails accessible along Asbury and Graham creeks, up the friendly little 2,200-foot peak that is Sonoma Mountain, around fine old vineyards, down to a charming little lake and to what was once Jack London's working ranch.

Of these, my favorite is the ranch trail, partly for the architectural surprises it offers, among them the actual cottage where London lived and died on the ranch, the remains of the pioneer Kohler and Frohling Winery, and oddly enough, a round sty of rock known as the Pig Palace, designed by London himself.

To make this walk, transport yourself north from San Francisco via Highway 101. Take 37, the Sears Point Cutoff, then 121 north to Big Bend to pick up Arnold Drive (which parallels Route 12) into the town of Glen Ellen. At the north end of the main shopping street, bear left following the State Park signs. Be prepared to pay your two dollar per vehicle fee, or half that if you are a silver-haired senior. If you bring Rover and Towser, there is an additional tail fee of fifty cents per dog, they must be kept on leashes, and you need proof they've had rabies shots.

At the outset, stop in Charmian London's House of Happy Walls, handy to the parking lot, to see how a writer actually lived, and to pick up a trail guide to the ranch. Mementos of his many travels and triumphs abound. Looking into the office, one can easily envision him writing the daily thousand-word stint, preparing lectures, reading proofs, answering the ten thousand fan letters per year, negotiating with his agents and publishers, drawing up plans to construct the piggery, generating new ideas. But it is when you peer into the viewer to see a motion picture film strip flickering as London rides one of his big horses or hugs a prize pig that the immense vitality of the man comes across. Then one sees him truly as he viewed himself, a sailor on horseback.

After you have looked upstairs to see the clever inglenook windowseats that could double as beds, go across the parking lot to find on the opposite side the trailhead for the ranch trail, a stroll of one kilometer under gracious old trees. Building 1, built of stone by Chinese laborers in 1884 was the Kohler and Frohling sherry building. The famous piano manufacturer, Charles Kohler, and his partner, John Frohling, acquired their Tokay vineyard in 1875. They were also the founders of Anaheim, Orange County, and came north because they heard it was better winegrowing country. In 1876, they pressed 45,000 gallons of wine in Glen Ellen. By 1888, they were growing 250 acres of grapes on the nearby hills.

Site 2 was built in 1914 by Italian stonemasons, and the stones protruding from the walls was deliberate, a style in contrast to the Chinese preference of stones flush with the walls. Although it looks charmingly rustic enough to have served as a guest cottage, London designed it for composting manure, much of it gathered from Site 3, the stone barn where six of the prize Shire workhorses dwelt.

From the barn swing southwestward toward The Cottage, built in 1862 by state supreme court justice Jackson Temple. Nearest wing was a winery building that served as dining room while Wolf House was abuilding. Go around to the far side to find the room, added on in 1914 after Wolf House had burned, where Jack wrote *Valley of the Moon,* and *Little Lady of the Big House.* "I liked those hills up there," he wrote. "They were beautiful, as you see, and I wanted beauty . . . I bought beauty and I was content with beauty for a while. It pleases me more than anything else now, but I am putting this ranch into first class shape and am laying a foundation for a good paying industry here." Look in each of the three directions the windows face to see the beauty he meant.

Then swing around to the front of the building to see the miniscule room where he died of uremia on November 22, 1916, two months short of his forty-first birthday. For a man who planned on mammoth lines, it is ironic that he died in a sleeping porch so small one wonders a bed would fit in it.

Wine buffs will find the huge foundation at Site 5 equally astonishing, for exactly the opposite reason — immensity. The huge building built by Kohler and Frohling to house their winery came down in the 1906 earthquake. London rebuilt it to house his guests, ranch hands, and carriages. A fire destroyed the wooden upper stories in 1965 during the time when London's nephew, Milo Shepard, was operating the big ranch and vineyard.

"Watch my dust," London wrote. "Oh, I shall make mistakes a-many; but watch my dream come true." Walk through the eucalyptus forest to see two of his mistakes, the forest itself, mistakenly planted to the tune of $50,000 in the expectation that it would be a hardwood crop, and the two abandoned silos — never necessary to California farming as they are to northern snowbound farms.

It is the Pig Palace that will dumbfound most visitors. The circular shape was to save labor, a central feedhouse surrounded by seventeen pens. Each family of pigs had its own quarters, including a front patio, private feed and water troughs, roofed pen, and backyard, all more spacious than many hotel rooms. The old Kohler and Frohling distillery, Site 10, and the blacksmith shop, which look rather like the home of the witch that baked Hansel and Gretel, were used by London to store farm machines.

When you have finished the loop, swing back along the service road to return by way of Wolf House. The dining room designed to seat fifty guests stands stark and open to the sky. It may not be the Acropolis, but it is the Bay Area's most romantic, bittersweetly melancholy ruin.

29

It has been a fancy of mine that botanists, like bobcats or lemurs, come out to sun on the west-facing slope of Russian Hill on pleasant afternoons. Or like rare wildflowers that thrive in one location, or one microclimate, or on one kind of soil, they have found a strip one block wide going west from Larkin Street most compatible with their needs in life.

Some of the garden buffs and botanists who have lived there include the Nobel prize-winning botanist, Alice Eastwood, who lived on Lombard Street, one block north of my own house; her protégé, John Thomas Howell, who lived one block south of us on Filbert; his colleague, Elizabeth McClintock, who lived in the 1300 block of Union; and of course, Imogen Cunningham, who lived in the 1300 block of Green—all within five blocks of one another.

It was from these locations that Alice Eastwood wrote her charming little Flora of the Nob Hill Cobblestones and Howell, his Doorstep Botany.

The Easy Way 'Round: No Hills to Home

L ET'S TAKE AN old-fashioned walk!" It could almost be my theme song, but some recent visitors from England didn't really expect walking as a viable solution one night after we'd

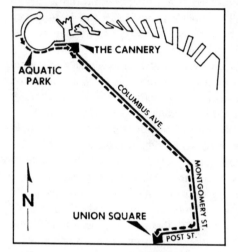

missed the last Hyde Street cable car and couldn't get a taxi to return them to their hotel near Union Square. Remembering the cable car climb up and over Nob Hill, they looked up the nearer slope of Russian Hill in dismay.

"Come on," I urged. "We'll go an easy way. No hills. It's an almost level route. Only two and a half miles."

The British are great walkers. After arriving comfortably back at the Sir Francis Drake, my guests gamely asked if I'd write out directions so they could walk our route again by daylight and pass it on later to friends.

As we all come to consider walking for transportation as well as pleasure, you too may want to know the "easy way" downtown from the northern waterfront. It is a romantic, historical way to go. Here's how:

To make this walk, transport yourself to Aquatic Park at the foot of Van Ness Avenue, preferably via the No. 19 Polk, No. 30 Stockton, No. 32 Embarcadero, or No. 47 Potrero Muni bus. Fort Mason is its western boundary. Before you take a step, look around.

Fort Mason, a military post named for Colonel Richard Barnes Mason, has sat on Black Point since 1851, although heirs of John C. Fremont who squatted here after spiking the guns of the Presidio in 1846, are still in litigation over it. Now the western half of the fort is a gigantic sandbox being reshaped into park as headquarters for the Golden Gate National Recreation Area.

Black Point Pumping Station, the emergency supply source that faces the water, has already been perked up, its tall smokestack truncated, and the little L-shaped "Alcatraz" pier on the shoreline across from it, once the place where prisoners embarked for the "Rock," has been gaily repainted as a fishing pier. From the end of the 1,850-foot-long Muni Pier, built between 1929 and 1934, which also serves as a sea wall sheltering this sandy cove, the view back at the city is almost as good as a boat ride on the bay.

When San Francisco was newly hatched as a city, cattle were driven to slaughter down a dusty road that has since become Van Ness Avenue. The water also ran red with dyes from the Pioneer Woolen Mill, now part of the Ghirardelli Square complex, as hired Chinese, housed in two high narrow buildings on the shore, would run each freshly dyed batch of wool down a redwood ramp to set the color in salt water. Looking at the elegant scene today, one finds it hard to believe it was once industrial, but Selby Smelter and Refinery once sat here with great smokestacks puffing out over the beach. Other old factories, canneries, and warehouses thriftily remodeled to house shops, galleries, theaters, and restaurants have become so popular with tourists that the trend to such reclamation of old buildings is now worldwide. Locally there is even new construction trumped up to look like reused buildings.

Start walking east from the tunnel with the tracks of the Belt Line Railroad as it cuts behind the ship-shaped concrete Casino Building housing the National Maritime Museum. Inspiration to its architect, William Mooser III, may well have been the revenue cutter *James S. Polk*, whose anchorage here long ago also helped give Polk Street the president's name.

Once past the three venerable rowing clubs and the Hyde Street Pier, whose museum ships, like the Haslett Warehouse, are now part of the national recreation area, follow Jefferson Street to the big glass wall of The Cannery. For fun, look underfoot to locate the brass surveyor's mark that indicates the exact point both the GGNRA and the Golden Gate Promenade begin. Then cut through the olive trees in The Cannery's sheltered outdoor mall to emerge across from the Wine Museum exactly at the end of Columbus Ave-

nue. This was only a path through the sand when banker William Ralston used to walk out daily from Montgomery Street for a lunch hour swim, much as runners and joggers do today.

As you start walking toward the Transamerica pyramid, try to envision water lapping at your feet as far as Francisco Street. North Beach really was a beach in 1850 when "Honest Harry" built Meiggs' Wharf and Sawmill at Taylor and Francisco. A prototype of the booster who believed North Beach could become what the northern waterfront is today, Honest Harry had run up debts to the tune of $750,000. He skipped town with $250,000 cash, to surface much, much later as the builder of Peru's spectacular railroad system in the Andes. Three years before his death in 1877, he paid off his San Francisco debts and the State of California exonerated him, but Meiggs never returned. Mourned as a national hero in Peru, he died a "splendid outcast" from San Francisco.

For thirty years after Meiggs left, the wharf was the romantic place to take your girl. You could stroll out and see Cockney White's Museum of monkeys and bears, or watch his educated pig play seven-up. If that palled, you could rent a bathhouse and swim, show off your marksmanship at Riley's Shooting Gallery, take in the fights at Doherty's Barn, climb the greased pole for the five dollar gold piece on top at Jimmy Kenovans, or stop at Abe Warner's Cobweb Palace for beer and free crab chowder.

North Beach Playground and Washington Square were "country" in those halcyon days. Broadway was the north end of town and stopped with a dead end at Russian Hill. Early arrivers at the Gold Rush of '49 would scramble ashore at Clark's Point at the other end of Broadway. The town grew so fast thereafter that three years later the Broadway wharf stuck 250 feet out into the bay and there were so many abandoned ships in Yerba Buena Cove you could walk the same distance using them for stepping-stones.

When you reach Montgomery Street, site of the old "Montgomery Block," the city's first fireproof building, you are once again at the original shoreline. When Henry W. Halleck built it in 1853, no one had ever tried to float a brick building on a redwood pad. Much of San Francisco's early financial history happened here. Pisco Punch was invented in the Bank Exchange saloon on the ground floor and editor James King of William (sic) assassinated on the sidewalk just outside, but before the building came down in 1959, the old "Montgy Block" had become a low-rent heaven for bohemians.

Banks and brokerages in the canyon that is Montgomery Street have earned it the nickname of "Money" Street and "The Wall Street of the West," but it was Jacob P. Leese, San Francisco's second resident, who built the first business establishment on it, a shop at Commercial and Montgomery. His first neighbor was Hudson's Bay Company, whose factor, William Glen Rae, was also San Francisco's first suicide. He used a gun.

When you reach Post Street bear right. Three blocks later, you will arrive at Union Square. Every running front foot of land on this route, every stone underfoot, indeed every twig, has enough tales to tell about San Francisco to write a book. It would be fun to find and tell them all, but ah, it is so much more fun to walk and see what is there now with one's own eyes.

30

When the summer fog pattern overwhelms sanguine San Franciscans, they cross the bay to walk, sun, or swim. This is one of the charms of living around San Francisco Bay that may not be readily apparent to the tourist or newcomer. Many towns surrounding the bay had their origins as summer resorts, so San Franciscans could escape the cool grey wetness if it persisted too long. After three or four days of fog, sunshine seems precious. Coming back, of course, is as refreshing as a whiff of bay leaves on a warm slope.

Contra Costa, Alameda, Marin, Sonoma, Napa, Solano, Santa Clara, and San Mateo citizens, conversely, come into San Francisco for summer walking, festival attending, night-clubbing, shopping, dining, and theater-going to enjoy the coolth when the days seem too hot too long in the hinterlands.

Of course, I like the going out and coming back equally.

Lake Temescal

LAKE TEMESCAL, ONE of the East Bay Regional Park District's oldest parks, has been the ole swimmin' and fishin' hole for most of the kids who have grown up in the Montclair neighbor-

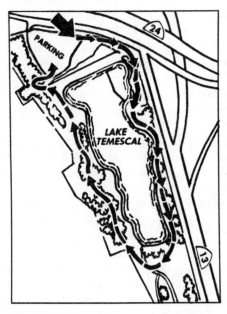

hood between Berkeley and Oakland. On a hot day, as many as three thousand happy swimmers may paddle and play along the pocket of Monterey sand at the north end. Almost as many fishermen regularly line the banks to pull in the rainbow trout that are stocked every two weeks during summer—along with some resident bigmouth bass, red-ear sunfish, bluegill, channel cats, and white cats. A ten-year-old boy came along with a string of five fish when I walked around the trail that encircles the lake one time. He said he had caught them using stale French bread for bait. Admiring tales of the man who caught a thirty-one-inch catfish in Temescal are sure to surface whenever fishermen start swapping yarns.

The walking around the lake, especially on the upper trail through the trees, is pleasant indeed. To make this walk, tuck your picnic and swimsuit into a tote bag, then transport yourself east from San Francisco via the Bay Bridge and Highway 24. Just short of the Highway 13 exit, take the Broadway Terrace offramp in Oakland and follow the frontage road signs to the big Lake Temescal parking area. There is also public transportation to the lake via the AC Transit No. 59 bus from Oakland and Montclair.

Once parked, pay the modest fee, then walk across the broad

lawn toward the south. If you suddenly have the impression you are walking on an earthfill dam, your archeological instincts are right on target. It was built in 1868 by Anthony Chabot, according to some authorities, in 1870 by William F. Boardman, according to others, to provide a reservoir for the tiny town of Oakland. Walter Wood, whose stepfather George Logan was the filtration plant superintendent, grew up on the farm that surrounded the lake early on. He recalled that it was known then as Hays' Canyon for Colonel Jack Hays who owned most of the surrounding land. A generous man, Hays gave the land off Morage Avenue where the Montclair firehouse now stands for the one-room wooden schoolhouse where Wood and his brothers and sisters went walking over dirt roads and open fields to reach it.

Bear left on the path along the weir to reach the beach and bathhouse, built during the New Deal days with WPA labor. Lake Temescal's debut as a forty-eight-acre park with the thirteen-acre gem of a lake in its heart was October 18, 1936.

If the gate is open on the left as you face the bathhouse, go up the steps to see the rose garden, pride of Eddie Collins, a thirty-four-year employee of the EBRPD. Thriftily, the bathhouse contains some of the park district business offices. Cross the broad patio to find a little recycling creek tumbling through rocks, then follow the steps down on the far side of the rock garden to see where it emerges near the lake level as a waterfall. Then continue south on the broad trail that skirts the water's edge. Boxes and plastic pipe near the little bridge over Caldecott Creek are part of a siltation monitoring project under way by the U.S. Geological Survey, Caltrans, and the Environmental Protection Agency to check runoff from Caldecott Tunnel, just uphill. Siltation was so great shortly after the tunnel was completed that it would have filled the lake within ten years if a dredging project hadn't been initiated. Dredging was completed in 1979, saving the local ecosystem and cleaning up the water for both fish and other swimmers.

The building you reach at the far end began life as the Kiwanis Hut. Expanded in 1963 by the Montclair Community Play Center, a nursery school older than the park itself, its model playground is used by nursery school kids on weekday mornings and everyone else the rest of the time. When you have looked over the area, follow the walkway into the trees to cross Temescal Creek.

The Juchiyunes Indians fished for salmon in Temescal Creek, long before the gringo came, and a sweathouse they built in this area gave the arroyo that now holds the lake its name, an Aztec word the Spaniards brought along when they first came to the Contra Costa. Jose Vicente Peralta managed this portion of the vast Peralta rancho for his father and later inherited it. His adobe home farther downhill at what is now the intersection of Telegraph Avenue, and Vicente and 55th streets became the nucleus of a little Mexican town called Temescal.

Stop short of the small parking lot at the south end of the lake and look for a footpath that goes uphill to the right. Start up on it and in a few steps you leave the meticulously groomed lake level of the park for a little wilderness, changed very little from the days when the Woods and Logan children played here. Later generations have enjoyed it just as much. Bill Malone, whom I met along the trail, has lived in the neighborhood since 1958. "My two sons grew up in the park," he says. "It was what made their childhood pleasant and it makes my day to walk here." Millie Luke, walking her dog, was equally complimentary. "I've lived all over the world and never found any other park that suited me quite so well. It is what made me choose to retire in this neighborhood."

As one rises with the trail, a powerhouse across the highway peeps from behind the trees. New houses on the hills beyond come into view, but so cleverly are they engineered, the two freeways 24 and 13, which define the north and east boundaries of the park, never seem intrusive.

Unexpectedly there is a little redwood grove on the trail. Farther along leatherferns, wildflowers, squirrels, warblers, and thrushes stud the surrounding area. All too soon one has made the mile circuit of the lake and is suddenly back at the weir. Climb the steps for quick return to your wheels. Better yet, get into your swimming suit and enjoy the lazy summer weather.

August

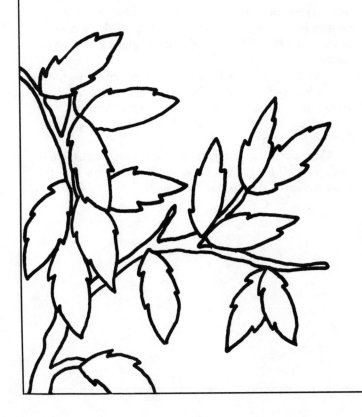

31

The flea, which long ago came up out of the sea, retains its ancient rhythms and breeds on a fourteen-day cycle at times of the new moon and the full moon, which are also the times of the highest and lowest tides. Newcomers to the Bay Area often complain about fleabites. "Pooh-pooh!" say the old-timers, who have become immune. "Fleas are no big thing."

It takes about a year for the average newcomer to reach a stage where fleabites don't seem annoying. Tots probably suffer more than most people, especially after a day at the beach. When our sons were young, we filled an old tractor tire with sea sand for a sandbox in the yard. They came in covered with bites. Our landlord then sprayed it with strong insecticide.

"We don't want the boys breathing that stuff," my pediatrician husband said later. So we dug up all the sea sand, hosed down the big tire, and refilled it with Number 2 river sand, which is available at most construction supply yards. No more fleabites.

Champers, our Alsatian, brings a few in after every beach walk. Then it's time to get busy on the rugs with the vacuum cleaner. And to give him a bath.

Daly City Trails

THE CALIFORNIA CONSTITUTION guarantees public access to the ocean.

As any walker who has been driven from the shore at gunpoint by a property owner who thinks you are trespassing on "his beach" can tell you, the reality for the last hundred years has been more like, "Yeah, but not over my land. Now, git!"

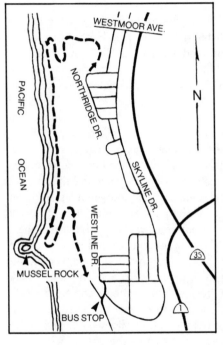

Constitution or no Constitution, you could follow Highway 1 for miles without finding a way to put your feet in the blue Pacific.

Now, thanks to shoreline access guidelines adopted by the State Coastal Commission, instead of drooling outside the fence like penniless kids at the candy store window, you and I, fellow citizen, are able to go down to the sea again.

Wildman's Gulch and Mussel Rock at Daly City are great examples. Not long ago, at the invitation of State Director of Resources Huey Johnson, Daly City Mayor Victor Kyriakis, and Frank Williamson of the Nichiren Shoshu Academy, it was my privilege to walk down steep Wildman's Gulch via the new Daisaku Ikeda Trail, stroll the beach, and return by way of Mussel Rock Trail.

It is a spectacular walk. The story behind the trail is almost as exciting as the terrain. To make this walk, which is for the agile only, provide yourself with lug-soled shoes, for the Daisaku Ikeda Canyon drops quickly from 450-foot bluffs to the sea. Take your lunch,

159

swimsuit, or fishing gear in a backpack. If you have an alpenstock, carry it. Then transport yourself south from San Francisco via Skyline Freeway 35 to Northridge Park at Northridge Drive west of Avalon Drive. Westmoor is the handy offramp. SamTrans Coastside buses 1A, 1C, 10A, and 10S from the Daly City BART Station leave once an hour on weekends.

Pocketsize Northridge Park shares its parking lot with the "chanting Buddhists" of Nichiren Shoshu Academy, housed like a hermit crab in the abandoned shell of a Christian church at 50 Northridge. Look toward the ocean between the parking lot and temple building to discern a hiker's stile of heavy logs and log archway, reminiscent of a torii gate, framing clouds or sky. This is the trailhead for Daisaku Ikeda Canyon, renamed for the president of Soka Gakkai, a Buddhist sect of 20 million people, mostly in Japan, who follow the Mahayana, or later teachings of Gautama Buddha. Dedicated to world peace, its members chant the Lotus sutra, beginning *Nam yo ho renge kyo,* daily in their homes and gohunzans.

Although the ocean may seem to be straight ahead, start down the trail through the brush heading toward your right. Soon it rounds the canyon lip to reach an area where academy members whacked out the trail and in one weekend planted two thousand Monterey pines and cypress along its undulating route. When you reach the first set of pilings, built to shore up a sliding slope, look across the canyon to locate the shelf where the Ocean Shore Railroad, whose slogan was "It Reaches the Beaches," used to run in 1909. The shelf below it is an old length of Highway 1. This is the area where the San Andreas fault reaches the sea, mocking the puny efforts of man again and again.

Climb down carefully and continue toward the center of the ellipse in this great horseshoe. Hundreds of Doelger-built "lemmings marching on the sea," as Herb Caen once described them, are visible above as you walk, all housing families whose children, like children everywhere, have longed for ways down to the beach.

Ignore the service road and bear left at the fork in the trail. You swing around the steep curve, enhanced with tie steps by Daly City engineers with the help of a grant from the Coastal Conservancy. The minute you turn your back on the development above the cliff-line, civilization seems to recede. By the time you have descended this steep slope, it becomes evident there are three big earthwork weirs and a standpipe across the canyon floor. Once highway ledges, they serve as siltation ponds for storm overflow for Daly City in the rainy season.

Follow the big Z made by the trail from the last of these hundred and fifty feet down to the beach. Cormorants, pelicans, sandpipers, willets, godwits, gulls, petrels, and sooty shearwaters may pass as you descend. Or a California gray whale, en route this time of year from the breeding grounds in Baja California may pass. When you reach the beach, play, bask, fish, or picnic to your heart's content. As you pause, look at the cliffs behind you. Geologists bring students here to point out the big slide that cut off the railroad, revealing both Pleistocene and Pliocene horizons of the San Francisco peninsula. Look underfoot and you may scuff up a fossil pinecone, fossil coal, avocado fossils, fossil shells, and sand dollars. They all wash out from the Merced Formation offshore.

The biggest of the sea stacks visible to the south is Mussel Rock, composed of greenstone basalt, bubbled up from the seabottom long ago, a product of marine volcanism. An hour before you are ready to leave the beach, take Mussel Rock as your landmark. Then stroll the mile of beach until you reach it. Originally part of Rancho Laguna de la Merced granted to Nicholas Galindo of Durango, Daly City was largely John Daly's dairy ranch when the earthquake of 1906 hit. Thereafter refugees from the great fire that followed the quake were given small portable two-room cottages, and many of them set the little homes on lots, sold at four hundred dollars each, in Daly City. Vegetable gardens and nurseries growing violets, gladiolus, dahlias, heather, and artichokes, all of which thrive on the coast, soon followed. Rampant development of commuter homes was next in the long history of the land uphill, just out of sight beyond the cliffs. Complete with trash.

When you reach a long uphill ramp from the beach, ignore it. It leads to what used to be the garbage dump. Now nicely covered with landfill, it is being rehabilitated. Instead, go as far as you can into the sea stacks facing Mussel Rock and look south to discern a tunnel, cut long ago to admit a stage but never used. Slides, sinking beach, erosion, and other faultline activity isolated it. Fishermen sometimes make their way out to Mussel Rock at low tide. Inviting as it seems, the going is treacherous and you take your life in your hands to risk it.

When you have marveled at this remarkable shoreline, take the ramp to your left, which zigzags up through clumps of rabbit-tail grass past the undeveloped 160-acre Daly City Park on the site of the old garbage dump. Like other shoreline property holders, Daly City is required by the Coastal Commission to provide public access. This one may become a model if plans to tap the methane gasfield underground are well coordinated with evolving park plans. "We've come a long way since garbage trucks dumped into Fog Gap," Mayor Kyriakis told me. "We're already nursing along a natural marsh back in the draw that supports deer, grey fox, raccoons, and maybe even coyotes."

Once site of a Costanoan Indian village, rare implements have also been found here by anthropologists. When you near the big blocky building, a transfer station for compacting garbage before transporting it elsewhere, look for a hiker's stile on the downhill side. Go through it and climb Westline Drive to Skyline Boulevard (west of Skyline Freeway) to find a SamTrans bus stop for return via public transportation. For walkers who left their wheels at Northridge Park, Skyline Boulevard to Northridge Drive is the route of choice. On the way back, you'll have the fun of passing the great parade of dracaenas, or dragon trees, that adorn Daly City front lawns.

32

A scientist has propounded the theory that rats have some sort of "force field" that enables rats all over the world to know instantly what is happening to rats every other place.

I wonder if we have a modification of such a force field ourselves, but consciously suppress it. Even before the days of radio and TV, ideas seemed to spring up in many parts of the human world simultaneously and spontaneously. The great vogue for preservation of a past that seems in danger of slipping away everywhere seems to be one of those ideas.

Benicia

WAITIN' ON THE levee, waitin' for the *Robert E. Lee. . . ."* Since 1962 when the U.S. Government Arsenal closed, that's been appropriate background music for Benicia, a deepwater port on the Sacramento River. Once it had so much river traffic, it could have been Hannibal, Missouri, by another name.

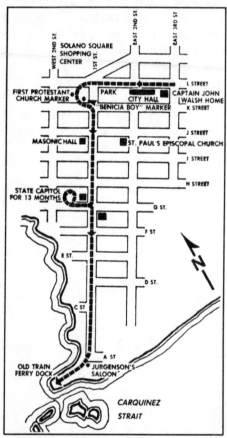

Benicia's waiting days may be over. A fresh new wind is blowing down First Street. Slowly, carefully, the long disused working port between Semple's Wharf and the old Pacific Mail Docks, an area immortalized by Jack London in *John Barleycorn* and *Tales of the Fish Patrol* is being transformed into a marina surrounded by park, wildlife, and a marshland preserve. At the moment Benicia Point may not be quite as pristine as Dr. Robert Semple and Thomas O. Larkin found it in 1847, but most of the big warehouses are down and the view sweep from town to waterway is more open than it has been in years. All of which makes for pleasant and nostalgic walking.

To enjoy this walk, transport yourself north from San Francisco using the Bay Bridge, Highway 580 to Walnut Creek, and 680 thereafter to Benicia, crossing the Sacramento River on the George Miller Memorial Bridge at Martinez. Once across the bridge swing east on 780 past Pine Lake to the East Second Street offramp. Drive south a block or so, until you reach the big Solano Square Shopping Center, then look for a place to park.

Once parked, seek out at L and East Third streets the home of Captain John Walsh, a handsome Victorian confection still in use as a private home. It was one of three identical houses prefabricated in Boston and shipped around the Horn in 1849. One of its twins, "Lachryma Montis," formerly home of General Mariano de Vallejo, is within the state park at Sonoma.

Bear west along L Street, passing City Hall, once the site of Saint Mary's of the Pacific Episcopal girls' school, whose most famous student was novelist Gertrude Atherton. "The Many Mizners" once dwelt on the site of the Police Department. Progenitor Lansing Mizner operated a mule stage line between Benicia and Sacramento in 1849 to make the money that let his talented sons, architect Addison and bon vivant Wilson shine in New York's Society. Today Wilson Mizner is best remembered for his bon mots ("A trip through Hollywood is like a trip through a sewer in a glass-bottom boat").

At First Street you reach the park and the dividing line for street numbering. One block in either direction is Second Street, one named East, the other West, Second, and so on, an old Mexican custom that can be a source of confusion to visitors. Cross to the city park, whose charming gazebo was a gift of Bill Turnbull. Some stunning stone picnic benches, a clown in a bowler hat from whose arms swings depend, and three historic markers also grace the park. One commemorates Mills College's first home and one the first Protestant church in California; the third is a tribute to John "The Benicia Boy" Heenan, who went thirty-seven rounds with British heavyweight champion Tom Sayres. After two hours, the referee awarded both men the title of World Champion. Heenan married actress Adah Mencken and was a lifelong friend of Charles Dickens.

Solano Square was the site of another of Benicia's historical firsts, the Dominican Saint Catherine's Academy, which evolved into Dominican College. The tragic Dona Concepcion Arguello, forsaken by her lover, the dashing Russian Nicolai Petrovic Reznikov, took the veil here. Another feather from History's wingbeats dropped in the form of Eliza Donner of the ill-fated Donner Party when she enrolled as a student in 1856.

Head south on First Street, renowned in our time as "Antique Street" for its fourteen purveyors of yesterday's throwaways. Across from the handsome Lundin House, at J Street, one comes upon one of the nicest of Benicia's amenities, the little park called Saint Paul's Square, which replaces an ugly service station that used to hide beautiful old Saint Paul's Episcopal Church, built in 1859 by Scandinavian shipwrights from the Pacific Mail and Steamship Company. Much like the Norwegian stave churches, it has "ship's knees" for strength. If it is open, go inside to see the ceiling and the Guildhall.

Across the street, the Masonic Lodge is one of three in which any Masonic group may hold meetings for conferring of Masonic degrees. Artist Manuel Neri has a studio in the old church beyond.

One night at the Bella Union Saloon, corner of First and H streets, a miner didn't like the music the pianist was producing, so he shot, but missed, him. Indignant Benicians ran the miner out of town, not for his murderous intent but for wrecking the piano.

At G Street bear west to visit the charming building that was California's state capitol for thirteen months of 1853 and 1854, now a state historical park, and the Fisher-Hanlon House, once a Gold Rush hotel, next to it. Flower buffs who come along here at 7:30 P.M. may find the night-blooming cereus in full splendor. The tree botanists seek out the unusual Australian cow itch, whose flowers look like champagne glasses. For more casual visitors, there are picnic tables near the carriage house.

When you have made the tour of this vestige of the Old West, continue down First. Almost every building has its story to tell, but those that pique the curiosity most are the skeleton of the big Kullman-Saltz Tannery, which once processed a third of the leather produced in California, and Jurgenson's Saloon, where "Curly-Headed Jack" London hung out while living on a houseboat nearby. Fish canneries lay east of the saloon in the area where the marina is emerging. Once past the depot, veer west on the old train ferry dock. As many as thirty transcontinental Southern Pacific trains daily were ferried from the dock by the big Contra Costa and Solano train ferries in the heyday of steam.

If you hear a whistle round the bend, as you gaze up and down our muddy old buddy, the river, it will be a lonely Amtrak train swinging over the bridge that put the ferries out of business. "Say, pardon me, boys. Was that the Sacramento choo-choo? Heading upstream? Or was it a dream . . ."

33

In the halcyon days, B.A. (Before Automobiles) when the air was pure and all things measured to the human stride, the emperor's court in Japan annually traveled from Tokyo to Kyoto on foot (now they have the Tokyo Express, the bullet train). On the other side of the world too, gentlemen customarily concluded their education at Oxford, the Sorbonne, or Munich, with a wanderjahr, a year of wandering Europe from inn to inn on foot.

The time may come when it will be possible to do that in Northern California, for we have an increasing number of fine "bed and breakfast" inns, hostels, small hotels, and other unplastic guest accommodations.

Rambles in the wine country could be made along the Russian River by canoe. Now if we only had a Hiroshige to record the journey from San Francisco to Gualala, say, in woodblock prints.

> Even the "Seven Sages"
> of olden time.
> What they longed for chiefly
> seems to have been wine.
> —Otomo no Tabito

Korbel

And we meet, with champagne and a chicken at last.
Lady Mary Wortley Montagu

C HAMPAGNE IS THE wine of romance. If the occasion is romantic, or celebrates a romance, a success, an achievement, or just the wish for one, you can bet your tastevin there will be heady bubbles in the glasses.

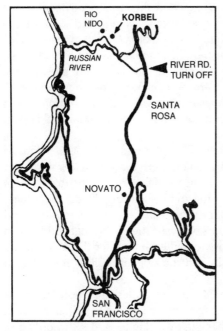

Couple the opportunity to stroll around a newly restored pioneer garden, a vine-covered old winery and a charming little train station and wind up with a taste of champagne, and you have the ingredients for a walk that can make your day.

The place to do it is Korbel Champagne Cellars, a venerable establishment overlooking the Russian River just east of Guerneville. To make this walk transport yourself north from San Francisco via Highway 101 to the Fulton-River Road turnoff just a little north of Santa Rosa. Follow River Road westward as it meanders past the little riverside resorts of Mirabel, Hacienda, Rio Del, Rio Nido, and Summerhome Park. You round a curve and there is Korbel's picturesque brick brandy tower and vine-covered winery framed by towering redwood trees. Park in the revamped parking lot near the new warehouse. Stroll up past the little picnic area near the tasting room, but for the moment don't stop here. Save the tasting room for the end of this walk and continue past.

169

The road you are on began as a roadbed of the Northwestern Pacific Railway in 1876, a spur created to carry lumber and cigar boxes, not grapes. Before the Korbel brothers arrived in California from Bohemia in the 1860s, two of them, Anton and Josef, had been working as master mechanics and the oldest, Francis, in the tobacco industry. He soon became aware of the need for a cigar box factory for California, established a sawmill, and came to own the six thousand acres of hillsides stretching from here to Rio Nido.

When the logging came to an end, they sought advice from the University of California Department of Viticulture and soon planted vines among the redwood stumps. Look to your left at the old brick winery building. The industrious Bohemian brothers made their own brick for the building, designed machinery for pressing the grapes, supervised the construction of oak cooperage, and even made the hand-forged hinges on the winery door. Tempting as it may be to go in, forbear and continue on to the small building on your right.

Once Korbel Train Station was the end of the line, extended from Guerneville by the railroad in return for the logs for ties. Later it rambled farther west to Duncan Mills. Except for this shelf of siding, River Road sits on the old railway roadbed. The winery bought the station in 1935 for five dollars. It is now a museum and starting point for winery tours. Go past the bench that surrounds a redwood tree where visitors forgather, and enter the little station. Early pictures line the walls and the original waiting room bench stands against one wall.

When you have looked them over, look slightly uphill from the station to find a tremendous section of redwood log. Standing by it, locate the brandy tower, then start walking toward it. According to local legend, Francis Korbel built the tower in imitation of one at Dolibor prison fortress in which he had been imprisoned after participating in a student uprising in Europe. His mother smuggled in women's clothing to permit him to escape as a visitor. Iron bands were strapped around the building to brace it after the 1906 earthquake. It is now used for storage. The weathervane on top survived the quake too.

Take a good look at the little building across the road from the brandy tower. In its time it served not only as a post office and as a

place where cigar box labels were printed, but also as the home of *The Wasp*, the famous satirical literary weekly magazine created by the Brothers Korbel in 1876. Because they had the label lithograph presses capable of printing color, *The Wasp* was the first American magazine to use color cartoons. Ambrose Bierce was *The Wasp*'s most famous stinger.

Barn buildings behind the little post office are in use and off limits except by formal invitation from winery president Gary Heck, son of Adolf Heck, who with his brother Paul took over the winery from the Korbel family in 1954. Beyond the barn is the Ridenhour Ranch bed and breakfast inn, one of the most charming of Russian River hostelries.

Continue uphill past the blacksmithy, now being restored, and bear left at the second roadway above the winery tower. It goes through a rose-covered gate. Pause a moment and look downhill here to count the cupolas. At one time there were so many, Korbel Station looked like a Bohemian village. As you walk, there will be a vegetable garden on the cliff on your right and winery machine shops on the left. Soon the road will take you to a towering grove of redwoods.

When you reach a fenced garden on your left, go in through the first gate. Old redwood stumps hide on either side of the garden walk. A viewing bench sits in a scrap of green lawn among the great trees, and just uphill is the white farmhouse that was the old Korbel family home, a landmark here since 1865. The Heck family used it as a summerhouse. Now it too is being restored.

The gardens have recently been renewed, saving old varieties wherever possible and reintroducing others that were known to have been planted here. Stroll around toward the front of the house on the first path leading uphill to your right to see the little round garden fountain and a gazebo overlooking the vineyards. The vineyard beyond the house still has one old redwood stump visible among the vines. The view out toward the Russian River is a classic of picturesque tranquility. Contemporary tea roses are mingled with the old Bourbon roses in the housefront rose garden.

When you have enjoyed the flowers, the coolth of the gigantic redwood trees, and the view to your heart's content, take the lowest garden path downhill to find a wrought iron gate that emerges back on the main winery street. Bear left again to reach the train station and take the winery tour. It includes cool rooms rich in fine cooperage and a fine slide show.

Then it's time to seek out the tasting room where a plat of the original patent to the land signed by President Polk in 1864 still hangs on the wall. If you brought along a cold bird, you can buy a bottle here to enjoy at the little picnic grove under the redwoods outside.

34

Earthquake tremors are not uncommon in San Francisco. We had two good ones the day a housecleaner recently arrived from Mississippi came to work for us. The first tremor shook out the dust she had just swept into the dustpan. Carefully she swept it up a second time, finishing just in time to have the aftershock shake it out on the floor again.

"Mrs. Doss," she said, shaking the dustpan at me. "Do you have another dustpan? There is something wrong with this one. It seems to have a built-in shimmy."

Noe Valley grew as a neighborhood after the San Francisco earthquake and fire of 1906.

Noe Valley

NOE VALLEY, NOE Valley, you are ringing in my ears/ like a slow sweet piece of music from the long forgotten years. . . . (Apologies to John Masefield.)

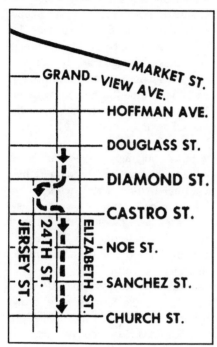

In a city once known for the neighborliness of all its neighborhoods, it may well be that Noe Valley led all the rest, for it is still neighborly. People speak to one another on the street, pass the time of day over the back fence, and now and again, borrow a cup of bulgur. Salespeople in the 24th Street shops pride themselves on their helpfulness and courtesy. The Noe Valley section of the East and West of Castro Street Improvement Club gets together to donate labor painting out any graffiti interlopers may leave. Walk the streets that nestle in that pocket east of Twin Peaks and south of Market and the esprit is easily apparent.

In February an annual History Festival is usually under way at the Noe Valley Library, sponsored by the Noe Valley Community Archives. Old San Franciscans dig in the family scrapbooks and shoeboxes for pictures, letters, journals, and clippings about Noe Valley, and the best are put on display.

To make this walk, transport yourself, preferably by Muni bus No. 48, to the corner of Douglass and 24th streets. The lively construction in the center of the lawn next to Noe Valley tennis courts, which looks like a frozen waterfall or a piece of contemporary sculp-

175

ture, is actually playground equipment, the gift of the Friends of Noe Valley. (What other neighborhood has quite so many groups devoted to its nurture, enhancement, and preservation?) Look south uphill on steep Douglass Street where the rich niche green with trees, formerly a quarry, is the Douglass Street Playground.

Twin Peaks, and this slope, were part of Rancho San Miguel, granted in 1845 by Governor Pio Pico to José de Jesus Noe, last Mexican *alcalde,* or mayor, of San Francisco. To avoid the humiliation of surrendering the town to General Montgomery, he retired to his then distant rancho at Twin Peaks where he passed the rest of his life. The city charter line of 1851 stopped in those days at his Castro Street border. After 1862, horsemen paid twenty-five cents toll to reach the beach via the new five-and-a-half-mile Mission and Ocean Beach Macadamized Toll Road.

Start walking east on 24th Street, originally named Park Street by John M. Horner because it led to the park surrounding Pioneer Racecourse. Horner and his brother bought 4,300 acres of San Miguel to lay out Horner's Addition, or "Horner's Corners" as it became known, one of the city's earliest subdivisions. Elizabeth Street, one block north of 24th, and Jersey, one block south, still retain the names Horner gave them, but John, which he named for himself, is now 22nd, and Horner Street became 23rd.

When you reach Diamond, walk one block south to Jersey to see a "tower house" as Queen Anne-style houses were known when they were built in the 1880s. According to a little leaflet prepared on Victorians in 1975 for Stanford Research Institute, "Depending on how fancy the tastes of the customer, cottages were $290 to $360 per room, residences cost $320 to $420 per room and a villa could cost from $450 to $700 per room to build." Today one could not build the front door for that price.

Bear left on Jersey to number 451, the Noe Valley Branch Public Library, a handsome example of the long-neglected Beaux Arts period of architecture. For architecture buffs, the library is "Spanish, with nice ceramic moldings and the classical Beaux Arts axial symmetry." If it is open, go inside to see the library's archival photo display, a handsome piece of sculpture by Ruth Asawa, and the community garden that surrounds the building. As part of the festival, neighborhood history walks are usually conducted free on

Saturdays by San Francisco's City Guides, a group of volunteers under the auspices of the library.

Once you leave the library, look for the Stick-style Victorians along Jersey. Artist Mel Moss, journalist Rasa Gastaitis, gerontologist Gerry Murphy, and publisher Donald M. Allen of Grey Fox Press are typical of the residents who now find this old neighborhood friendly. "Come in here," Don Allen, who conducted me on this walk, said, steering me into Small Press Traffic bookshop at 3841-B 24th Street, a block over. "It is exclusively devoted to publications on poetry, drama, fiction, and literary criticism. They have more than two thousand titles in stock from three hundred small presses in the United States, Canada, and England. Most of the books are printed right here in the Bay Area. If there is a new literary frontier emerging in this country, the small presses are in the vanguard of it."

Next stop was Star Magic, 3995 24th Street, devoted to "eclectic objects of Science and Spirit" including some of the most remarkable telescopes, microscopes, ion generators, and other adult toys yet devised. Down the street at Ver Brugge Meats, the clerk pointed out that the fish was caught fresh daily on their own boat. Books Plus, Noe Valley's General Bookstore, is also in this block.

Name phreakers can chuckle over "A Cut Above Castro," which turns out to be a barbershop, "Quiche and Carry," just what it sounds like, and "Kidstuff," which has both new and used toddler's clothing for sale. The Frog Shop sells — surprise! — frogs, largely ornamental, while the Meat Market is a coffeehouse. The Yellow Cavern at Vicksburg Avenue told me, "We don't have nothin' fancy in here, Lady." It is an old neighborhood pub.

In the Glen Five and Ten, an old-timer along the street, manager Ella Melendy told us, "The building was once one of the three theaters along the Noe Valley section of 24th Street. The Acme Nickelodian, I think. For awhile there was a basketball court here too, used by the California Boys Club. The community used to be mostly Irish, I think from Saint Phillip's parish or from Saint Paul's."

The diversity is so great both in shops and people today that the walker can find almost anything civilized along this well-aged vintage of a street, so end it where you please. The best discoveries are the ones you make yourself.

35

One of my favorite walkers of all time is a man named John Francis who vowed, a few years ago, to go nowhere except traveling under his own power. At that time John lived in Inverness.

One day he was invited to participate in an ecological seminar at University of California, Berkeley, to be held three weeks in the future. John began planning his route at once, for he was honored to be invited. It would have been a matter of an hour or forty-five minutes by car using either the San Rafael or the Golden Gate and Bay bridges. On foot it was another matter. Walkers were not permitted on the Bay Bridge.

He arrived at the San Rafael Bridge, unaware that walkers were not permitted on it, either. Doggedly he headed north on foot, skirted the bay, and arrived at the Carquinez Strait Bridges, only to be told walkers are not permitted there either. Fortunately, that day one of the twin bridges was closed for painting, and after much persuasion, he was allowed to cross. He finally made it to the conference. It took him three days and he had to walk 110 miles out of his way.

When he wrote to the Governor to call to his attention the need for permitting walkers on bridges, the letter was bounced to the Director of Transportation who assured John Francis that the state was planning to put a motorized walker's shuttle on a bridge in San Diego. As though that would solve John Francis's—and every other walker's—need in Marin.

The New York Times *Sunday crossword puzzle reminded me of John again yesterday. Nineteen down's clue was: "What bureaucrats give." The answer: "The runaround."*

Johnstone Trail at Tomales Bay State Park

Dear Margot,

Every time my mother visits from Newton, Massachusetts, we have one of those Mark Twain summers. Fog, fog, fog. Her idea of fun as a grandmother is to lie at the beach getting tanned while little kids dig in the sand and big ones chase through the woods playing Indian. She says she won't visit us again unless we can guarantee her a warm sunny beach for sunning and swimming. Any ideas?

Desperate

Dear Desperate,

How lucky can you get. Tell Nana Bay Area summers are always foggy and let her entertain you on Cape Cod. On the other hand, if you like to have her come here, invite her for the sunny months, May, June, September, and October.

On second thought, the kids would be in school (though why California schools still stick to vacations timed long ago for the convenience of eastern farm families who wanted help with weeding and harvesting from the child labor of their own begetting, Heaven only knows).

Well, no one can guarantee sunshine, but there are some fine, sandy, shallow swimming beaches in Tomales Bay State Park where the water is dependably warmer than the ocean. Located on some shell mounds, it has great trails for playing Indian where Indians used to play.

Yours truly,
Margot

DESPERATE ISN'T THE ONLY one to suffer from that "fog along the coast" summer pattern. Many a summer visitor to the Point Reyes National Seashore finds the place socked in and retreats before that thick gray blanket of fog. That's when a little local knowledge can save the day.

179

My special walk for such an occasion is a two-and-a-half-mile loop that uses trails named for conservationists Willis Jepson, the

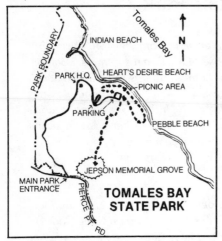

botanist who founded the School of Forestry at University of California, Berkeley, and Bruce Johnstone, who was the persistent planner who created this jewel of a park. Along the trails there are some breathtaking views through Bishop pines that make the short ramble to the beach pleasant indeed.

To make this walk, transport yourself four miles north of Inverness (past Inverness Park) via Highway 101, the Sir Francis Drake Boulevard, and Pierce Point Road. Take your swim gear and picnic in a daypack, wear lug-soled boots if you have them, and anticipate a modest day use fee the state parks are now charging. The entrance to Tomales Bay State Park is about a thousand yards north of the junction on Pierce Point Road after you leave Sir Francis Drake Boulevard. Drive to the big parking lot at Heart's Desire Beach.

Find a place on the granite sand to enjoy your first swim of the day before lunching on the beach. If you see clammers, they will probably be seeking *Paphia staminea*, also called the Tomales Bay cockle, the rock clam, the ribbed carpet shell, the littleneck clam, the hard-shell clam, and the rock cockle. Fifty is the limit and each must be more than an inch and a half long. Sportfishing licenses are required but are not for sale in the park. If you long to try the raw clam, before setting out, buy a measuring ring at the bait shop at the same time you pick up your tide table and license.

Long before either Juan Rodriguez Cabrillo or Sir Francis Drake sailed along the Marin coast, Miwok Indians clawed among the rocks of this shore for clams, much as people do today. The Miwok name for the water that had filled the San Andreas rift zone was Lake Olemas. Since Tomales means "bay," we now use a redundant name meaning "Bay Bay" for this long narrow inlet.

When the beach has revealed its charms and you feel the urge to explore some more of this 1,018-acre playground, look at the southern end of the scallop of sand for the 0.6-mile-long Pebble Beach Trail. It leads through oak and bay forest, past hidden picnic tables, to another crescent of surf-free pocket beach, whose granite sand relates Point Reyes to the Farallones. Millions of years ago, both were part of a great land mass known to geologists as Salinia.

Before you go down to Pebble Beach, observe the junction with the Johnstone Trail. Return to it after you have explored this little cove. Constructed by Ranger Pete Orchard to honor Bruce Johnstone, who served five years on the Marin County Planning Commission and worked unceasingly to see these beaches become a park, the trail has been extended around a private holding surrounding Shallow Beach to reach Shell Beach, the southernmost of the Tomales Bay State Park beaches.

Thirty years ago when the park land was being acquired, Carolyn Livermore of the Marin Conservation League, who also fought diligently for the park, advised her public-spirited colleagues to take what they could get their hands on, leaving inholdings for later acquisition if possible. When you reach the trail, bear right, uphill on it. Sometimes you will see through trees an occasional car that goes down to cabins around Shallow Beach.

Once you are in sight of Pierce Point Road again, look to your right for the marker for the Jepson Trail. It soon leads to the Jepson Memorial Grove of Bishop pine, one of the few remaining virgin groves in California.

Follow the trail as it meanders downhill, stopping at each of the cleverly sited view points. At that unexpected broader vista, the great sandy slope you see across the waters of Tomales Bay is at Dillon Beach, the continuation of a dune to be found on the tip of Tomales Point as well. Bay, madrone, wax myrtle, and oak bend and sigh over the trail. Sticky monkey flower and three hundred other varieties of wildflower have been identified along these trails by botanists. Unusual ferns wave their lush fronds and at least half a dozen kinds of berries grow along the trail, all the product of sunny summer languor.

September

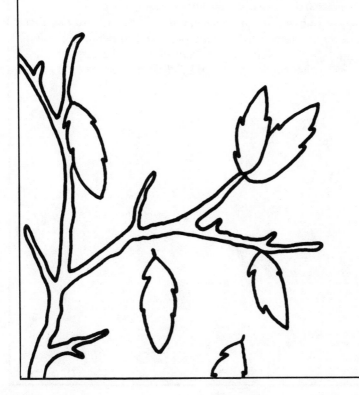

36

Villages—take Pleasanton if you need a genuine village to consider—customarily had one general store, one post office, one smithy (today it would be a gas station), one saloon, one hardware and feed store, one hotel, one school, one barbershop, a doctor, a dentist, a church, and if the village was centrally located, a theater. These establishments were enough to supply the basics of life in the days before automobiles. All were located within walking distance of everyone who lived in the village. After the railroad appeared on the horizons of the world, these basics were within walking distance of arriving train passengers.

Suburbs, on the other hand, assume at word one that every homeowner has a motorcar and so perforce, there is nothing at all planned "within easy walking distance." Indeed, there are many suburbs without sidewalks at all.

Pleasanton

STROLLING DOWN PLEASANTON'S serene streets, one finds it hard to believe this was once called the most desperate town of the West. Today it may well be the tamest. Yet there

was a time when desperadoes and bandits—Joaquin Murietta, Narcisco Borjorques, Tiburcio Vasquez, Juan Soto, Manuel "Three-Fingered Jack" Garcia, to name but five—found a haven there. The adobe barn that Judge John Kottinger pressed into service as the first county jail stands in mute evidence of "The Bandit Era." Around the bar at the Pleasanton Hotel, they still tell the story of the Chilean midwife, Donna Pilaria, hiding "Joaquin the Terrible" under her hoop skirts, following the sheriff all the while he searched her house for him.

Walkers who come to explore this deliciously bucolic old town will find it in the forefront of true progress. It got there by steadfastly resisting the urge to modernize, by using and re-using its beautiful old buildings. Second Street, where *Rebecca of Sunnybrook Farm* was filmed, could serve as a set for that picture tomorrow. Jack Pickford in the role of Huck Finn would find fish in Arroyo del Valle Creek today. Lillian Gish, Clara Bow, Tom Mix, Buster Keaton, or Abbott and Costello could come back anytime with a camera and find scenes they remembered.

If you have never been to the pleasant town named, not for its ambiance but for General Alfred Pleasanton, pick a day when San Francisco is socked in with fog. By the time you reach Dublin on Route 580, you will probably be in sunshine. If you come when Pleasanton is celebrating its annual Heritage Days, dress in clothes of the 1880s or you may find yourself in the rolling jail. Fines go toward a worthy cause.

Hopyard Road just past Dublin is the offramp to take from Interstate 580. It will take you south, right into town. Watch where you park. There is a tough parking ordinance. Once parked, head for that wonderfully nostalgic arch that carries the name of Pleasanton overhead across Main Street. In its heyday as a winter center for harness racehorse breeding, five gracious old hotels stood along Main. Of them, Farmer's Hotel on the west side of the street, twice burned, twice rebuilt, survives today as the restaurant and saloon called the Pleasanton Hotel. At the outset, go up its wide veranda to find the historical marker. If you plan to return for lunch, make your reservations early. The creek where Huck fished is just north of the hotel. Check it out if you wish, but walk south to peek through the gate into the hotel garden, a favorite place for weddings and receptions for more than a hundred years.

Immediately beyond, the Victorian home of Jerome Arendt now houses the Hacienda del Sol. In another re-use, it housed the district school office. The police station next door was formerly City Hall. At the corner of Ray Street, cross Main and walk north to locate another much-loved Pleasanton institution, the Cheese Factory, which makes many of the cheeses sold here. My favorite, known as hot jack, is a spicy version of Monterey jack to which I was introduced by local resident Salle Larson. If you go in, notice the mousetraps at three for a dollar and the windows that let shoppers see the cheese during process of manufacture. Outside tables, heated from above, are used all year round.

When you have enjoyed this unusual factory, walk south again on Main to the first driveway and bear left along a row of boutiques, among them the Hairhouse, the Clothes Tree, and upstairs, the Frilly Dilly. Just beyond, look to the left to discern a tremendous mural that depicts Pleasanton's long agricultural history as a center for raising grain, hops, vegetables, cattle, and horses. Four railroad tracks enfold the downtown area. The racetrack in the mural is now the county fairground. The firemen's muster in the foreground still happens regularly.

Do an about-face and walk south through the alleyway along-side the neat white Victorian cottage to reach Ray Street, then bear left. The next Victorian houses a dentist's office. History walks with you on this street, for it was here that Judge John Kottinger lived in

1852 after he married Maria Refugio Agosta Bernal, daughter of Juan Pablo Bernal, who generously gave the newlyweds 4,500 acres of his massive Rancho el Valle de San José. When you spot the black walnut trees, cross Ray Street to Adobe Plaza to find the barn nicely fenced jutting into the parking lot. Look on the east side of it to locate an E. Clampus Vitus historical marker commemorating its service as a jail. To foil escapes, a tunnel went underground between the judge's home, now gone, and the barn jail. Local historians are hopeful it will one day be restored as a museum.

Near First Street, when you cross the Southern Pacific Railroad tracks, look to the right. Huge wooden warehouses used to store hay and grain once lined the tracks. An old depot and a brick firehouse are visible far down the track. Bear right on First Street and look along here for an unusual shop, the Old Schoolhouse, open only after school, which supplies educational materials for teachers. The First Street next door has music Friday and Saturday nights, as well as commendable food.

As you approach the park, look across First Street to locate Arendt Way, once an extension of narrow Division Street. Both were formerly known as Stingy Lane because pioneers Kottinger and his brother-in-law, Joshua Neal, each gave up as little as possible of their property for a street at the point where their lands met.

The Senior Citizens Kitchen Band plays in the Lions Bicentennial Bandstand at 2 P.M. on Sundays. When you are abreast of the little Chamber of Commerce Building, look across the tracks to locate the old depot, now boarded up, alas. Cross First at Neal Street and walk past the grey house, formerly the manse of the neighboring United Presbyterian Church, vintage 1876, whose architectural embellishments include a fanlight, a cupola rather like one on a midwestern barn, and shutters on the choir loft windows. The deodar tree next to it is more than a hundred years old. Like other trees, it is protected by Pleasanton's Heritage Tree Ordinance. Bear right on Second Street. If you feel you've seen the charming little houses, rambling roses, picket fences, and fine old trees before, you probably have. They were in more than one early film. Notice the porches where people really sit and the swing that has half a baseball bat for a seat.

At Angela Street, bear right on the path. Number 110, a pink

Victorian, has vegetables among its flowers. On First Street, bear right again, passing John DeLucchi Memorial Park, which commemorates a truck farmer who was also the chief of police. Bear left on Neal and as you pass the depot, look toward the Meadowlark to locate a former saloon-cum-whorehouse that thrived in the railroad's heyday of passenger service.

Before you reach the Amaral law offices at number 62, look upstairs at the display window where Mrs. Babbitt places noncommercial displays. Pleasanton also has a bank president named Warren Harding.

At Main Street, notice the 1890 building that says H. Arendt and Co. General Merchandise. The green building catty-corner from it originated as an early Bank of America. Former mayor Jim Trimingham, who conducted me on this walk, pointed out that Canadian and American horse breeders used to winter at the old Rose Hotel on this spot when Pleasanton was the center of winter harness racing.

Bear right on Main Street. If you come this way about noon, the carillon from the Lutheran church will lift your spirits. So will the white Queen Anne building that houses Kolln's Hardware. If it is open, go in for the classic flavor, and to see the cash register and safe that have been here since Cruikshank and Kolln was founded seventy-five years ago. Urban cowboys may want to end this walk instead across the street at the Tack Room of Christensens, where they sell everything but the cayuse.

37

Fire, like laughter and language, is one of those remarkable ladders that has helped boost civilization to its present eminence. It is also a sometime thing.

What may be a pleasure at the campsite, or a comfort on the hearth, may, in a moment, become a disaster—a few flicking tongues of flame shooting out from the embers can rise and in an instant destroy everything in its path.

San Francisco has had her share of these catastrophes, which is one reason the Fire Museum is so fascinating. The city has also had some famous fire buffs, among them Lillie Hitchcock Coit (Coit Tower) and Louise Davies (Davies Hall). But even if you do not have a tower or performing arts center named for you, you can enjoy the fireman's lore in which the town abounds.

For Fire Buffs

I sing the bold fireman, whose true sturdy stroke
Always turns every fire which we have into smoke.

THE MEN OF the San Francisco Fire Department had reason to sing that rousing old song to the tune of "King and Countrymen" in 1883. The Pacific Coast Guide of the Knights Templar Triennial Conclave had written of them: "This is one of the most efficient Fire Departments in the world." It went on to list the force at that time as "320 officers and men, seventeen steamers, nineteen hose reels, eight hose carriages, seven hook and ladder trucks, seventy-one horses . . . 24,000 feet of carbolized hose, 1,371 hydrants and fifty-five cisterns with a total capacity of 2,011,856 gallons."

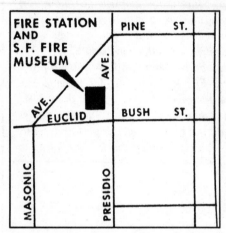

What this accolade didn't tell, the men all knew—how at big fires their tiny streams of water went up into the air as powerless vapor. They had learned it during the five great fires that plagued San Francisco between 1849 and 1851. According to Bancroft, at the last of these six firemen were lost, three known to be crushed by one falling wall from which twelve others narrowly escaped and "how many more were killed and injured no one can say."

They also discovered at that fire that "more effectual than water was the pulling down and blowing up of buildings . . . voluntary destruction went hand in hand with the inner devastation, the boom of explosion mingling with the crackling of timbers, the crash of tumbling walls and the dull detonation from falling roofs. A momentary darkening, then a gush of scintillating sparks, followed by fiery columns, which still rose, while the canopy of smoke sent

190

their reflection for a hundred miles around, even to Monterey. It is related that the brilliant illumination in the moonless night attracted flocks of brant from the marshes, which, soaring to and fro above the flames, glistened like specks of burnished gold."

Strong stuff to experience. When the city of the Gold Rush found that these fires had been deliberately set by looters, it's small wonder they formed a Committee of Vigilance to string up "the miscreants" or run them out of town. It also beefed up the volunteer fire companies, which ultimately became the city fire department.

If a childhood thrill of combined fear and excitement still goes through you whenever the sirens shriek or the engines clang past on the street, consider a walk through San Francisco's Fire Museum, which is open to the public four days a week—from 1 to 5 P.M. Thursdays through Sundays.

To make this walk, transport yourself to Presidio Avenue (once Cemetery Street) between Bush and Pine. There in the north wing of the firehouse occupied by Engine and Truck Companies No. 10, City Guide volunteers, many of them former firemen, walk the visitor through "reminders of the horse drawn era of fire fighting in the city."

It's an unusual experience. The San Francisco Hook and Ladder Society, founded to preserve the fire history of the City, has refurbished the ten-year-old museum with some striking displays. Go in, past the appropriately fireman-red geraniums, to discover just inside the door San Francisco's first fire bell, cast in Boston in 1853. Journalists, proofreaders, and those born under the astrological sign of Virgo can amuse themselves by looking for the typo on the bell. (Clue: it isn't in the first chief's name. He really was George N. Hossefross.) The rhythm and pattern of clangs on the bell were a code to indicate to volunteers the location of fires. As you walk around the museum, signals coming in next door indicate location today, alerting men when the "masheens" are to go out.

For a look at the equipment early "vamps," or "salamanders" as firemen were known in the 1850s, used, look at the case on your right. Many a collector would give his eyeteeth for one of those blue glass "bottle-bombs." Nearby is the James Smith hand-drawn hand-pumper, built in 1810, repainted and redecorated at Tehachapi for the big annual fire muster in Benicia.

At the case demonstrating the changeover from the volunteer companies to a paid municipal department, volunteer Barney Leinart, a retired fireman whose grandfather was clerk of Broderick Company Number One, pointed out the Exempt certificates, so called because they exempted the fireman from jury or military service.

"The Steamer keeps blowing her whistle and throwing a stream from a three-cornered nozzle./ The Exempts in a pipe of old fashion delight, then beat her five yards horizontal," wrote the poet laureate of "The Exempts" after they had successfully bested a rival company, possibly using the same steam pumper and hand-drawn cart that stands hard by.

Take a little time to look at the big hand-drawn hand-pumper, a double-decker with double end stroke, which could accommodate fifty men manning her. A fireplug nearby is about the right height for a mastiff or Irish wolfhound. Beyond it, the 1897 La France steam engine is also a prize.

Unexpected at the back of the hall is the "Lady of Progress," that sat on the San Francisco City Hall that tumbled down in the big earthquake and fire of 1906. Lights were put on her wreath at San Diego where she had been on loan for an exposition. Not surprisingly there is a section devoted to Lillie Hitchcock Coit, San Francisco's most famous fire buff of all time.

38

"Oh the sounds of the earth are like music . . ." but only when you separate them out in a city. Otherwise there is, according to my electronic-whiz son, Rick, a bassy rumble, the wild sound or brown noise that forms a constant mechanical background to a city dweller's life.

Both he and I came into this world with the ability to hear dog whistles, alas. These are usually beyond the range of human hearing. It can be uncomfortable, embarrassing, even painful, to possess such hyperacuity. Kids in Baltimore used to stick pins into automobile horns as a Halloween prank when I was pregnant with Rick. One night such a prank kept me from sleeping. My courtly spouse, then a medical student at the Johns Hopkins, couldn't hear the car horn, but he volunteered to go find it when I told him the sound came from the direction of Patterson Park. He took the pin out of an open car's horn parked near the fountain more than a mile away.

Baltimore had pleasanter sounds too, the street cries of hucksters selling merchandise from horse-drawn wagons. "Hey! Annarannel cannalopes. Getcha Annarannal countee cannalopes," one street arab would sing out.

"Hard coal," another called in a voice sonorous as a fog horn. "Hard coal!"

My favorite was the peach seller, "Oh I got Alaberta peaches. Twenty cents a big pail, yep."

Unfortunately we came to San Francisco too late to hear the shrimp sellers with their baskets slung from a yoke, crying, "Schlimpy! Schlimpy! Fi cent!" on the streets.

A Sound Walk

"SNICK SNICK SNICK snick snick" comes the rhythmic rush of footsteps of a weimaraner approaching in the grass. Over it is the "sussurrussurrus" of wind in the trees.

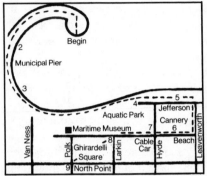

"Beeeeeeeeeeeeeeee" goes a deep foghorn, to be answered contrapuntally in a few seconds by the restrained "OOOOOOOOO" of another near it. "Ah ha hahahahaha," a lady cascades out a laugh in the middle distance.

"Sputter sputter sputter sputter." A nervous lawnmower up the hill? No, it's a little yellow service vehicle coming this way.

"Gurgle ga-gurgle swoosh spash." Water surges around the sea stack just below us. Beyond a pilot boat goes purring by almost as silently as the Phantom of the Opera.

Consider yourself tuned in to the soundscapes of the city if you can identify from these few clues where we are in San Francisco . . .

Waterfront. Right! It is about 11 A.M. Monday on that length of the Golden Gate Promenade within Fort Mason. We are walking east toward Muni Pier. The occasion is a "soundwalk" that anyone can do, suggested by the Exploratorium in its bimonthly magazine.*

"Sightseeing is what attracts most tourists to the San Francisco wharf area, but there's a very different way to tour this popular part of the city—sound-hearing," suggested editor Diane Hales, who took me on the walk she had described "as an experiment in raised *aural* consciousness."

"All you really need to make this walk," she said, "is two ears and two feet." Read the article first, if you choose (you will find it printed in its entirety on pages 197-99), and then transport yourself to the watery end of Van Ness Avenue, that curved hook on the far end of Municipal Pier.

*The Exploratorium, Vol. 2, No. 3, August/September 1978.

"We start at Municipal Pier, where waves break against the rocks. Wind blowing hard from the west intermittently swooshes past our ears. In between the swooshes the afternoon is quiet, and our feet make the loudest sounds we hear."

After duplicating the walk on a sunny morning, my own notes say: Add the mewling of gulls, the efficient snicker of a fisherman's reel tossing out a baited line; the happy squeals of children, mellowed across the sheltered water from the apron of sand in Aquatic Park.

The Exploratorium's soundwalk goes on to suggest that as an experiment we put on blindfolds. It is amazing how all sounds become exaggerated once the sense of sight is blocked. Don't try it unless you have a friend along to steer you away from that raised curbing behind the benches. Diane tied a scarf around my eyes. Suddenly, with sight gone, the volume seems amplified for every sound. A poptop-can opened was like a frightening little thundering out of proportion to its size. Gull conversation that had seemed casual emerged as a wrangling argument — the peck order jockeying for a favorite piling on the nearby Alcatraz pier. Happiest sound of all was the song of the Hyde Street cable car bells across the water.

"You can hear fog," Diane said. "It is different from wind, a strange sound." To me it seemed most audible by the changes it makes by muffling other sounds.

As we walked she explained that all the world is an Exploratorium to director Frank Oppenheimer, who has developed a whole new museum section on language and sound. Already popular at the museum is "The Vidium" in which one can see patterns of one's own speech, or the tree that lights up when one stands nearby and claps hands or speaks to it. "Little kids say 'I love you' a lot to that tree," Diane commented, "but my favorite experience with the sound exhibits was to come upon a deaf boy teaching himself to modulate sounds with The Vidium." Another popular display is The Cocktail Party, in which two conversations are happening, one at either ear. When one presses a button, they mesh, resulting in total aural confusion. In the exhibit, you can speak into it, turn a dial different ways, and hear yourself as a cackling witch or a low-moaning monster.

We went past the Maritime Museum, with its whipping flag, past the bleachers where a steel-drummer often holds forth, and were passed, in turn, by the clickety clickety clickety click of a skate-board with increasing, then diminishing, music. At the Cannery's Jefferson Street entrance, we turned into the Mall as Item 6 directs. "We hear exotic sounds: A tambourine and a bird cry. Nearby, we find a guitarist and a woman, each with a parrot perched on a shoulder, playing and dancing." On our replication of the walk, a juggler dropped a soft, grey, felt top hat with an interesting hollow sound. There was a heavy contrast of the natural noises we had heard out over the water and the surge of man-made crowd noises as they appreciated the performers in the mall.

Coming out on Beach Street we turned right toward Hyde Street and picked up the humming of the cables under the cobbles and metal plates, the snort of buses, the noisy click of a Hasselblad camera lens as a tourist snapped a picture. As we mounted the Larkin Street steps to Ghirardelli Square, we could sort out the splashes of five jets of water in the Ruth Asawa fountain while a string quartet played Haydn in the background.

By then, tuned in to the sounds of our environment, we were ready for a noisy lunch, the kind that would make us salivate in anticipation with the very sounds of it. The Exploratorium's sound-walk ends at Polk and Northpoint with the disagreeable snorts and coughs of municipal buses "lined up like circus elephants holding each other's tails." We ended instead at Gaylords, to the happy slapping of paratha, the baked Indian bread, to the sizzle of tandoori hot from the oven, to the rhythmic chopping of vegetables and the soothing sound of a raga.

If that isn't your dish of tea, one of the most interesting sounds in all of San Francisco is available only under the rotunda back at the Palace of Fine Arts. Stand exactly in the middle and clap your hands. You should hear at least four (count 'em, four) echoes of that hand clapping.

Soundscapes: A San Francisco Soundwalk*
Diane Hales

Sight-seeing is what attracts most tourists to San Francisco's wharf area, but there's a very different way to tour this popular part of the city—"sound hearing." As an experiment in raised aural conscious-ness, some of the Exploratorium's staff took our ears on a soundwalk. To follow our footsteps and tune into an area whose sounds are far less familiar than its sights, you need only two ears and two feet. You also might find some notes from our trip helpful:

1. We start at municipal pier, where waves break against rocks and the pier. Wind, blowing hard from the west, intermittently swooshes past our ears. In between the swooshes the afternoon is quiet, and our feet make the loudest sounds we hear.

2. On a foggy day, you might listen for a foghorn's bleat or a tanker's five-note warning. During our walk, the bay is peaceful, with only an occasional motorboat or circling helicopter cutting through the natural sounds.

3. As an experiment, we put on blindfolds. Without eyes to distract us, we notice sounds we hadn't heard before: a gull chuckling, the clacking of a sailboat's rigging, fishermen sorting through their gear. Without visual clues, other sounds are exaggerated: a peanut shell scraping along the concrete sounds like a paper bag being tossed in the wind.

4. As we leave the pier, we encounter more people, more cars, more sounds. The waves, lapping the sandy beach in Aquatic Park, provide a gentle contrast. The chatter of tourists blends together in a multi-lingual collage of syllables.

5. Along the wharf, street musicians add their songs and music to the laughter of tourists. We listen carefully to hear the cracking of a crab shell and the rustling of paper bags of sourdough bread. We walk past a panhandler, sing-songing of money won, lost and wanted.

6. Along the Cannery, street artists silently sketch portraits as families and friends of their subjects whisper and giggle. We hear exotic sounds: a tambourine and a bird cry. Nearby, we find a guitarist and a woman, each with a parrot perched on a shoulder, playing and dancing.

7. At Hyde Street, we listen to a unique San Francisco sound—the hum of the cable car line. At the cable-car turn around, we hear the bells clang as the the car is pivoted around for its downtown trip.

8. As we approach Ghirardelli Square, we notice unusually loud and shrill bird calls. Finally we see the singing "birds," plastic

whistles being played and sold on the corner of the square. We walk through Ghirardelli, which is filled with an excited blur of voices, and stop at the soothing gurgles of the fountain. The wind sets a chime swaying and playing. Recorded music spills out of stores. The broom of a janitor makes an odd, grating sound. As we leave, we pause at a store filled with music boxes and listen to their tinny trills.

9. The final sound we hear is the loudest — and most disagreeable — of the day: the coughing of four municipal buses, lined up like circus elephants holding each other's tails, as they chug through rush-hour traffic.

* Reprinted with permission from the *Exploratorium,* Vol. 2, No. 3/September 1978. Edited by Diane Hales

39

It hasn't been easy to find roses with a sweet aroma in Northern California. Cecile Brunner and Harrison's Yellow are two great exceptions. The hybrid tea roses seem to have had the perfume bred out of them. Fog seems to steal the odor away from others. But when the perfume of Harrison's Yellow in my neighbor's garden comes wafting across the fence, it's time for a walk. There are some fine old roses in unexpected places on Russian Hill.

Along the Russian Hill Ridge

WATERFRONTS, HILLTOPS, AND open spaces are what give San Francisco its exhilarating quality. The perception of space, interpreted as freedom, is what we all especially

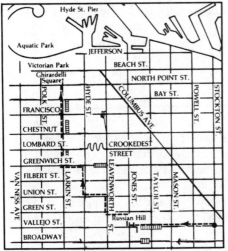

enjoy on a walk. Given the choice, almost anyone will opt for the clump of green trees or the glint of blue water visible in the distance as a destination to walk toward.

Coincidentally, it is also one of the things San Francisco is famous for, that tourists remember and talk about back home—those unexpected glimpses of the bay framed between buildings, the ever widening perspectives as one climbs a hill, the sense of achievement at the top, the breathtaking reward of a distant vista from a summit, the rounding of a corner to find the whole horizon open.

Ideally, the route for any such city walk offers at least two such sensations. One of my favorites touches two hilltops, a beach, and four small parks; has at least seven surprise vistas; and goes through Russian Hill, our most civilized neighborhood.

To make this walk, get off the Powell and Mason Fisherman's Wharf cable car at Vallejo Street. Look around for the green oasis, then start uphill toward it on Vallejo. In a trice you leave the barren urban desert of stark buildings to find the lush informality of Alta Vista Terrace. Take the steps alongside that lead up to Ina Coolbrith Park, a memorial to the famous librarian who inspired Jack London. Once in it, sit a moment on one of the park benches to look back at North Beach below before crossing Taylor Street for a climb to even loftier heights.

With each ten feet you climb on the Vallejo Street steps, pause briefly to assess the widening vista. To Ambrose Bierce, Will and Wallace Irwin, Gelett (Purple Cow) Burgess, Charlie Dobie, and Frank Norris, who often climbed this flight, this was an aerie of Bohemia. It was also the site of San Francisco's first gallows. The Mediterranean-style balustrades at the top of the hill were designed by architect Willis Polk, who lived on the south side of the 1000 block and walled off half his house rather than sell it after his divorce. For one of the all-time fabulous views of the East Bay, punctuated by Telegraph Hill, walk over to the end of the parking circle.

Russian Hill Place and Florence Place are so entrancing a country-style neighborhood, you may want to linger forever, but walk west again to the balustrade opposite at Jones Street, the site of the Russian graveyard that gave Russian Hill its name. When the ramps and balustrade were built in 1912, road cuts revealed skeletons.

Bear right down the ramp to Green Street, ignoring the Eichler Summit if you can, and cross to the north side for another of those great surprises. Then zig west on the "Paris block of Green Street," the most variable in the city, to enjoy its architectural mixtures of firehouse, octagon, farmhouse, Beaux Arts, Art Nouveau, and French and Italianate Victorian buildings. Zag right again on Leavenworth and walk on the east side for the fun of a glimpse down Macondray Lane, one of the hill's best-kept public secrets. The Union Street corner view north is another sheer dropoff whose steepness gives the thrilling glimpse of infinity. Bear left on Union, and at Hyde Street there is another distant vista, this one revealing Pacific Heights and the Presidio as a backdrop.

A cable car may rumble past as you approach Hyde Street. If you can resist Swenson's ice cream shop, follow the car tracks to the right until you reach Greenwich Street. Look east for a great vista of Coit Tower, but bear left instead up the red brick ramp past the tennis courts into George Sterling Park, named for a poet whose home overlooked it. On the northern steps, start down and go through the gap into a broad, tree-lined *alleé*. Short of its end, bear left through another gap in the hedge to the next lower terrace and look for the concrete staircase in the northwest corner of the park, a great place to see the mountains of Marin or watch a fall sunset.

Follow the steps down to Lombard Street. The open space to the right, the site of the old Rolfe estate, is soon to accommodate a small group of townhouses conforming to neighborhood standards.

Follow Larkin toward the trees on the west side of the street. Another surprise! Hidden steps go down, with a look at the whole northwestern waterfront as you descend. Look both ways as you come to the curve of Larkin before crossing to reach a middle lap of the steps that lead to Francisco Street's lower section. You soon arrive alongside the lower Hyde Street reservoir, whose unpaved pathway borders the upper edge of the Bay Street park, a favorite dogrun for all of Russian Hill.

Near the delightful vegetable garden, look for the lower level of the steps that parallel North View Street to end at Bay. Cross Bay Street with the stoplight, continue one block downhill on Larkin, and you will reach that instant vacation known as Ghirardelli Square. Linger for lunch, browse, shop, or rest, for every bench has been placed with a masterful eye for the stimulating outlook. Then work your way downhill to Beach Street, cross it, and lo! there you are at Aquatic Park, the Hyde Street Pier, the National Maritime Museum, and the beginning to our grandest waterfront walk of all, the Golden Gate Promenade.

October

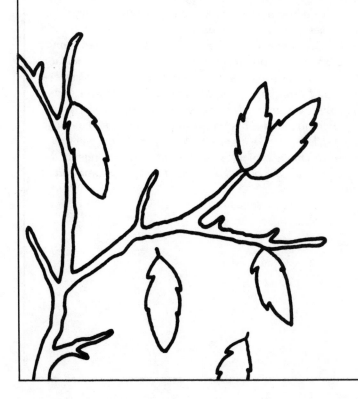

40

Hanging on the doorknob like a May basket when I answered the bell some years back, there was a gnarled blackthorn stick with a note and a small bouquet of carnations attached to the handle. "This cane once belonged to Sir Harry Lauder," the note said. "I thought you might appreciate owning it." It was signed, "A reader."

It's a humorous walking stick, the work of a sculptor manqué, and I do enjoy owning it. The handle looks rather like the head of a cairn terrier, while the lower third of the staff is a cruikshanks, two branches naturally entwined to resemble a pair of crooked legs crossed nonchalantly. It's a stout stick that cries for moors, heather, for horizons, and October's bright blue weather. Either a clever gardener must have trained a thornbush for many years to reach this unlikely shape or some astute woodsman with an artist's eye separated it from a tangled wild brier with great effort. In any case, time, wit, and skill went into the making of it.

Perhaps it did support the legendary comedian on stage as he rolled out, "Oh it's nice to get oop in the mornin' when the sun is shinin' brrright . . . " His spirit seems to linger in the stick. No one ever picks it up without assuming some sort of comic stance.

Hidden Canyon

YOU WAKE ONE morning and the air is a bugle call, blue and cold, with golden promises of warmth as the sun climbs. Suddenly fall is in the air. If you find yourself longing for that

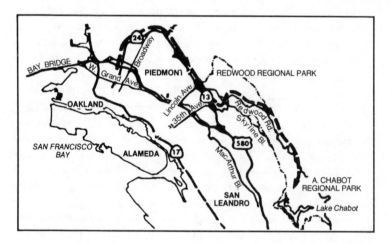

pungent, currylike flavor of chaparral, for the pleasure of dry leaves underfoot to scuffle, for the reds and golds of frost-lit trees, brilliant as torches in the sun-dappled woodland, then a walk through Hidden Canyon is for you.

Hidden Canyon lies in the lea of Lake Chabot, within the 4,934-acre regional park named for Anthony Chabot, the engineering genius who provided the East Bay with water by creating its earthfill dam in 1874. Some of the vast park is within Oakland, some in Castro Valley, and some in San Leandro. For almost a hundred years, fishermen would look down hungrily from high points in these cities and dream of the ten-pound bass and six-pound trout reputed to dwell in the 315-acre lake. Came the day in 1966 when the East Bay Municipal Utility District opened the gates and lo, it was true! There are still big fish in Lake Chabot and every so often a fisherman catches one.

Anthony Chabot Regional Park, the second largest in the EBRP District, has another well-kept secret. Its Las Cumbres Campground is the East Bay's closest woodland for family camping. There are sites for campers, vans, tent-trailers, RVs, tents, and backpackers, all at reasonable rates, first come, first served. Hidden Canyon Trail begins near the campground, so the way to embark on this walk is to transport yourself to Oakland, to the junction of Redwood Road and Skyline Boulevard along the ridge of the East Bay hills. Drive southeastward on Redwood Road for 6.37 miles to the Marciel Gate of Anthony Chabot Regional Park. Drive as far as you can and park just past the Rifle Range access road near the locked gate to Las Cumbres Campground.

Once parked, look on the south side of the parking circle for a broad trail that takes off at a slight downhill grade. Soon you will round a curve and vast views of Coyote Hills and the Hayward shoreline open up across the western horizon. At the junction with the Brandon Trail, a length of the National Skyline Regional Trail, bear right downhill on the Coffeeberry Trail. It soon brings you up to the group recreation area of Las Cumbres Campground. At this point, leave the trail, and follow the road past Hilltop Vista, a pay phone, and Canyon Vista camp areas. Look for the trailhead at the triangle of roads. It begins on the right-hand side of the main road and goes downhill into eucalyptus woodland. Until they run out, self-guiding trail maps are posted on the trailhead box.

As we went through the woods, Ranger Jane Morehead, who conducted me on this walk, pointed out the web patterns of three unusual spiders. One was the tube made by the doorless trapdoor spider, whose very name seems a contradiction. Another was the inverted pyramid of the funnel-web spider. The third is the dropped handkerchief of the filmy-dome spider. All three are valuable bug catchers. The hillsides you are walking through, incidentally, represent the largest concentration of eucalyptus anywhere in the world outside of Australia. Native vegetation, including bigleaf maple, wild rose, ocean spray, goldbacked fern, monkey flower, and bracken, grows in the draws.

Past the amphitheater, which has been slightly disassembled to allow log benches to decay into soil, bear right at the fork, and right again at the next fork. Shots you hear in the distance along this length of the trail may come from the rifle range in a neighboring canyon. The sudden view of Oakland, visible for a moment through a gap, is around 73rd Avenue. Bear right at the bench and right again at the next fork.

Although you will have to look for it, Campsite 54 will be just uphill on your left above Post 6. Posts and benches were installed by Boy Scouts, among them Lance Brocchini as part of his Eagle Scout project. A new self-guiding trail booklet has been prepared to match. Number 9 is an especially nice touch with the oakplank bench, showing wood in cross section, under the coast live oak tree.

When you reach the Toyon Hut at Number 11, pause a moment to look it over. This three-sided stone shelter was built by the Senior Boys Crew of youthful offenders assigned to work off sentences by local judges. After the 1958 fire that roared through here when it was still known as the Grass Valley Regional Park, the Boys Crew built the huts and picnic tables, laid trails, and installed water lines in the park.

Take the old ranch road around to the left. It will soon bring you uphill to a stile. Before you go through the stile, walk over to the western edge of the hill you are standing on. There, below in all its glory is Lake Chabot, cool, still, and beautiful. When Anthony Chabot built it, he washed tons of earth downhill into San Leandro Creek, using the gigantic water hoses perfected for hydraulic mining in the gold country. He then ran herds of wild horses back and forth over the loosened dirt to compact it into an earthen dam. EBMUD, which still uses the lake as an emergency reservoir, lowered the water not long ago to earthquakeproof the dam.

When you have enjoyed the eagle's-eye view sufficiently, let yourself through the stile and follow the road downhill through the Las Cumbres Campground to complete the loop back to your wheels. If you are game for a longer walk, look for the Lakeside trailhead near the hot-shower facilities. Backpackers who come under their own steam will also find that by crossing the footbridge over the lake in Opossum Cove, they can follow the Cameron Trail back to the Chabot Park entrance and pick up AC Transit bus No. 91 for Hayward, Castro Valley, and BART.

41

"Oh won't you lead me to that smell of penny candy, although I may not have a penny handy," went a line from "Needles and Pins," the great Depression Broadway musical. For thousands of San Franciscans, the smell of penny candy is also the odor of the Cecile Brunner rose, used by gay blades during the Gay Nineties as a boutonniere.

The Cecile Brunner is a miniature pale pink rose that grows on a large hardy shrub, blooms almost all year, and makes a charming nosegay when surrounded with blue forget-me-nots and a bit of paper lace.

A lot of those Gay Nineties dandies sporting the boutonniere came from down the Peninsula, including William Ralston. Of course, they didn't use the word "gay" the way it's used in the Gay Eighties.

Belmont's Twin Pines Park

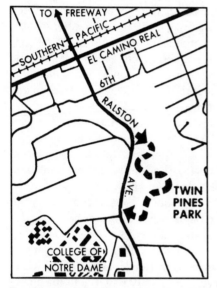

T HE INDIANS CALLED it Cañada del Diablo—Devil's Canyon. The Spanish, discovering it was the easiest route across the peninsula between the bay and the coast, renamed it Cañada de San Augustin. The citizens of Belmont call it Ralston Avenue today, but many a hasty commuter, who finds himself slowed on it by a Southern Pacific freight may still think this canyon is pretty devilish.

Not nearly so devilish, however, as Belmontians think the motorists are who use their main street for a chute. Along Ralston the stoplights are few and far between. A walker takes his life in his hands to cross it. For this reason, I have resisted walking or writing about Belmont for years. With this warning, however, I would like to invite you to walk in the gracious old estate that is now Belmont's Twin Pines Park, a little oasis of sanity that shuts out the speeders, the smog, and the sounds with big old oak, bay, and buckeye trees.

To make this walk, transport yourself to Belmont, preferably the way William Chapman Ralston, riverboatman, banker, horseman, Comstock millionaire, and "one-man chamber of commerce for California," used to transport his dinner guests. He raced the diamond stack steam locomotive on the San Francisco and San Jose Railroad in a horse-drawn carriage—often winning. A few people re-enacted this race one year at the invitation of the San Mateo Historical Society, a few in a demi-break, the rest on the train. Amtrak trains leave the San Francisco Fourth and Townsend Station. If you must burn fossil fuel, take Bayshore Highway 101 south to Belmont, turn west on Ralston, and after you cross Sixth Street, a short walk from the station, look for the Twin Pines parking area. It is just beyond the Wells Fargo Bank on the south side of Ralston. It is safest to cross with the light at Sixth if you are on foot.

Within the park, walk to the big palm that adorns the lawn in the carriage turnaround fronting the mansion built for George Center, cashier of the Bank of California, in 1910. It now houses the San Mateo Arts Council and a handful of compatible organizations. At the outset, read the historical marker, which reveals that this park was created in 1976 on the site of a Costanoan Indian settlement, camped on by Captain Fernando Rivera and Fr. Francisco Palou, granted in 1790 to Don José Arguello, and at one time grounds of the home of California's second governor, John McDougal. It was later the site of Carl Janke's biergarten, Belmont Park, where picnickers by the thousand came on chartered trains. The longest brought seven thousand Oddfellows here in seventy-five railroad cars to dance, roister, and drink Janke's sarsaparilla. The grounds later belonged to a gracious Lady Bountiful, Mrs. Annette S. Alexander, who ran a remarkably modern sanitarium. Her home is now the Belmont Hills Psychiatric Center, farther down Ralston Avenue. The mansion across the driveway became Twin Pines Sanitarium under the management of Dr. William Rebec, father of the California Humane Commitment Act, around 1930. Go into the building to examine the galleries that now adorn walls patients once stared at.

Tempting as it is to enjoy this sophisticated recycling of a fine old home immediately, for this walk return to the front of the building and walk east past the police station to the Wells Fargo parking lot. Notice the shortcut path cutting through toward the Safeway, a bucolic wisp of straw that reveals Belmont's proclivity to resist Tomorrow in favor of Yesterday. Old foundations from an early barn or milk house are still visible under the fallen leaves. Walk south on the road that soon comes to a log cabin on the creekside, once Ye Old Cabin Inn stagestop at La Honda.

Follow the creek to your right as you face the cabin, and beyond the little tack room, used now oddly enough for poison storage, you reach the creekside kilns and studios of several members of the Twin Pines Art Center. Many of them also use the upper level of the mansion. Next building along the creek is a Senior Citizens Center where inexpensive lunches are served occasionally. From it, bear right and walk between the lodge, which contains meeting rooms, and the Belmont Park office. On weekdays, a guide to the native plants in Twin Pines Park is available here. Numbers along the nature trail are keyed to this booklet. When you reach the two bollards where the nature trail begins, bear left. Follow the nature trail through the trees. As close as it is to Ralson Avenue, the difference in elevation almost shuts out traffic noise.

All too soon you are back up on the busy thoroughfare. Belmont, the steamboatlike mansion of W. C. Ralston that gave the town its name, is the heart of the College of Notre Dame, halfway up the canyon wall on the opposite side of Ralston Avenue. Now renamed Ralston Hall, its ballroom is the chamber in which "The Ralston Series" of chamber music is held Sunday afternoons during October. If you are planning to walk up, go all the way to Chula Vista to cross. Although the Belmont Exercise Trail on the campus beckons invitingly, don't be tempted to cross when you see it. The exercise trail is free to walkers at any time, but tours of the campus are given by appointment weekdays only, and arranged by calling 593-1601, extension 6.

42

The turkey vulture is your friendly neighborhood undertaker. He patrols his territory with conscientious regularity, usually three times a day, looking for fresh kills. His collection system is infinitely faster, quieter, and cleaner than any city garbage system. Without him and the banana slug, the dung beetle, and a few other scavengers, the woods would reek of carrion.

One cold morning while living on the upper slope of Mount Tamalpais, I went into the utility room to find a rattler coiled around the water heater. I retreated quickly and closed the door. How to get rid of the invader before the children came home from school? Like many another suburbanite, I telephoned the exterminator. When he learned how far I lived from town, he refused to make the trip, but he asked me if we had a fire extinguisher. We did. "Read me the ingredients," he ordered. I did. "Fine," he said. "Have you got a hatchet?" We had. He then commanded me to turn off the gas outside the house before spraying the snake with the fire extinguisher.

"You'll have to chop him off the pipe," he instructed. "Wear gloves and be careful how you pick up the head. Use fire tongs if you have them. Then throw all the pieces out for the vultures to clean up. It will all be gone in minutes."

He was right. Six turkey vultures did a better job of cleaning up the debris than any yardman could. It was spectacular to see those big wings alight at close range. A five-foot spread. Thereafter they got our meat scraps and I came to be grateful to them as the garbage can smelled sweeter.

Today I wouldn't kill the rattler. Rattlers are afraid of us, with good reason, and will hurry away to hide, given half a chance. You may not see any on the Skyline-to-the-Sea Trail, but if you do, please give them the chance to escape.

Skyline-to-the-Sea Trail

SARATOGA GAP! THE name has a flavor of the mountains, of wilderness, of solitude—an adventurous, pioneering, shades-of-the-Old-West ring to it. As well it might, for at an

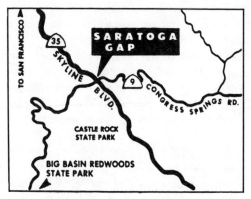

elevation of 2,634 feet above sea level it was one of the few places in the late 1800s where a road could go between some of the Santa Cruz mountains from San Francisco Bay to the sea.

Located where the southern tips of San Mateo and Santa Clara counties meet the northernmost point of Santa Cruz County, today it is still a crossroads. Half a dozen hiking and/or riding trails originating in state, county, and regional parks and open space districts meet here. Of them, the most significant is the dramatic thirty-eight-mile-long Skyline-to-the-Sea Trail, a longtime project of the Sempervirens Fund, an outgrowth of the founders of Big Basin Redwoods State Park, which challenges Yosemite as the first state park in California and Muir Woods as the first redwood preservation effort in the nation. Sempervirens also has had a hand in establishing Castle Rock, one of the newest state parks in the system, thanks largely to the remarkable inventor, Dr. Russell Varian, his widow Dorothy, and their many friends, who helped purchase the land. After years of trailbuilding by the Santa Cruz Mountain Trail Association, the two parks are now linked by the Skyline-to-the-Sea Trail.

The trail has been cleverly routed to be usable for long or short walks. For the outdoors enthusiast in great physical shape, it can be a long weekend or week's backpacking excursion with camps conveniently located en route. If you are planning to do this at any season, register in advance by calling Big Basin (408-338-6132) or writing Big Basin Redwoods State Park, Big Basin, CA 95006.

Since this is a year-round trail, camps are always in use, but less so during the winter months, of course.

For the Sunday walker who spends the rest of the week at a desk, it is possible to walk several separate sections as a one day outing. For starters, a pleasurable section is the Summit Meadows Loop.

To make this walk, pack your daybag and canteen, take a jacket, and wear lug-soled boots. Then transport yourself about forty miles south from San Francisco via Skyline Boulevard, State Highway 35, to its junction with Highway 9, the Big Basin–Congress Springs Road out of Saratoga. The vista point at their meeting place, Saratoga Gap, has been enhanced with paving and landscaping by Caltrans in cooperation with the state park system to provide trailhead and view parking.

Once parked, look around you. Just across Highway 9 to the north are trails leading to Palo Alto, to Saratoga, and to Upper Stevens Creek County Park through lands of the Mid-Peninsula Park District. To the south are trails that lead to Castle Rock State Park and to Sanborn Skyline County Park. Other trails lead west. To pick up the Skyline-to-the-Sea Trail, cross Highway 35. A Cal-Trans maintenance station will appear directly below the shoulder of the highway. Follow the direction arrows indicated on state park signs about fifty yards along the dirt shoulder, and enter the trail, which immediately drops below the highway level.

After half a mile, the trail heads uphill and crosses Highway 9, plainly marked by signposts. Once across the highway, the trail heads west along the upper flank of the Oil Creek drainage along an old wagon road that made its way down to the confluence of Oil Creek and Pescadero Creek. "Tony" Claude Look and Joyce Leonard, of Sempervirens Fund, who conducted me on this walk, cautioned against following this old road beyond the wooden post that designates the Skyline-to-the-Sea Trail; it soon goes into private property.

At this point you are actually in Big Basin State Park in a trail corridor purchased by Sempervirens in 1915 to connect the sea and the mountains. Long known to seasoned hikers, it was little used by novices until trail workdays began a few years ago in which thousands of Peninsula young people volunteered their time to create connections between old logging roads through the trail corridor. Redwoods were cut out long ago through here, but the gigantic bay trees and Douglas firs have never been touched. Vista points along this portion of the trail show the high meadows and wooded hills to the west of Skyline Ridge. At one opening in the trees the blue Pacific is visible near the town of Pescadero; at another, near Waddell Beach.

A mile along, you will again reach the shoulder of Highway 9. Look for the highway paddle marker number 26.00, a white metal stake with the numbers in black on its flat surface. Leave the Skyline-to-the-Sea Trail and cross Highway 9 again at this point. Head toward the wire gate leading to Summit Meadows, an area acquired by the Sempervirens Fund and the state as an addition to Castle Rock State Park. You can enter the trail to Summit Meadows through an opening about fifteen feet to the right of the metal gate.

Follow the trail markers from the Summit Meadows Loop along the dirt road that runs toward the walker's right. The open meadows once supported a homesteader whose cabin has long since disappeared, and later a Christmas tree farm, which left the Coulter, lodgepole, and Monterey pines growing here. Soon the trail swings into dense stands of red-bark madrone, Douglas firs, and a few redwoods. Wildflowers that pop up here after the rains are so remarkable, a flora, *Plants of Big Basin Redwoods State Park and the Coastal Mountains of Northern California* written by Mary Beth Cooney-Lazaneo and Kathleen Lyons and illustrated in color by Howard King, has been published by Mountain Press Publishing Company.

As the mile mark draws near about twenty to thirty minutes into the Meadows Loop, watch on your left for a square block of concrete, a wellsite. The trail leading off uphill to your right reaches a vista point in a quarter of a mile so spectacular it is worth the digression. The blocky face of Varian Peak above the drainage basin for the San Lorenzo River is the eye catcher. On clear days Monterey and Moss Landing, Ben Lomond Mountain, Monterey Bay, and Santa Cruz are visible, with Eagle Rock State Forestry Lookout and beyond it the Scott Creek drainage heading west. Pine Mountain, the southern boundary of Big Basin Redwoods is to the north. Closer at hand are the Waddell Creek drainage, identifiable by the white-patched ridge known as "the chalks," and Pescadero Creek drainage basin, which flows northward toward Portola State Park before veering west to the ocean.

Retrace your steps to the wellsite and continue along the pathway to the next vista point. From grassy meadows it offers a closer look at the San Lorenzo River basin, revealing the forests, rocks, and ridges of Castle Rock State Park.

From this second vista point, take the lower pathway below the level and walk around the hill, dropping down gradually to an area adjacent to Highway 9. Cross 9 once more and head toward the trail, which winds around a well-rounded grassy knoll. This leads to Sempervirens Point, the spot where motorists along Highway 9 often stop to view the vista the walker has been enjoying for the last mile.

Look for the green metal gate where the Skyline-to-the-Sea wooden trail marker appears. Turn right at this point and begin the gradual ascent along the Skyline-to-the-Sea Trail. You will rejoin your turnoff spot at the same mileage marker, 26.00, to retrace your steps back to Saratoga Gap.

43

Sometimes when I am walking trails in the Bay Area, the feeling of other, earlier presences that inhabited a place is strong in me. Oakwood Valley is like that. The feeling overwhelmed me the first time I led a group of walkers in a University of California Extension class up the Oakwood Valley Trail. We stopped to lunch on a high point overlooking Sausalito. The trail had only recently been completed, but the spirit of Indians was as tangible as water.

Our culture scoffs at mystical impressions, so instead of telling the class how I felt, I said, "This might be a good place to look for arrowheads."

Before we finished lunch, Angela Eassa, one of the class members, had found an arrowhead, the first to be found in the Headlands since it became a national park. It is now in the archeological collection of the Golden Gate National Recreation Area. Such finds are valuable to the archeologists. If you have comparable luck, please take your find around to Fort Mason, the park headquarters, or to one of the regional ranger stations. You'll get it back if they don't need it.

Oakwood Valley Trail

When "OCTOBER'S BRIGHT blue weather sets the gypsy blood astir," it is time to take to the hills and dales, to smell the pungent chaparral, scuff a few fallen leaves, marvel as the quail duck into the rich lavender coyote mint, and admire the hawks riding thermals far overhead.

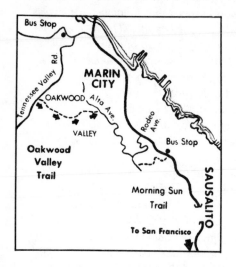

You can drive fifty miles into the country for the experience, but short of that, where do you find that kind of country walk in these energy-conscious days? Would you believe that you can now do it within five miles of San Francisco and reach it by public transportation?

The Oakwood Valley Trail is the secret. Just off the Tennessee Valley Road in the Golden Gate National Recreation Area, its short mile and a half could make any urban cowboy feel like a son of the Golden West. It offers a pleasant ramble through a sheltered valley, up through woodland on a gentle climb along the side of Hershey's Hill, to end at Alta Avenue with a sensational view overlooking Sausalito and all of San Francisco Bay beyond it.

To make this walk, put on your lug-soled boots, stock your canteen and daypack, and bring a windbreaker. Then transport yourself north via the Golden Gate Bridge, Highway 101, and Highway 1. Turn west off Shoreline Highway, Route 1, on the Tennessee Valley Road before you reach that busy crossroad in Tamalpais Valley. If you pass Le Camembert Restaurant, you have gone too far. (Golden Gate Transit buses stop at Tamalpais Junction.) The produce truck on the creekside is one landmark for Tennessee Valley Road. About three-quarters of a mile past the truck you will be at

Oakwood Valley. As soon as you spot the first big GGNRA sign, park under the trees on your right.

Once parked, cross the road to the open meadow and look for a path that goes uphill through the grassland west of the willows that hide the creek on the valley floor. Follow it along the trees. Soon you become aware of that rich currylike odor—part mint, part pearly everlasting, part fallen leaves—that gives the salubrious air of autumn its distinctive zest. Inhale and enjoy it.

As the trail rises into the coastal scrub, look on your left for mounds of sticks. These are the haunts of the dusky-footed wood-rat. When the Citizen's Trails Committee that has helped the park create its trail system during the last eight years explored this trail, we discovered five woodrats' nests along this lower length. Bright-eyed Elizabeth Terwilliger, one of several naturalists who are members of the committee, found one in a low-growing tree. Usually woodrats nest on the ground.

The trail swings through a marsh, dry at this season, then goes westward through a little virgin forest. When the path returns to the east side of the valley, cross the creek to emerge at the old Oak-wood Valley Ranch Road. At this broad flat area, the walker has several choices. One is to amble downhill on the gentle grade of the road, looping past old farm sites and one remaining residence to return to the starting point.

The upper trail is steeper, but the panorama revealed at its cli-max makes the climb worth it. Bear right and follow the road as it meanders upward through the trees. Old orchards, leveled barn and homesites, and occasional introduced plants such as periwinkle and calla lilies, attest the long use man has made of this land. Origi-nally part of old Rancho Sausalito, it was granted to William Antonio Richardson in 1838.

In his reminiscences published in the San Rafael *Independent* in 1916, Charles Lauff, a Bolinas pioneer, wrote, "We slaughtered twelve elk in one morning on a wild game hunt with Richardson," and described the ground as white with the bones of deer, elk, and wild cattle killed here and in Tennessee Valley for their hides. Grizzly bears and wildcats also roamed here 150 years ago.

Next owner of Rancho Sausalito was Samuel Throckmorton. Most recent private owner of the upper part of Oakwood Valley was Marin school executive Virgil Hollis. As you approach the old stock pond on the Hollis tract, watch nearby trees and power poles for the great horned owls that nest nearby. They often hunt small animals that come to the watering hole.

Soon you round the bend to discover new trail work on the right. The road that seems to continue toward the left doubles back to meet the trail about twenty feet higher. Climb onto the path on the right and in a trice you are out into open country again. Red-tailed and sharp-shinned hawks often soar over the valley on your right. Indian paintbrush, mule ears, and California poppies bloom along here.

All too soon the trail comes up over the ridge. Walk through the open gate and you are at Alta Avenue above Sausalito. Civilization as we know it in the Bay Area is spread below at your feet. Pause as long as you like at this aerie, but if you picnic here, please pack out your own debris.

To return, if you came by bus, bear right on Alta Avenue, and right at the Y going uphill. When you reach Gracie's Forest of eucalyptus trees, watch on your left for the trailhead of the Morning Sun Trail, which will take you downhill to Highway 101 and a handy bus stop north of the Spencer Avenue overpass.

To reach your own wheels, if this is how you came, go back downhill on the Oakwood Valley Trail or follow the Oakwood Valley Ranch Road. The views of the forest canopy with its alternating dark shadows and windows of flickering sunlight always look different on a return trip.

44

Mourning doves nested in our Russian Hill garden for the first time in 1972 and have been returning yearly. That year I became aware for the first time of others nesting at Fort Mason, Lafayette Square, and Golden Gate Park. Survival is a powerful instinct. Perhaps the mourning doves suddenly realized that cities were safer than rural nesting places. Pigeons have always liked cities, possibly because a haven from guns and small boys is easier to find amid many people.

Herb Caen has called the Union Square pigeons "rats with feathers." He doesn't like them. I find them more attractive than the rats that also seem to increase in the city. Like those of Hyde Park, Saint Marks Square in Venice, and almost any other great city, our pigeons are so much of a fixture, we do not think of them as wildlings. Yet the "blue rock" pigeons hunted in Sonora, Mexico, that still fly wild in great flocks are much the same bird.

San Francisco has many interesting bird populations. Best of all I love the exotics that make it here. One little flock we see in the fruit trees on Russian Hill is the East Asian laughing thrush. A neighbor heard one calling for a mate some years back and sent off to an importer for one. Instead he received a mated pair. He released both and out of that trio has grown an ever-increasing flock, whose songs are more melodious than the nightingale.

For years there was a big green Amazon parrot living in the palm trees near the fine old Victorian houses on California at Franklin. A mynah bird hangs out at Aquatic Park near the Sea Scout Base. My favorite of the exotics are the budgies and parakeets who have joined forces on Telegraph Hill. When the flock, which may number thirty birds, lifts off, it rises in the blink of an eye like a sprinkle of confetti in an updraft. In the next blink it is gone.

Any number of jays, robins, song sparrows, house finches, geese, ducks, osprey, hawks, and other native and migrating birds pass through the city twice a year. I don't recall seeing eagles at Eagles' Point, but once I watched a great air battle between a gull and a red-tailed hawk over the channel there.

Eagles' Point

EAGLES' POINT, SAN Francisco, is an aerie with one of the boss views of all time. "A superb Marine View in a frame of bold hills," Frank Morton Todd called it in his 1914 *Handbook*

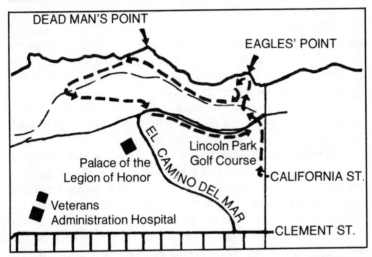

for San Francisco. In the days when the Ferries and Cliff House Railroad chugged along 33rd Street rounding a curve at what is now El Camino del Mar, it was the first breathtaking view passengers in the open air cars had of the Golden Gate Straits. Instantly one forgot City Cemetery, the potters' field that antedated Lincoln Park, and was swept up in the stunning panorama of blue water and sky, distant hills, and rocky cliffs. In its time, it was the counterpart of the Hyde Street cable car plunge downhill just past Lombard Street, or the great widening of landscape northbound on Panoramic Highway on the third curve above Stinson Beach, when all of Bolinas Lagoon is revealed below.

Hidden for years by Monterey pine and cypress planted by Park Superintendent John McLaren in 1924, it emerged from the woods in 1981's storms when twenty-eight of the trees came down. Now part of the Golden Gate National Recreation Area, it has been enhanced with sturdy retaining walls, footpaths, stairways, erosion control plantings, benches, and safety railings. Thanks to the work of the dedicated youngsters of the Youth Conservation Corps and the Young Adult Conservation Corps, once again for anyone on foot the view is as spectacular as ever it was.

Wait for one of those scintillating days of autumn when the air is like wine to make this walk, then transport yourself to the northwest corner of the city. If you go in your own fossil-fueler, park along El Camino del Mar just west of 32nd Avenue. Via public transportation, take the No. 1 California bus, whose number is a legacy from the old Cliff No. 1 trolley of the United Railroads-Cliff House Electric Line that supplanted the steam dummies between 1905 and 1923. Disembark at 32nd Street and walk west, mounting those imposing steps at the end of California Street. Bear right at the top of them. You will then be on the old roadbed of Adolph Sutro's Ferries and Cliff House Railroad, built in 1888.

About parallel to what is now Miss Burke's tennis courts, the sixty-passenger open excursion cars would begin their swing toward Eagles' Point. Cross El Camino del Mar in the crosswalk designated for golfers. Then look for a gap in the trees, as yet unsigned, but marked by two posts and a trash can. This is the start to the Lands' End Trail, a length of the longer Pacific Coast Trail. Follow the trail about one hundred feet along the border of the seventeenth hole of Lincoln Park Golf Course. Just about the time you spy two stately pines and a lofty bench, you will become aware of the familiar brown and white GGNRA signs cautioning against the dangers of cliff and surf for those who leave the designated paths. Go up the tie steps, made of recycled material like all the other reclamation work along this treacherous headland. Soon you are standing on a cobbled circle, with Sea Cliff and Phelan Beach immediately apparent on the right and the Golden Gate Bridge soaring like a harp of the winds in the distance. Go down the steps to the next bench, and suddenly the Transamerica pyramid and the dome of Temple Sherith Israel are visible on the horizon. The U.S. Public Health Service Hospital looms out of the Presidio greenery. So does a whole little city of enlisted men's Wherry housing.

Go down another set of steps and pass under the gnarled tree for even closer acquaintance with the famous strait. At the lookout barrier, once again look to the right to see Lime Point, Fort Point, Belvedere, Angel Island, and on a clear day, the Richmond tank

farm through Raccoon Strait, framed by the bridge. As breakers crash on the rocks below, a kittiwake may cry, a freighter pass, a tour boat come under the bridge, a surfer bob in the waves, or a nearby bluff, cracked by repeated waves, shudder at the impact. It is a thrilling proximity.

Try the more westerly viewpoint before you return. It looks across the strait at Kirby Cove, Point Bonita, Mount Tamalpais, Bolinas, and Point Reyes. Pause a moment on the bench whose graffiti labels it for stoners. Swirls and eddies around Mile Rock sometimes seem alive with birds. If you don't suffer from fear of heights, go down to the lowest barrier to glimpse the beach below the dangerous cliff. Steep as it is, native rabbit grass, lupine, lizard-tail, and seaside daisy cling tenaciously.

When you have feasted your eyes long enough on this lovely aspect, return to the Lands' End Trail and bear right. On an average day, this is sweat city, as runners, racewalkers, and joggers pass on the soft sandy surface. (When was the last time you saw a jogger pass smiling?) Tracks were removed during World War II to make guns. Below the greens, vegetation is little disturbed, but beware the hooker—the golfer, that is, who misdrives a hooked ball.

When you emerge from the tunnel of greenery, you are approaching Dead Man's Point, named by the Coast Guardsmen who have fished many a body out of the surf below. Tempting as it seems don't go up on the point. Instead follow the main path through a narrow defile and bear left when the path narrows. The cove below is the slide area that ultimately closed the railroad. Steps in this area were made from old granite and basalt crossing blocks, dumped here as fill long ago, park technician Jim Milestone, who supervised the trail project, told me. Notice the spring, outlined on your left in dark tufts of bunch grasses. When you climb out of the little sea of seafig, bear right toward the water. At the foot of more tie steps, beyond the odd post tied with plastic, elastic, and string, the trail broadens again. Now one seems to be approaching Mile Rock Light, automated and topped with a helipad instead of the three-tiered residence and lookout tower it had when the wickies manned the light.

After you pass the second cautionary sign, you will be walking toward a great white slash of paint, which looks like a free-fall by Jackson Pollock. Look uphill to find the color echoed by a pylon — both aids to navigation in the channel.

When Veterans' Hospital looms overhead like a monster at the next curve, bear left on the asphalt road. It will bring you past the fourth hole of the golf course back to El Camino del Mar across from the Palace of the Legion of Honor. Bear left on "The Road of the Sea" for a quick return to your wheels or to public transportation.

November

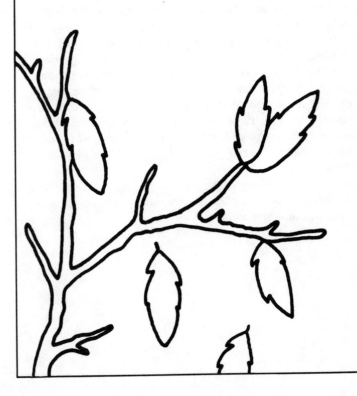

45

Reaching for the citywalking shoes in my closet that show the most wear, and hence must get the most use, I find them to be neutral-colored suede ghillies by Bally of Switzerland. They have a 1¼-inch heel and laces that stretch. For having rubber soles, they are surprisingly dressy. Another pair, camel-colored leather British walkers, is custom made, sporty, but ladylike. On this shelf there are also knee-high boots of Spanish leather with a half-inch platform sole that keeps the foot up out of the wet.

Only the mules, the house slippers, have wedge heels. Fashion notwithstanding, on San Francisco's hills a heel to dig into the concrete striations on steep streets makes good sense. There are no high spike heels, those symbols of male domination. Nor are there any clunkers. Those tragic thick-soled Kothurni, or cothurnus, first worn by actors in ancient Greece so they could be seen from the back of the amphi-theater, are fashionable along Fillmore, Polk, and Castro streets (come to think of it, those streets are stages). My orthopedist says more broken bones than he cares to count have resulted from exaggerated platforms with high heels on steps.

There are plenty of steps on this sky walk. Most of them are beautifully curved like the "keyhole" staircases in ante-bellum Southern mansions.

Embarcadero Center

THE LAST LINK in San Francisco's convenient trail-system-in-the-sky is finished. With the completion of John Portman's 4 Embarcadero Center, it became possible to walk from Ferry Park at Steuart and Market streets to Sidney Walton Park at Pacific and Front streets safely removed from traffic all the way. This remarkable walk, fourteen years a-building, connects three parks by means of a festive upper-level promenade designed to be strolled. The amenities must be seen to be believed. Monumental works of public art, fountains, sidewalk tables for brown-bagging it or just lingering in the sun, greenery, comfortable benches, open courts, ramps, bridges, streetside restaurants and watering holes, galleries, bookshops, trendy boutiques, and entrancing vistas of San Francisco Bay make the mile-long walk unique.

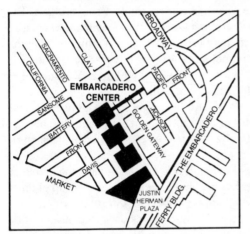

There are several good times to make this walk. For art lovers and architecture buffs, it is Sundays, when the crowds are diminished. For shoppers, it is Saturdays or the midweek hours before and after lunchtime. For romantics, it is twilight. On a clear day, when the sun slinks slowly into the west as in an old travelogue, there is nothing to compare with sitting at Lily's or Scotts or La Fuente, watching the pink afterglow deepen while twinkling lights around the bay wink on one by one.

To make this walk, transport yourself to Ferry Park via the California Street cable car, BART, the Marin ferry, any Market streetcar, or any of fifteen bus lines that converge near that wedge of streets that fans out from the foot of Market. Early franchises granted origi-

nally to serve the Ferry Building have created better public transportation here than anywhere else in the city.

Walk into Ferry Park and bear southeast to examine the berms,
benches, street furniture, tall trees, and sculpture. The equestrian is
Juan Bautista de Anza. The bus turnaround is another legacy from
a time when San Francisco had perfect public transportation. The
first turnaround was below street level on the Embarcadero where it
was possible to walk into the Ferry Building via a ramp, or from this
level, via a bridge. If you make this walk on a weekday, go into San
Francisco's best loved landmark to visit the Mineral Museum of its
oldest tenant, the California Bureau of Mines.

Then return to the park and bear right to experience the celebration of rushing water in the Vaillancourt Fountain, designed so
the walker can go under the falls without getting wet, by walking on
big concrete stepping-stones.

As you emerge, look up at the big tulip-in-outline, the architect-
designed sculpture that has become a symbol for this group of office
buildings, hotel, and sky-bridges. Walk across Justin Herman Plaza
toward it. An outdoor theater is part of this wide expanse of brick.
Go up the broad steps toward the double line of zelkova trees.
When you reach the handsome staircase that spirals upward, you
are at Commercial Street. Like Market Street, it has always had an
open view to the Ferry Building clock tower and the booklike slabs
of office buildings were designed to keep that openness clear.

Tempting as it is to go up the stairway immediately, look
around this level first. Clever planning has placed such winners as
Huckleberry's Ice Cream Parlour, the Expresso Experience coffee
house, Mrs. Fields' Chocolate Chippery, and the San Francisco
Boulangerie handy to the park. Some other surprises worth seeking
on street level are the Nature Company, where everything for sale
delights the nature lover without exploiting the natural world; Christian Bernard, a French jeweler where jeweled gold-handled tooth-
brushes and razors are an ultimate status treasure; the World of
Cutlery, which has Samurai swords; Waldenbooks; and Richter's,
where one can choose from a library of three hundred the song for
your music box.

Walk up the spiral ramp when you have discovered these and
other unusual shops to reach the lobby level, where almost all of the

clothing shops, including Livingston's, feature designer clothes. Two of the important pieces in Embarcadero Center's remarkable fiber-works collection hang through this level. They are big soft sculptures by Sheilah Hicks. Go past the escalator to find them. After you enjoy their depth of color and texture, look for the hundred-year-old wooden Indian at Somerset General Store, then go in to discover the store lives up to its name, selling among other unlikely things, shoestrings and nails. Also worth seeking out on this level is Peck & Peck's, which has antique French pressed-tin wall panels.

The bridge leading west over Drumm Street promises more enticements, but for the moment return to the big spiral ramp around the tulip, which, incidentally, is lighted in rich pink at night, to reach the podium level of 4 Embarcadero Center. Unusual on this level are Applause, where the desk embellishments would suit a czarina; Games Women Play, where everything is designed by women for women's comfort; and Pastabella, which makes its own pasta and offers a choice of sauces.

When you have admired these, walk toward Lily's Restaurant, a branch of the famous Philadelphia establishment, to find another sky-bridge, which leads into the lobby level of the Hyatt Regency Hotel. Go in, bear left through the lobby for one of this new mini-city's great visual experiences, then go down the steps at the eastern end to find you have made a little loop bringing you back to Justin Herman Plaza.

If you are game for more walking, go back to the circular stair-case at the end of Commercial Street, climb to the lobby level, and explore all those other enticing shops. Or to see twenty or more additional public sculptures, cross Drumm Street via the sky-bridge. Following the upper level along the line of Commercial Street across Davis and Front streets will reveal the other three Embarca-dero Center buildings, each of which has its own collection of un-usual restaurants and shops to explore. Turn north in 1 Embarca-dero Center to cross sky-bridges over Sacramento, Clay, Washing-ton, and Jackson streets. En route you will pass through Maritime Plaza surrounding the Alcoa Building, and Golden Gateway, to reach Sidney Walton Park. The return trip is just as much fun.

46

The telephone rang. It was Stanleigh Arnold, then Sunday editor, at his Chronicle desk at Fifth and Mission streets. "A flight of Canada geese just flew over the Mint," he said. "They're coming your way, northwest. Ought to be there any minute."

"Hang on, let me look."

Sure enough, there they came. A long straggling V of streamlined geese winging their way toward Point Reyes in search of a marsh where they could feed and rest. Awed at this little fragment of wilderness over the city, I thanked him and asked, "Do you suppose anyone else saw them?"

"Maybe a hunter or two," he said; "nobody else expects to see wild geese over the city."

I've never forgotten the thrill of that V flying framed by the Golden Gate Bridge. Ever after, I have sought out places where migrating birds might be seen—especially marshy waterfronts.

Waterfronts have been badly treated by our culture until recently. Most of them were preempted long ago by industry as dumping grounds or filled for building. In 1966 there were less than six and a half miles out of the roughly four hundred miles of shoreline on San Francisco Bay where one could walk to look for birds, or just enjoy the freshness of marsh air. By 1976 there were sufficient "Public Access and Recreation Areas" for the San Francisco Bay Conservation and Development Commission to publish a handy little guidebook by that name to such places in the nine counties that touch the bay.

We still have a long way to go, of course, but now when a flight of Canada geese wings past the bedroom window, it's reassuring to know they'll have a place or two to rest. A place that's good enough for the birds is good enough for us.

The Oakport Trail

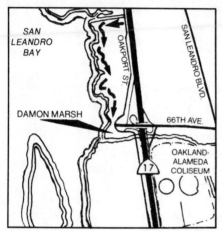

SAN LEANDRO BAY

OAKPORT ST.

SAN LEANDRO BLVD.

DAMON MARSH

66TH AVE.

OAKLAND-ALAMEDA COLISEUM

17

FOR THE POET Sidney Lanier, "the freedom that fills all the space 'twixt the marsh and the skies" was one of the natural world's great inspirations. When he died a little over one hundred years ago (1881), there were plenty of marshes for poets and everyone else to enjoy.

Today marshes are a rarity, to be prized for their oxygen-producing richness, for their food chain base for all of life, for their protected feeding places for migrating bird flocks, for their resident fish, and for their wilderness and solitude. If you can find a marsh where the hand of man lies lightly, that untrammeled, untroubled sense of freedom the poet appreciated is still there. Fortunately for all of us, scraps of marsh surrounding San Leandro Bay are being rescued and restored, little by little, by a dozen or more agencies cooperating with the Port of Oakland and the East Bay Regional Park District. One addition is a mile of shoreline between East Creek Slough and Damon Marsh. The multiuse Oakport Trail along it, paved with asphalt and supplied with benches, is flat enough for wheelchairs. It is a wonderful place to watch migrating birds twice a year, and shorebirds anytime.

To make this walk within the San Leandro Bay Regional Shoreline, transport yourself to Oakland. None of it is in San Leandro, despite the name. From the San Francisco Bay Bridge, follow Route 17, the Nimitz Freeway, south to the 66th Avenue-Coliseum offramp. Turn right on 66th Avenue for about a block and right again on Oakport Street. Follow Oakport north, parallel to the freeway, past an EBMUD facility to a hundred-car parking area along the roadside just south of the East Creek Slough bridge. (If you reach P G & E's Oakland Service Center, you have gone too far. Turn back.)

Wooden, country-style fencing surrounds the hiker's stile about a hundred feet west of the bridge. Walk in, and immediately on your right there is a familiar brown EBRPD rules sign forbidding hunting and such, with the tidal slough just beyond it. The trail takes a turn to follow the water. Cross the Southern Pacific railroad tracks, little used on weekends. Eventually the path will line both sides of the slough.

As you walk toward San Leandro Bay, the old lumber company sawdust burner visible to the north beyond the mudflats gives a clue to past uses of the surrounding land. Once it all belonged to pioneer William Tyson, who learned to be a carpenter, joiner, and wagonmaker in his native Scotland before coming to California by wagon train from Iowa in March of 1849. Joe Gomez, who has worked there for fifty-four years, says East Shore Lumber & Mill Company and its neighbor along Tidewater Street, the White Brothers Forest Products, have both been here in the mudflats since 1872 when this area was known as Clark's Landing within the town of Melrose. Melrose, since incorporated into Oakland, was once famous for its fine rope walk at Pacific Cordage Company.

When you reach the bench overlooking East Creek Slough as it empties into San Leandro Bay, pause awhile, especially if it is low tide, to try to imagine waiting on the tide to board Henry Clark's schooner to make the trip from Melrose to San Francisco. Alameda, off to the northwest from this vantage, is easy to discern by its featherduster palms. The bridge leads past Mount Trashmore, once the Alameda city dump, to Bay Farm Island, now the Harbor Bay Isle development. In the foreground, godwits, kittiwakes, sandpipers, and sanderlings may flit along this shallow watery reach. Despite the annual quarantine, sometimes they have to compete for food with human clammers. Fifty one-and-a-half-inch clams is the legal limit when quarantine is lifted.

If it is high tide, thousands of ducks, brant, and geese may bob in the surf during the annual migrations in fall and spring. Cormorants find the old ship hull far out in the flat a natural perch. As you continue southward along the Oakport Trail, at certain times fishermen may be bringing in stripers or rubbermouth or silver perch.

Picnic tables and barbecues have been placed near the shoreline for the angler who likes his lunch to jump into the pan.

While he was conducting me on this walk, Park Supervisor Ray Dawson and I startled great blue herons, American egrets, and a jackrabbit. The bandbox of the Oakland Coliseum looms off to the left. The Coliseum Drive-In Theatre makes another easily discernible landmark north of it, whereas new yellow warehouses, a big oil tank, and an office building rising in the distance seem almost like anachronisms beyond the chaparral.

The trail swings inland toward the railroad tracks at Damon Creek. Along the tracks a flock of more than a hundred mourning doves rose, sounding like creaky machinery much in need of oiling as they flew. An odd herringbone pattern on the creekbanks, made originally by a dredge, is reinforced by the tide as it comes and goes, Dawson told me. A sharp-eyed birder, he has reported sighting the endangered clapper rail along here. White-crowned sparrows and meadowlarks sang as we neared Damon Marsh.

There were two thousand or more acres of pickleweed marsh here when the tidal inlet on Damon's Landing brought passengers to the Pacific Racetrack at what was hopefully to become the town of Fitchburg. "This," according to Munro-Fraser's 1880 *History of Alameda County*, "like Martin Chuzzlewit's Eden, is simply a town of the future, at present it has only a prospect."

The prospect across the arm of San Leandro Creek today is Arrowhead Marsh, which has fifty acres protected within the San Leandro Regional Shoreline. When you reach the little paved circle, just broad enough for a warden's patrol car to turn around, you are parallel to 66th Avenue, just across the channel from Bay Park Refuge. Ultimately Edgewater Drive will be extended and a walker or bicyclist can continue along the water to Arrowhead Marsh, nine miles farther. For the present, the Oakport Trail ends at Damon Marsh. It's the same distance back as it was out to this point — nine-tenths of a mile — but on the way back there are always things to see you missed. The changing tide, the changing hour, the changing light all have their revelations to make, for those who have the eyes to see.

47

The old mythical Ixion was tied to a wheel, but no more so than those who live in the automotive age. Shuttling back and forth as we do behind the wheel, we miss the ambiance, the primal, even the penumbra of the scene through which we pass, whether it be urban or rural.

It is not until one sets out afoot that the pleasures of the real world are with us. Have you ever tried to look at a painting at fifty-miles an hour? To observe the subtleties of sculpture at the same mileage? Hardly. It is the walkers who see the artistry of architecture, of nature, indeed of a single flower or leaf as much as of the tree; it is not the Ixions.

Civic Center Lagoon, Marin

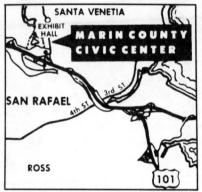

WHEN WINTER RAINS turn the tawny hills of autumn green, one of the pleasantest urban walks in the Bay Area is around Marin Center Lagoon, designed, like the Civic Center it fronts, by America's most famous architect, Frank Lloyd Wright.

Wright thriftily availed the county of the water offered by the site itself, a broad tidal pond in the South Fork of Las Gallinas Creek, which had drained this valley long before it became the 22,000-acre Spanish land grant known as Santa Margarita y las Gallinas, or Saint Margaret and the Hens. Indeed its blue water was the inspiration for those stunning roofs of the California blue-and-gold Civic Center buildings.

Level enough for senior citizens, toddlers in or out of prams, and wheelchairs motorized or otherwise, it is an ideal walk to enjoy the great architect's last great masterpiece, usually glimpsed all too fleetingly from Highway 101. Your dog is welcome, too, on a leash.

To make this walk, transport yourself two and a half miles beyond downtown San Rafael to North San Pedro Road, the off-ramp for Civic Center. Public transportation is good on weekdays only. Once there, ignore the Administration Building for the moment and follow Civic Center Drive past the post office, also designed by Frank Lloyd Wright, and past the fire station. As you approach the big triangular lagoon, look for a right turn on the downhill side to find plenty of parking screened by trees. Once parked, walk toward the grove of willows by the water's edge, where a large gaggle of domestic gray geese and resident mallard ducks is often joined by migrating waterfowl. Picnic tables are spotted in sheltered places near trees and on lawns.

At the water's edge, bear right, away from the buildings. In the next clear vista look across the lagoon to see the 172-foot-tall golden aluminum spire of the Administration Building looming like contemporary sculpture. A smokestack ventilating the building's cooling system hides inside. The great arches of the ground floor, topped by the smaller arched windows on the second and the ever-diminishing circular motifs on each of the next two floors give the building a happy, almost festive look from this aspect. The biggest circles, of course, are the round hills the two main horizontal buildings, totaling 15,500 feet in length, together bridge at the lowest level. From this east shore of the lagoon, Marin Veterans Memorial, the concert hall off to the north, third major structure on the 160-acre site, makes a nice counterpoint in the landscape.

Walking toward it, one becomes aware of the tule rush and cattails on the near shore which often shelter entire flotillas of birds at some seasons. The big descending rounds on the opposite shore are rock filled and known as the lagoon cascades. Wright and his disciple, architect Aaron Green, who finished the complex after Wright's sudden death in 1959, envisioned them as shallow waterfalls, linking the big pond and buildings beyond it. The curve in the roadway to the building carries out the illusion of a river.

The bare space on your right was intended to contain a fairground pavilion in the Wright master plan and includes eighty acres added to the park for that purpose. During the Marin County Fair that is held here annually, it contains the carnival. When you reach the bridge, you are at Las Gallinas creek and marsh, which dries in the summer, but may run full and strong in the rainy season.

As you cross the bridge, pause again to look back at the center to see how the buildings seem to float from hill to hill, fitting into the landscape and enhancing it all at once. The cost for this beautiful building, which has 140,000 square feet of space, was almost a dollar less per square foot than San Francisco's mediocre Hall of Justice, built about the same time.

Following the shoreline soon brings you to the Exhibit Hall and Showcase Theatre building, fronted by a parking lot that badly needs trees to shield service trucks. Those tall poles are designed to take many light bulbs when an event is in progress, while the pipe rounds become circular tents when colorful canvas is hung on them. Wright had planned for a children's zoo to occupy this area as well and the island offshore to be a children's playground. It came close to his plan as a gamefield during the 1981 county fair.

When you are in front of Veterans Memorial, the scene of symphony, ballet, and other concerts, look across its lot, furnished with trees and hedges, to spot the Hall of Justice building, almost a twin to the Administration Building. The bronze "doughboy" statue is a World War I memorial moved here from its earlier location on the old courthouse square on Fourth Street in downtown San Rafael.

As you swing southward on the waterside trail, look into the next group of benches to locate a plaque on a boulder that announces the lagoon park and trail as a county bicentennial project. When you are abreast of the Administration Building, cross Civic Center Drive and go in, if the building is open, to enjoy the continuation of the parklike ambiance indoors. Boulevardlike interior gardens open to all four floors are in the center of the building. If it isn't open, Civic Center still has another surprise for the walker willing to climb a hill. It is a low maintenance, drought resistant garden level with the fourth floor of the Administration Building. Look for the path that leads up at the south end, whether you are interested in gardens or not, if only to enjoy from the top the panoramic view of San Pablo Bay.

48

There is an unusual television biography of John Muir that has been produced by B. Ziggy Stone, the genius who made Evening Magazine *the great success it became. Mr. Z, as he likes to be called, has shown the remarkable conservationist as he was, as much as a producer can in half an hour. What can't be shown is Muir walking fifty miles cross-country in a day. The country isn't the same, for one thing.*

Muir thought nothing of walking from his home in Martinez to the peak of Mount Diablo in a day. Or taking off from Martinez to walk to Tahoe or to Yosemite. He often walked from Martinez to Point Richmond to catch a ferry to San Francisco and walked back from Point Richmond on the return. Ironically he couldn't do that in our time. Even if Muir managed to arrive in Point Richmond by boat, three freeways he could not cross would "lie between him and his hame." One of them bears the name of John Muir Parkway.

John Muir's Orchard and the Martinez Adobe

IN ONE OF the several biographies of John Muir, there is a famous four-color photograph by Galen Rowell of a pinnacle in the Sierra Nevada. On its peak there stands a hiker, shepherd's

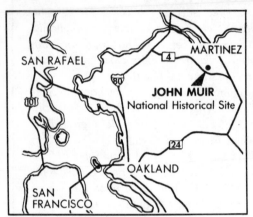

crook in hand, backlighted by a rising sun against a blue sky to look like a saint on the great altar of the world. It is in this light that conservationists today regard journalist John Muir, co-founder of the Sierra Club.

"They come into his 'scribble room' and are appalled that he kept a drawer full of peppermints to hand out to young visitors." Historian P. J. Ryan, of the John Muir National Historic site in Martinez, says with a wry smile, "In this time of health foods, peppermints don't seem compatible with his conservationist image." Public images, of course, are made up of preconceived notions, some of them legendary, some apocryphal, and not all necessarily true.

Orchardist, successful and astute businessman, inventor, magazine editor, patron of the arts, horseman, efficiency expert, and pioneer of factory automation are some of the many roles John Muir played in life. The better known and more revered ones of conservationist and national park and forest service founder were a second choice. Of himself, Muir said, "I could have become a millionaire, but I chose to become a tramp."

The choice was brought about by an industrial accident that left him blind for six weeks, so ever after he would "no longer study the works of man and money but rather the works of God and nature." The first thing he did in 1867, six weeks after the accident and life choice, was to go for a walk. It is the famous "A Thousand Mile

Walk to the Gulf" recorded in his journal published in 1914. The walk, or tramp as he called his expeditions, began in Jeffersonville, Kentucky, and went to Cedar Key, Florida. It finally led him by boat to Cuba, to California, to the Sierra, and ultimately to Martinez. Ten years as an orchardist in Martinez left him financially independent and able to return to being "a tramp."

Most of the 840 acres of orchards he tended in the Alhambra Valley are now housing tracts, but the National Park Service has created an orchard trail through the 8.7 acres surrounding the wonderful old Victorian-cum-Georgian Muir-Strentzel ranch house and the nearby Martinez Adobe, a two-story home built by Don Vicente Martinez in 1849. It is a pleasant walk at any time.

To make this walk, transport yourself east from San Francisco via the Bay Bridge. The fastest route is via Highway 24 to Walnut Creek, north on 680, and east on Highway 4 to Martinez. From 4, the Alhambra offramp goes directly to the John Muir home. Park alongside the visitor's center. (If it is crowded, on Sundays there is also space next door north for overflow parking by the Martinez Post Office.)

Go into the visitor's center, formerly a veterinarian's hospital, nicely remodeled in 1975. The little Japanese garden comes as a surprise until one discovers that the chunk of redwood log is from Muir Woods; the granite from Cathedral Peak, where it helped as a key to the puzzle of glaciation; and the fragment of wood from the famous Wawona tunnel tree so often pictured with a buckboard of visitors passing through it. Look on the walls to find photos of parks Muir helped to create. What seems to be a gravestone pictured among them is actually a memorial to Muir that stands near his childhood home near Fountain Lake, Wisconsin. Muir is actually buried in the Muir-Strentzel family graveyard in a pioneer pear orchard only a few blocks south of where you are standing.

Pause a moment to look over the book rack where a good collection of books relating to the great preservationist is displayed, then pay the modest fee and pick up a copy of the guide booklet. Movies are shown for those who wish to wait for the guided tours, held around 10:30 A.M. and 2:30 P.M. If you'd rather do it on your own, go out the far door into the orchard and look uphill.

"I hold dearly cherished memories about it [the house] and

fine garden grounds full of trees and bushes and flowers that my wife and father-in-law and I planted — fine things from every land," Muir wrote. The first trees you see as you go out are incense cedars, his favorite tree, which he planted in the 1880s.

Bear left to the trail and right at the walkway, ignoring for the nonce the big Victorian home where Dr. John Strentzel practiced as a country doctor. Instead stroll past the peach orchard, full of John Muir peaches, and the windmill. (The John Muir who developed and hybridized the famous peaches was an Iowan, and no relation, incidentally.)

As you walk you will pass orange trees, Bartlett pears, Queen Anne cherries, pomegranates, fig trees, and tokay grapes. The numbered stakes correspond to the text of a booklet. The original Mission grape vineyard planted here by Don Vicente was removed early on by Muir, who planted zinfandel, muscat, and tokay. "The padres ought to have known better, such good judges as they were in most things relating to the stomach," Muir said of the Mission grape. His grandson, John Hanna, a Napa County viticulturist, replanted the present vineyard to tokay grapes in 1975.

Continue across the creek toward the adobe house visible at the end of the walk. The little creek, wildest part of the grounds, was named for Edward Franklin, the first of a series of owners who followed Don Vicente Martinez in the husbanding of this land. It was Muir's father-in-law, Dr. John Strentzel, often called the Father of California Horticulture, who switched most of the acreage from cattle ranching to fruit trees because of the rich soil. He used the adobe to house his foremen. Although John Muir never lived here, he was often a dinner guest in the adobe after it became the honeymoon cottage, and later the home, of his oldest daughter, Wanda, and her husband, Thomas Hanna. Picnic tables behind the adobe are open to all on a first come-first served basis.

Inside the adobe, notice the fine old pictures, and in the dining room, the early Contra Costa County map that shows where Muir's own original twenty acres of orchard were located, the Muir railroad station, and the location of the Dutch Colonial house where he lived while managing the Muir-Strentzel ranch. Upper rooms in the adobe have "listening chairs" to hear tapes of Dr. Rioza Azuma, often called the John Muir of Japan.

Before you head up the knoll to inspect the interior of the John Muir home, look across the John Muir Parkway to locate a length of the California Riding and Hiking Trail that goes below this freeway. The dream of many East Bay walkers is to link via an extension of this trail the Martinez Regional Shoreline with Briones Regional Park and ultimately Mt. Diablo State Park, a walk John Muir would have made unencumbered in a day.

Enjoy the house as you will, but don't miss the attic and bell tower. The telegram in which the famous walker learned that Muir Woods had been named for him by Senator William Kent lies on a trunk in the attic. In the bell tower, you get a chance to pull the bell.

December

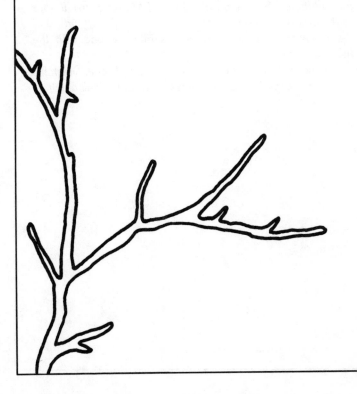

49

Once, in Baltimore, I was privileged to handle the citified walking stick of the famous physician, Sir William Osler. It was an elegant gold-topped ebony cane, quite obviously intended to go with cutaway coat and kid gloves. A gold-headed cane is also the badge of office to the Surgeon to the Queen of England. It was first held by Dr. John Radcliffe and, for the 250-odd years since, used by the outstanding physicians who have succeeded him serving the crown.

That stick has a counterpart in San Francisco—the gold-headed cane given each year at the University of California Medical School on the slope of Mount Sutro. It goes to the graduate who seems to embody the highest virtues of the medical profession, not necessarily the one with the highest grades.

Urbane is the word for the gold-headed cane, which fits the scene at the Louise M. Davies Symphony Hall anytime.

Civic Center Area, San Francisco

THE GALLANT MADNESS that is San Francisco had a great new cultural infusion with the opening of the exciting Louise M. Davies Symphony Hall, whose impact, better than any

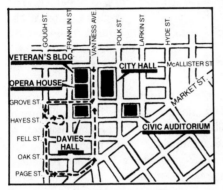

redevelopment agency, is already manifesting itself in neighborhood renewal for blocks around. The walker who goes to hear music from *The Bartered Bride* or *Scheherazade*— or just to admire the monumental Neo-Baroque auditorium with its tremendous people-roundabout facade—will discover there are new places nearby to dine, new galleries to explore, new shops, new courtyards, and new parking lots.

The ideal way to go of course is by limousine on an opening night, swathed in furs, diamonds, and champagne. Barring that, pick a scintillating winter afternoon when the air is as fresh as bugle notes. Then transport yourself, preferably by the "opera bus," No. 47, to Civic Center. Disembus at McAllister Street and take a look in all directions as though you had never before seen San Francisco's "City Beautiful" city hall, often described as the outstanding example of Beaux Arts French Renaissance architecture in the United States. Arthur Brown, Jr., and John Bakewell were the architects, winners in a 1912 design competition. To play the compleat tourist, stop in the Veterans' Building on the west side of Van Ness to see the redesigned Herbst Theatre if it is open. A little reprise on the melody that swells at the Opera House next door, it has four murals interpreting earth, air, fire, and water by Frank Brangwyn gracing the side walls. The startling high-tech bookstore in the lobby is an introduction to the San Francisco Museum of Modern Art, quite possibly the best in the West, upstairs. The museum is open ten to five weekdays for a modest fee.

If the gate is open on the Thomas Church-designed Opera

Court between Herbst Theatre and the Opera House, a formal little green oasis behind a handsome picket wicket, step inside to see how adroitly the $5 million addition containing rehearsal hall and library has been tagged onto the back. It is almost indistinguishable from Arthur Brown's original design. Winthrop Sargeant of *The New Yorker* magazine raved about its "atmosphere of great elegance" and called it "one of the great opera houses of the world."

When you reach Grove Street, stop on the north side for a breathtaking perspective on the new Louise M. Davies Symphony Hall. When a symphony is about to happen, the great three-story expanse of curved glass looks as though it was dreamed up by F. Scott Fitzgerald. Actually Charles Basset of the hometown firm of Skidmore, Owings & Merrill, with an assist from Pietro Belluschi of Portland, was the architect. Sculpture is by Henry Moore.

Bear west on Grove Street to see where Zellerbach Rehearsal Hall is located. First hint of the neighborhood "gentrification" comes at Franklin Street, where Kimballs' restaurant and bar reuse a handsome old brick building enlivened by a new skylight. Cross both Franklin and Grove to discover All About Music, a bookshop whose title tells the tale. "Have you found the historic marker in our neighborhood yet?" lawyer Dick Wirthimer asked as I walked past his offices. "I'll give you a clue: It salutes a labor union."

At Vorpal Gallery, 393 Grove, the vorpal blade may not be going snicker-snack when you pass, but the nicely revealed redwood beams of this resurrected warehouse, the whirligig fire escape slide, the Shrine, a conversation pit-cum-casting couch, and the Textile Gallery would make it worth a visit, whatever artists are being featured.

When you reach the freeway, notice how the stark lines have softened now that the eucalypti tower above them. Bear left on Gough. At Ivy and Gough, the handsome gold Victorian whose window boxes spill red geraniums is the Barrister's Chambers, one of several such imaginative reuses in this long-neglected corner of the city. Another is the Gough-Hayes Hotel. Looking west on Hayes, mark down for future reference Pendragon Bakery, which also serves meals, Martha's Mexican Food, and David's House, but bear left at Ivy Court. Ivy Restaurant, its neighbor City Picnic, Hardcastle's, and Ed Brown's Gallery all open into the garden as well as into the street on this lively complex. The Hayes Street Grill, a little farther along, has become so famous for its food, it is expanding. Next door the Mandarin Opera Restaurant is on the site of Cremona Violin Makers, only loss to musicians of the neighborhood since the symphony hall opened.

Double back on the south side of Hayes to Gough to find the historical marker—acclaiming the San Francisco Laundry and Dry Cleaning Union, which started here in 1901—and to discover Dorothy Starr, whose music stand has been supplying opera scores for twenty-one years. Another longtime landmark on the street is City Hall Market.

Look west to locate Golden Gate Costumes before you head south again on Gough. Victorian Press and Blackstone are small book publishers; Alex's Impulse is a gift shop. Steve's Coin Shop has been here at Linden Street corner for fourteen years.

Keep walking toward Market and you will discover at Fell, the Toyo Pottery workshop and Christina's Golden Bowl, washbasins imported from Mexico. Supersub takeout sandwiches and Our Kitchen reveal the distance the ripples have spread from the music center. When you reach the Bessie L. Smith Children's Center, bear left on Market, and left again on Van Ness, to pass the old Masonic Temple, a delightful Bliss and Faville building just crying to be turned into a music school or rehearsal studios. The Federal Greek Revival building next door, which old-timers recall as Godeaux Funeral home, now houses a credit union. For fun, look across the street to see reflected in the mirrors of the AAA the old school building that houses San Francisco's education department. In a trice you are back at Louise M. Davies Symphony Hall, having beaten the bounds of San Francisco's newest hotspot of civic renovation. It is all happening so fast, there may be three new places open before you return a second time.

50

An injury has brought me to a new appreciation of the walking stick. A gnarly country-style stick, the Christmas gift of a former editor, is my choice. It sets images tumbling through the mind when I pick it up. One is the cartoon of the cave-man dragging his mate-to-be along the ground by her hair. There is always a shillelagh or cudgel, a weapon that is an uglier version of a country walking stick, in his other hand.

Another image is Robin Hood and Little John or Friar Tuck fighting on the footbridge with longstaffs — walking sticks elongated. Other staffs evolved a crook and served the shepherd to snag an errant sheep, or sprouted a crown and became the mace or scepter, the staff of office. You can find a counterpart at Grace Cathedral or Saint Mary's any Sunday as the verger precedes the ranking cleric up the center aisle.

The finest collection of walking sticks I have seen are in the whaling museum at Nantucket. Intricately scrimshandered, they seem to call for the hero of Life With Father, who "wore a silk hat and carried a cane, like his friends. When he and they passed each other on the street, they raised their canes, touching the brims of their hats with them in formal salute." Clarence Day concludes, "I admired this rich and splendid gesture and wished I could imitate it, but I was too young for a cane."

Young as he was, he recognized the cane as a status symbol. So did Thorstein Veblen, who had the fop or dandy in mind when he said, "The walking stick serves the purpose of an advertisement that the bearer's hands are employed otherwise than in useful effort and it therefore has utility as an evidence of leisure."

It could also beat off bandits.

Palace of Fine Arts and Exploratorium

I love the Christmastide, and yet ...

Carolyn Wells

IT'S THAT "AND yet . . ." that gets many of us down at Christmas. The realities somehow never seem quite to live up to the expectations.

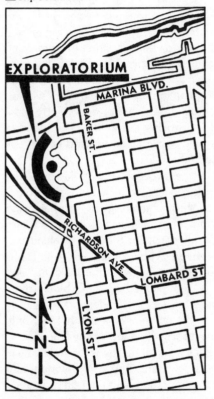

If this feeling threatens to overwhelm you, consider a walk to renew your childhood wonderment. The place to do it is in San Francisco's biggest toybox, the Exploratorium, in the Palace of Fine Arts. Here, within one of San Francisco's finest restored and recycled architectural treasures, Science, with a little help from Dr. Frank Oppenheimer, has provided more magic, marvels, and mysteries than one can comprehend in a day, a week, or a month.

"I intended a kind of woods of natural phenomena that were organized and selected in some way so that people could take many constructive paths," Dr. Oppenheimer says of his collection of four hundred hands-on exhibits. "This is not a museum, it's a curriculum." It has also been called "a large highly sophisticated school . . . in which the surface offers the appearance of random activity but is actually undergirded with a dense web of interrelated stimuli."

Don't be put off by this high-flown rhetoric. First and foremost, as the lucky kids who have discovered the museum since it opened in 1969 can tell you, it is FUN! Where else can you shake hands with yourself, elude your shadow, bend your voice, walk on tiles that make musical notes, light up a tree with the clap of a hand, see yourself multiplied into infinity, jump into a ton of birdseed, or crawl sightless through a score of textures almost as though being reborn?

To experience some of these sensations, transport yourself (preferably by Muni bus No. 30) to Northpoint and Broderick streets. For openers walk west one block to Baker Street to view the Palace of Fine Arts as its architect, Bernard Maybeck, intended, mirrored in its own reflecting pond. Largest structure remaining from the Panama-Pacific International Exposition of 1915, it was so loved that philanthropist Walter Johnson, and hundreds of other local citizens, refused to let it disintegrate. According to Hans Gerson, who directed the reconstruction and who was formerly Maybeck's partner, the architect took Brocklin's painting, "The Island of the Dead," as his inspiration. The construction method was in use two thousand years ago in the Baths of Diocletian.

Pause a moment to enjoy the sweetly melancholy scene, the rosy dome surmounting a semicircle fronted by a handsome colonnade, all set about with trees, shrubs, green lawns, fountain, and mirroring water. If you had come this way in the late 1800s, a steam dummy would have come along tracks in the street, taking picnickers to pioneer Rudolph Herman's Harbor View Park and Baths at the waterfront. The line of eucalyptus trees that borders Lyon Street at the end of the Marina were planted originally by Herman. Harbor View, the first of several recreational endeavors to occupy this land, once gave its name to the entire area, a site that had only recreational uses since the time it became an Indian shell mound.

The south end of the Palace of Fine Arts is occupied by a theater, often the scene of film premieres and of the annual film festival. Walk to the shore of the pond and bear right on the paved walkway that borders it. Come this way by night during the holidays and traditionally *son et lumiere* lighting transforms the whole sweetly melancholy scene into a deliciously romantic nighttime confection.

Swing with the path to the north end of the building (locate the exterior rest rooms in case you have a child or two along) and go between them through the main entrance into the museum. As you enter, the shops where exhibits are created will be on either hand, with work in progress visible for all to see. Immediately within, look up over the door to perceive the clock that has lighted mirrors for hands. "Meet me under the clock," is an old San Francisco tradition that has easily made a transition here from downtown.

Patterns are the clue to the first exhibits. The sun is the key to the next one, where a beam from an opening in the roof goes through prisms. Stand in front of the fractured light, and you find the separated colors change as you move. Concerts, films, lectures, and such are often under way in the theater just beyond the Exploratorium office.

Christmas shoppers may find themselves attracted by the store on the opposite wall, but save its goodies for your return trip. Old or young, you are sure to leave it burdened with a bag of scientific playthings. Instead, make your way along the right aisle to the far end. When you reach the Tactile Dome, come back along the left, or east, aisle.

With the red combination map-bookmark that was given you by one of the teenage "explainers" as you entered, check out the Color exhibits first. Humming a happy little tune as he walked me through the museum, Dr. Oppenheimer paused to point to a group of children at one exhibit playing in colored shadows. "It always makes the kids dance," he said.

At another exhibit, a cluster of boys were trying to "stop the differential." Farther along, young people were taking the temperature of their hands on a block of ice. At another gallerylike area, the work of cartoonist Saul Steinberg has been dissected with overlay panels to show how artistic balance suffers if one component of the drawing is elided.

We stood awhile beside a giant kaleidoscope that people duck under to get into. "This would be a great way to film a movie without extras," a man said as he emerged. "Go on in, it's a party," a woman told us.

Don't be disappointed if you can't get into the Tactile Dome. It is so much in demand, it must be reserved months ahead. If this is your first visit to the Exploratorium, you won't even care that you've missed it. You'll want to come back again anyway. Again and again and again.

51

There was a virtuoso of whistling in my neighborhood when I was a child. He liked to whistle while walking. You could hear his high, keen, true trills and arpeggios long before you could hear his footsteps. They were often elaborate symphonic music, worthy of a concert stage. Sometimes one would hear him going to work on a cold clear morning at 5 A.M., whistling so marvelously each note would sparkle like an icicle in sunlight.

Late at night one could sometimes hear him coming home from a date with his lady love, whistling happy romantic tunes. Then all the dark night would seem friendly, no matter how ominous dark trees and shadows tossing before the moon outside a little girl's window might have seemed the moment before he passed.

When George Dean, the moving figure behind the Fort Point Museum Association, told me his fellow officer Herbert Batz wondered why nobody whistled while they walked, I thought I'd give him a treat by suggesting in print that readers whistle an old Civil War tune, "The Girl I Left Behind Me," as they approached Fort Point for a special walk around it.

"We must build our museum. We must show our friends in Washington that the people here and our visitors are genuinely actively interested in Fort Point," George Dean later wrote in the July 1969 Fort Point Salvo. "If I had any doubts about this I forgot them on October 22, 1967, when Margot Patterson Doss wrote about the fort in her Sunday newspaper column 'San Francisco at Your Feet.' That day over 16,000 people came to see it. I had to run up the hill and turn back several hundred more at dusk."

Thousands of them came down to the Fort whistling that day. The Presidio sent up emergency helicopters to direct traffic (and subsequently asked me never to write about a place within their borders again without notifying the Sixth Army in advance).

The happy ending to this story, of course, is that Congress did approve Fort Point as a museum site and twenty-eight acres around it, including Andrews Road. Soon after, it became the very first part of what is now the Golden Gate National Recreation Area.

But I don't think Major Batz ever quite forgave me. He never could stand to hear "The Girl I Left Behind Me" whistled again. Those thousands of whistlers, alas, were not the walking virtuosos that Verne "Red" Hendershott, the whistler of my childhood, was.

Andrews Road

THOUSANDS OF PEOPLE daily pass within a few hundred yards of the drowsy little half-forgotten country lane called Andrews Road. It is a charmer. Tall eucalyptus trees line its narrow width. Birds flit and chirp among their graceful branches. Vines line the roadside on either hand. Flowers bloom nearby. At any moment one might expect a horse and carriage to come clip-clopping along the lane.

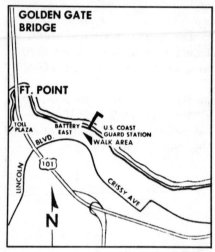

All this lies within a few hundred yards of the southern end of the Golden Gate Bridge; yet ask almost anyone crossing to tell you how to get to Andrews Road and you'll draw a bewildered "Where?" Yet the views along this lovely lane are superlative, and around the end of April the calla lilies cascade along its swale, the roses bloom on great mounds of shrubbery, and shy wildflowers raise their modest heads.

If you'd like to walk it, come any unfoggy time to the big parking lot on Lincoln Boulevard at Battery East Road just below the Golden Gate Bridge toll plaza. Better still, use public transportation to the toll plaza. Disembus from the No. 28 Muni bus near the statue of Joseph B. Strauss, designer of the bridge. Walk past the statue into the garden, and turn right at the Y. Walk downhill, go through the chain link gate, and bear right again on Battery East Road to the big parking lot at Lincoln Boulevard.

Lincoln Boulevard, incidentally, is part of U.S. 40, the military route known as the Lincoln Highway. Bear left on it, staying within the white line that has been painted to mark off a pedestrial walk.

Just past the water tank, notice the tremendous shrub rose, a Cecile Brunner, on your left. This was planted, Miriam Nagel says,

260

by her grandfather when he was keeper of the Fort Point lighthouse. Go past Scott Hall, the army guest house with the handsome pillars, almost to the junction of Long Avenue. At this point the view of the Bay Bridge, with the Coast Guard marine rescue station and its palm trees in the foreground, is so commanding one could easily overlook the turn.

But there, just before Long Avenue, is Andrews Road, closed off to vehicles by a cable. The cable, by the way, is exactly one meter from the ground. Numbers along the trail are keyed to a Fort Point Ecowalk designed for San Francisco schools' environmental science metric program by staffers working with the Golden Gate National Recreation Area. Teachers using ecowalk pamphlets direct their pupils to measure a meter on themselves as a way of estimating tree and log size farther along the route.

Take twenty steps along Andrews Road, round the bend, and suddenly one can shrug off a hundred years. Like Fort Point, the road was begun around 1853. Originally it led to the home of Col. R. E. DeRussy, the engineer who built the fort. The two-story house he built for his wife subsequently served as home for a succession of Presidio post commanders until the Golden Gate Bridge was built.

Glimpses of red roofs sometimes visible through the trees on the right are the army motor pool that backs on the Golden Gate Promenade along the bay.

When you reach the calla lily glade, pause a moment to look down it. Steps built in this draw by the Young Adult Conservation Corps lead to park headquarters of area manager Charley Hawkins, a former regular army man who has made Presidio history his lifetime hobby. Small as it is, the boxy little conduit that carries a rivulet downhill here is a prototype for the U.S. Army Corps of Engineers flood-control channels along Corte Madera Creek and Alameda Creek. Calla lilies bending on either side planted by Mrs. DeRussy more than a hundred years ago have naturalized here. Each spring they transform the gala swale into a bridal veil.

When you have enjoyed the aspect, walk into the clearing toward the second big Cecile Brunner rosebush on this trail.

Leave Andrews Road on the next path that goes uphill to the right. From the clearing overlooking the bay, Mrs. DeRussy could watch Fort Point as it grew. Today the walker sees a spectacular and intimate view of the bridge.

Walk away from the cliff, ignoring the side paths, and take the broader one that leads up through trees over a little ridge. Soon you are abreast of the first of three beautifully arched brick powder magazines. After the Civil War, gun emplacements for large muzzle-loading cannons stretched along this ridge. Climb up the stairs to the platform on your right to enjoy both a view and a little history.

When you return, bear right along the line of fortifications to the large brick heptagon where a cannon once stood. If you are spry enough, climb up on it for a wider view of the bay below. Then return to the trail and head west about twenty feet for one of the thrills of this walk—a tunnel. Go through it. Alice in Wonderland fans may wish they had a small piece of cake labeled "Eat Me" to make them grow smaller as they reach the far end, for the tunnel seems to shrink. Its low bridge out the far end was deliberately built this way to deflect cannonballs. Pop out the far side and you are in an intimate and different world.

Picnic tables, a barbecue pit, and a fantastic view of the bridge makes this a choice place to watch ships coming and going. After enjoying this secret spot, climb up the ridged concrete walkway. When you see a flag looming overhead, you have a landmark for the toll plaza. At the top of the ramp you are back again on Battery East Road. Fort Point is visible below on the water's edge with the path laid out like a map as it snakes its way along the hillside beside the bridge. The upper fork takes one under the bridge to batteries west of the bridge.

Bear left instead, and you soon reach the toll plaza again or the parking lot for a quick return to seven-league wheels.

52

Lighthouses are being automated. In the San Francisco Bay Area, the last to be manned was Point Bonita. Admiral Jim Gracey was the Coast Guard ranking officer at the time and he was kind enough to invite me to attend. We stood, fewer than one hundred souls, on the green lawn on that beautiful headland with San Francisco's skyline as a backdrop. It was a fine clear day. When the flag came down with appropriate pomp and a simple ceremony, Bill Whalen, as superintendent of the Golden Gate National Recreation Area, received the custodianship of the grounds on behalf of the people of the United States. It was a moving scene and more than one of us reached for a handkerchief, aware of an era passing.

It is the nature of lighthouses to be romantic as well as picturesque. Their locations insure both. Point Reyes Light boasts more steps, and it overlooks the best whale-watching shore of all, but Bonita Light has an unexpected tunnel and a bridge that is said to be a miniature replica of the Golden Gate. Winter is the best time to visit either one.

Whale Watching at Point Reyes Light

SINCE IT IS the farthest out to sea of Bay Area promontories, Point Reyes Head offers the best whale watching in the Bay Area. Not long ago, from the nice little overlook above the Point Reyes lighthouse, I saw thirteen spouts in quick succession, the sure sign of a passing pod of gray whales.

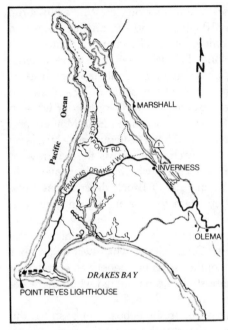

The migrating pods, as groups of whales are known, start their southward wave from the Arctic oceans in November, reaching California around January on their way to the breeding grounds at Scammon's Lagoon in Mexico. Northbound whales are sighted in increasing numbers through February and sometimes into March. Gray whales, more than any others, skirt the coast as they swim, moving about six or seven miles per hour and surfacing every six or seven minutes. Entire pods of whales sometimes surface, blow, and dive together, one of the clues that has led researchers to believe whales communicate with one another.

About twenty whales a day have been reported passing Point Reyes lighthouse. Since the weather at Point Reyes is sometimes warm and spectacular while the rest of the bay lies hunched under cold stagnant fog, winter is a great time to make a visit to Point Reyes. To make whale watching even easier than does the natural conformation of the land, the National Seashore sometimes runs a free weekend shuttlebus from Drake's Beach to the lighthouse.

To make this walk, dig out your down jacket and sturdy boots,

pack a picnic lunch with hot thermos, then transport yourself north
from San Francisco via Highway 101 and Sir Francis Drake Boulevard to the Kenneth C. Patrick Visitor's Center on Drake's Beach,
named in honor of the ranger who was shot by poachers a few
years ago.

Once at the beach, park in that spacious lot. Whale buses run
every fifteen minutes from 10 A.M. to 4:30 P.M. on Saturdays and
Sundays usually from November through February, and into March
if migration continues that long. If a bus just left, step into the handsomely designed complex, where an educational map is on display,
a food dispenser operates, and a little museum of local flora and
fauna can fill the short waiting time. It's also worth your while to
walk the beach and look for whales in Drake's Bay. Mothers and
young calf whales have been sighted here, distinguishable by a large
and smaller spout. From the beach, look across the bay toward
Chimney Rock, below Drake's Head, where whales have been
sighted in the maneuver ranger Leroy Brock describes as "sky-
hopping." This is when they seem to be standing on their tails,
almost out of water.

Once you board the bus, if your eyes are sharp, watch on the
Pacific side for whale spouts. Great Beach, which will be on your
right as you approach the lighthouse, is the dependable stretch of
shore where whales can almost always be sighted when there are
none visible from elsewhere in the Bay Area.

Though everyone else on your shuttlebus may dash for the
lighthouse steps, if it seems mobbed at the overlooks, a cooler way
to do your whale watching may be to visit the Sea Lion Overlook
first. Watch for a single path uphill on the left to this fence-enclosed
vantage. Breezy as it is, there may be low-growing wildflowers in
bloom underfoot. I have never visited this headland when there
wasn't something in flower. Sea lions and their pups are often visible
on the offshore rocks below or cavorting in the water nearby. Whale
spouts can be equally discernible here.

When you have explored this charming glimpse of shorelife
sufficiently, follow the looping trail back to the road, then use the
shelter of the old cypress windbreak to lead you to the lighthouse.
Great Beach will be visible on the right, framed through trees as you
walk. The *Sea Nymph*, the *Novick*, the *Warrior Queen* and the *Tai*

Vin are the more notable ships that were wrecked on this long strand. Another thirteen ships and an airliner were wrecked on the headland itself.

When you reach the lighthouse visitor center, you will be on top of a flight of 429 steps, a staircase equal to the thirty-story building. Handrails and several rest stop platforms were installed by the Park Service after they took over the lighthouse from the Coast Guard. The upper concrete pad on the right gives a splendid overview of the whole complex. Murres and puffins are sometimes among the cormorants on the rocks below. Bodega Head is the landmass to the northwest.

If you don't see a whale spout, the pineapple-shaped first order Fresnel lens in the light tower itself is worth the trip. More than a thousand hand-ground pieces of glass make up the lens, to give the appearance of gigantic glistening diamonds in the sunlight. Lit with oil lamps when it was established in 1870, the light has been electrified since 1916 and automated since 1970.

If you tire of watching for whales to pass, look over the railings at those dramatic cliffs below. Mariners have long referred to them and the eddies below as "the most dangerous shore on the west coast."

Epilogue

THE FEELING OF going some place in order to be *some-where* important, or at least meaningful, is what we all seek in a destination.

Not long ago the lead article in the Home Design section of the Sunday supplement of the *New York Times* was entitled "International Living," and touted the increasing "similarities that modern thinking has brought to home design worldwide." Claude Levi-Strauss is harsher. He once wrote, "The first thing we see as we travel around the world is our own garbage, flung into the face of mankind."

The result of monoculture is a kind of worldwide placelessness, such as airports and chain hotels, which everywhere look the same; or pseudo-places—the theme parks and Disney-style mockups. Writer Anatole Broyard has offered what may be the only solution for travelers: "If there truly is *no place* to go then perhaps we will have to learn to travel differently, not so hungrily, not in such a desperate spirit. We may even have to learn to love, or at least to live with the place where we are, to see ourselves as picturesque."

We are fortunate here in the Bay Area. There are many large pockets of place that still have natural individuality—federal, state, county, regional and city parks, open space preserves, water districts, farms, natural land unspoiled by the heedless misuse of man. Beginning with John Muir, thousands of people have seen these riches for what they are and fought to keep them so. I am proud to be one of their number. Trails for walkers run through all these special places.

It is in such places that the journey and the destination become co-equal. An area which has, as does the region around San Francisco Bay, destinations that are worthy of any walker's time, anytime of the year—ah, then that is a blessed land indeed.

Index